EXPLORATIONS IN POETICS

EXPLORATIONS IN POETICS

Benjamin Harshav

Stanford University Press
Stanford, California

Stanford University Press
Stanford, California

©2007 by Benjamin Harshav.

This book has been published with the assistance of Yale University's
Frederick W. Hilles Publication Fund.

Printed in the United States of America on acid-free, archival-quality paper

Library of Congress Cataloging-in-Publication Data
Harshav, Benjamin, 1928-
  Explorations in poetics / Benjamin Harshav.
    p. cm.
  Includes bibliographical references and index.
  ISBN 978-0-8047-5514-6 (cloth : alk. paper) -- ISBN 978-0-8047-5516-0 (pbk. : alk. paper)
  1. Literature--Philosophy. 2. Literature--History and criticism. I. Title.

PN49.H342 2007
808.1--dc22   2007002558

Designed by Bruce Lundquist
Typeset at Stanford University Press in 10/14 Minion

CONTENTS

FRAMEWORKS

PREFACE

To the laborers in this hard and immense field
in the twentieth century: philosophers, theoreticians,
literary critics, poets, students and colleagues,
I dedicate this book.

The essays collected in this book aim at developing a systematic, comprehensive theory of the work of literature. No matter what the interests of literary scholars today may be—political, cultural, ideological, national or thematic— we must be able to understand and rationally describe the basic unit of literary communication: the work of literature. Otherwise, the study of literature becomes the study of the world.

These chapters have been written at different times, yet they come together in one coherent perception of the literary text. I have now edited them thoroughly and agree with most of the ideas. I am trying to present an argument about the topics, as I see them today, to offer a model of the literary text and its major aspects, without burdening my essays with discussions of other theories and endless lists of references. I have read extensively in the philosophy of language, linguistics, literary theory and criticism of several generations. I looked into more, and, I am sure, overlooked much more. I benefited from many of those writings, and was influenced by phenomenology more than by structuralism, yet I believe that the science of literature, like any discipline in the humanities, must not be an applied philosophy or ideology, but must develop its own system of theory and research. Indeed, I learned mostly from carefully looking at how literary texts are made.

The chapters are arranged in a thematic rather than a chronological order. In several cases, there are considerable repetitions. I have left those as they were, because I needed the same conceptual framework for different purposes (e.g., fictionality, representation, and metaphor). Each essay can be read independent of the rest. A list of sources at the end of the book indicates the latest printed version of the collected articles. Some essays were written in Hebrew years ago and published in several versions in English. I stand behind the text as it is today.

The last section, "Frameworks," clarifies the assumptions underlying the specific studies. Chapter 9 discusses the pluralistic nature of the study of literature and was published first in 1968. Chapter 10 formulates the basic notions of my theory, as developed in seminars at the Hebrew University in Jerusalem and at the new Department of Poetics and Comparative Literature at Tel Aviv University, first presented outside of Israel in a Semiotics Seminar at Urbino, 1969, and summarized in English at Berkeley in 1972.

Some of the chapters refer to scholars of that time—it was a shorthand way of talking to my contemporaries about the issues. There is no intention to promote those names above others. The book is about ideas, no matter who articulated them first.

Benjamin Harshav (Hrushovski)
Professor of Comparative Literature, J.&H. Blaustein Professor of Hebrew Language and Literature and Professor of Slavic Languages and Literatures, Yale University
L.&S. Porter Professor Emeritus of Poetics and Literary Theory, Tel Aviv University

EXPLORATIONS IN POETICS

1 FICTIONALITY AND FIELDS OF REFERENCE

A Theoretical Framework

PREFACE

1. Works of literature convey meanings and meaning complexes as well as rhetorical and aesthetic import; they require of the reader some kind of "experience" or "concretization" and call for interpretations and elucidations. However, the experience and interpretation of literary texts are not a matter of language alone: language in literature can be understood only as embedded in fictional or projected constructs—situations, characters, ideas—no matter how partial or unstable these may be. On the other hand, the fictional constructs in literary texts—the situations, characters and ideas—are mediated through language alone. This is one basic inherent circularity of works of literary art.

It is not necessarily a logical "vicious circle," but can be understood as a detailed interdependence between the two domains: language and fictional constructs. We cannot simply build up or deduce the one from the other "objectively," as it were. An interpretation involves making certain hypotheses on aspects of this interdependence.

2. Let us take a simple example. The sentence "Everything changes" appears on the first page of Joyce's short story "Eveline." What does it mean? Can we understand it from the language itself, from the two simple English

---

For a different description of the theory, with additional sections on the reader, the concept of junction, and the hierarchy of patterns, see Chapter 8.

words? Does it convey the same thing as a similar idea uttered by an ancient Greek philosopher? What is the scope of the word "everything" and how serious is the commitment behind this assertion?

Indeed, this sentence may refer to permanent changes in nature, the destruction and recomposition of matter; or changes in society; or to biological changes in the lives of people.

The immediate context is:

> That was a long time ago; she [Eveline] and her brothers and sisters were all grown up; her mother was dead. Tizzie Dunn was dead, too, and the Waters had gone back to England. Everything changes. Now she was going to go away like the others, to leave her home.

Here, the sentence "Everything changes" can be taken as a generalization of the facts stated in the neighboring sentences. It may then either apply in a general way, as a characteristic of life: people move, grow up, die, leave home; or, in a more limited scope, as a summary of the destinies of the people around our character, Eveline. If we enlarge the context somewhat to other things described in the opening of the story, we may assume that "everything changes" applies to Dublin and its traditional world: a man from Belfast "came" and built new houses, foreign workers appeared, red brick houses were built, etc. Furthermore, Eveline's own leaving home is seen as a deduction from a general principle, and the story itself becomes an example of it. (The cover of the Penguin Modern Classics edition of *Dubliners* says: "The incidents he [Joyce] relates are small in themselves but of universal interest.")

In any case, to understand what the sentence conveys, we must consider the fictional "reality" to which it is applied, and the scope of things it may cover. Indeed, as we saw above, we may apply it in turn to several frames of reference, in the fictional as well as in the real world, as part of interpretation hypotheses.

When we read the whole story, however, it turns out that Eveline does not leave. She, who tried to escape the destiny of her mother, "becomes" her mother. In her life, at least, *nothing changes*. To the extent that Eveline can be seen as representative, as some readers would see her, the story epitomizes in Joyce's words, the "paralysis" of Ireland. Indeed, we may assign the interpretive construct "nothing changes" to the position of the narrator (or above him, to the implied author). This conclusion—nothing changes—is not stated in explicit language but results from a summary of the plot. Such a summary, however, contradicts the statement "everything changes" as understood before. To resolve the contradiction, the assertion "Everything changes" must be limited to Eveline's own point of view and to the circumstances, the time and place when it was uttered (or experienced), i.e., when Eveline thought that she, too, was leaving. This statement underlines the discrepancy between Eveline's understanding of her situation and the real state of affairs; or between her youthful "revolt" and its defeat. It represents the ironic distance between the constant *present* time of the character's experience—moving with the story and ignorant of the future—into which the reader is temporarily drawn, and the *past* of the narrator's perspective, which the reader grasps fully only at the end.

This dependence of language on "reality constructs" (which, in turn, are built from elements of language), as seen in such a simple utterance, is even more crucial in the "difficult" and figurative language of poetry, where words may be wide open for ambiguities and must be limited by fictional constructs (see Chapter 2 on metaphor).

3. This is not the only basic circularity, or interdependence, inherent in literary texts. Circularity in a logical argument is considered a negative feature. But in real life and in literary texts it is essential to human existence and to our understanding. Every person depends on his/her circumstances and shapes them at the same time. Ideas and characters, psychology and history are interdependent. Interaction theory of metaphor is based on this principle.

A similar circularity can be found between any part of the text and its *Regulating Principles*, such as irony, point of view, genre, etc.: we construct such attitudes from the text and then read the text as directed by them. Thus, a satirical text constructs the satirical tone and then reads the text in a satirical light.

Similar, though more diffuse, is the very difficult relation of "representation" between literary fictions and the external "world" upon which they are modeled on the one hand, and which they represent as typical, deviating, critical, etc., on the other.

Such interdependencies may occur in every aspect of literary works. A meter is constructed from certain distributions of syllables and stresses in verse and, in turn, imposes a certain reading on the verse lines. A plot is constructed from several events presented in the text and then, in turn, imposes certain readings, selections and interpolations of other events, often not explicitly stated in the text. Hypotheses of interpretation involve hypotheses on such interdependencies and may be refuted when one of the terms is exposed as wrong.

I shall not deal with the other kinds in this paper, but merely point out that ours is not an isolated case. Indeed, interdependence between constructs is at the very heart of representations of reality and of works of literature.

To return to our starting point: the problem of fiction and "fictional worlds" cannot be isolated from the problem of language in literature.

WHAT IS FICTIONALITY?

4. On the face of it, fiction can be described as language offering propositions which make no claim for truth values in the real world. Thus, the philosopher John Searle explains "fictional" utterances as opposed to "serious" utterances in the same way as he analyzes the opposition "metaphorical" versus "literal." According to him, "fictional utterances are 'nonserious'." "For example, if the author of a novel tells us that it is raining outside he isn't seriously committed to the view that it is at the time of writing actually raining outside. It is in this sense that fiction is nonserious" (Searle, p. 60).

Searle's analysis makes the important link between fictionality and commitment to the truth of a proposition. Fictional worlds are presented to us in language, often in the form of propositions. Yet somehow those propositions are not really "true." In this respect, he joins a venerable tradition, including such concepts as I. A. Richards's "pseudo-statements" and Roman Ingarden's "Quasi-Urteile."[1]

In the sense of his analysis, Searle is right: the novelist, indeed, makes no commitment that it is actually raining "outside" (wherever he is) "*at the time of writing*" (my emphasis—B.H.). But neither do we if we talk about an *absent frame of reference* in real life. The problem is that the truth value of propositions can be judged only within specific *frames of reference* to which they are—or may be—related. A person using the expression "it is raining outside"—in a novel or in a letter—may refer to his immediate surroundings, to the fictional situation in the novel, or to any other frame or reference that he recalls or tells about (such as India or the town where his mother lives).

5. In the case of a work of literature, we are not dealing with isolated sentences or propositions, but with an *Internal Field of Reference* (IFR)—a whole

---

1   The standard English translation of this term, "quasi-judgments," should be taken not in an evaluative sense but as equivalent to "quasi-propositions." Urteil, in German logic of the early 20th century means "proposition" or "assertion."

network of interrelated referents of various kinds: characters, events, situations, ideas, dialogues, etc.[2] The language of the text contributes to the establishment of this Internal Field and refers to it at the same time. For example, in the passage from Joyce's "Eveline" quoted above, an assertion is made: "Tizzie Dunn was dead." The text *projects* a new referent, not mentioned before, the person "Tizzie Dunn," and, at the same time, refers to it, asserting her/his death.[3]

Within this Internal Field of Reference, we judge the truth values of propositions using whatever other information for the same Field that we may have. This holds both for assertions made in the language of the text itself and for descriptions emerging from readings and interpretations of the text as in the case of "nothing changes" in the example above, which is not a statement in the text but a necessary construct in its interpretation.

There is no interpretation of the "meaning" of a text without such constructs, just from the language of the sentences, as it were.

6. Let us define our terms.

A *referent (r)* here is anything we can refer to or talk about, may it be a real object, an event, an idea, or a fictional, non-existent object.

A *frame of reference (fr)* is any semantic continuum of two or more referents that we may speak about: it may be a scene in time and space, a character, an ideology, a mood, a state of affairs, a plot, a policy, a theory, psychoanalysis, the wind in the autumn trees, the mountains of Corsica, etc. We know things in the world through such frames rather than through logical arguments. This mode of knowledge may be called *situational cognition*, which is the mode of operation of literature.

Any referent named in one word can be opened up into a frame of reference, if further details are given.

We may distinguish *fr*s of various kinds. An *fr* may be *present* to the interlocutors or *absent*; if absent, it may be *known* or *unknown* to one or both of them. It can be *real*, a concrete scene in time and space, or *ideal*, a theory or

---

2   The argument here is based on my theory of "Integrational Semantics" (see Chapter 3 below).

3   A few lines earlier in the story, the name Dunn is mentioned for the first time: "the Dunns" are listed among "the children of the avenue" who "used to play together in that field." The reader may conjecture that Tizzie Dunn is one of those children or their mother (which would parallel her own mother's death mentioned in the same sentence). No decisive evidence for or against such an assumption can be made from the text.

an abstract concept (e.g., "existence" or "triangle"). An *fr* can have a unique description in time or be iterative ("they used to play"), or have any other undefined or unusual reality-relations; it may be a typical situation ("autumn") or highly individualized ("the crazy party in my garden on the 6th of October last year"). It may be existing in reality, hypothetical or fictional; its ontological status is unimportant for semantics—it is anything that we can speak *about* or project in our imagination (an "intentional" object in Husserl's sense).

The various kinds of *frs* pose different problems for the theory of understanding. Thus, in a *present fr* (sitting in a room), some details of information will be supplied by the non-verbal situation and need not be spelled out in words, while in an *absent fr* many details are left out. In a *known fr* we may appeal to the hearer's knowledge or memory ("it is like in the picture on the left wall in my study," or: "it's Vietnam all over again"), whereas in a story we have to construct the missing parts or leave them indeterminate.[4] The problem of projecting a fictional world in literature depends on this contradiction. The story "Eveline" is largely presented from her point of view, but she sits inside the *fr* and doesn't need to explain what she observes, whereas the reader is outside that *fr* and somehow needs to know various facts: how old is she, what is her last name, her profession, etc. The writer has to find special ways to fill in such information. In other words, in the techniques of showing, the character is in a *present fr* while the reader observes an *absent fr*.

7. A *Field of Reference* (FR) is a large, multidimensional, hypothetical universe, containing a multitude of cotextual, crisscrossing and interrelated *frs* of various kinds. We may isolate such Fields as the USA, the Napoleonic Wars, Philosophy, the "world" of Tolstoy's *War and Peace*, the world today, cultural memory, etc. I use the term "isolate" advisedly, since a Field or a frame in this conception are not fixed ontological entities; their delimitation depends on strategies of reference, understanding and explanation. Any *fr*, e.g. "a party" in *War and Peace* (see my analysis in Chapter 8) can be composed of many smaller *frs* (characters, groups, dancing, drinks, etc.).

There is no essential difference between a large *fr* and an FR. Both project a hypothetical continuum, only parts of which are given in the text. There can

---

4   For some further descriptions of *frs*, see Chapter 2 below on poetic "Metaphor and Frames of Reference," especially sections 4 and 5.

be a whole hierarchy of frames within frames. An *fr* evoked in an utterance or a text is represented by several *r*s and never in full, while an FR is represented by several *fr*s and never in full. Thus, in a novel, the hero may appear at age two and then at age nineteen—we fill in the rest, if needed. The only difference lies in the convenience of understanding things within scenes or problems or continuities, that are all included in a larger, hypothetical whole.

When reading a newspaper, we get information about a large number of heterogeneous, disconnected *fr*s: segments in the economy, politics, trade unions, a literary prize, gossip, a description of an accident, predictions about the next day's weather, etc.—all in one page. We do not perceive them as isolated, disconnected objects, floating in a void, but rather as spots on a vast map, a Field of Reference, which has a hypothetical (though fuzzy) scope and coherence: "the World," "the USA," "Modernity," etc.

We know we shall never be able to connect all these *fr*s in their full continuity, fill up the full map of, say, "the USA today," but we do know some *fr*s on that map and have notions about some relations between them, and we know, in principle, how to go about finding out about other facts and connections or filling in missing information: by reading *The New York Times* or Norman Mailer, studying economics or geography, referring to an encyclopedia, talking to experts, etc. There is a network of relations there, the precise nature of which is not fully and explicitly known to anyone, but various approximations, generalizations, theories, combinations of those, as well as contours and concrete examples make the nature of the network clear to an extent that we think we know what it is and how to find out more about it.

A Field of a different kind is a science, such as Physics or Sociology. Here, too, we have to confront huge conglomerates of a great variety of theories, concrete studies, experiments—spots and approximations on a large map which is neither fully presented nor evenly filled in.

8. The unique feature of a work of literature is that it projects its own *Internal Field of Reference* (IFR) while referring to it at the same time; to use a well-known simile: a literary text builds the boat under its own feet while rowing in the sea. The "outside" in Searle's example is not an actual place but a frame of reference projected in the novel (the outside in relation to a house) at the same time as something is being predicated about it (that it rains there).

In other words, a work of literature projects its own "reality" while simultaneously describing it. The problematic nature of various "existents" in that "reality" (characters, objects, events) is closely related to the contradictory sources of our informants and information about it, the indeterminacies and gaps in the presentation, and the changing faces of language in shifting contexts.

Hence, when the author of a novel tells us that it is raining outside, we must assume that he or his character *is*, indeed, "seriously committed to the view that it is [. . .] actually raining outside" (Searle), though not, as Searle suggested, "at the time of writing," but *in the frame of reference he is speaking about.* On the other hand, he is not committed to the view that this *fr* itself exists in the real world. Thus, in a novel, as in the real world, if during that rain a visitor arrives, he or she must either be wet or was not really outside, or we must assume that the narrator or his character was either mistaken in his assertion, or is lying on purpose, or is altogether an "unreliable narrator."

Needless to say, an author rarely tells us anything directly, he does it through various speakers and narrators, who are committed to the same truth within the Internal Field of Reference or are exposed as being ironical, ignorant, lying, or unreliable.

9. In this respect, the use of language in a literary text is basically similar to that in real life situations which are outside our direct experience at the time of communication (*absent frs*): we cannot judge the truth value of utterances about them by means of direct observation; we can only confront them with other utterances—or images and other non-verbal evidence—relating to the same frames of reference. We can combine them, oppose them or subsume them under other *frs* that we do know. We have at our disposal not an "objective" world but only some information about it, mediated through different sources, speakers, texts, ideologies and points of view as well as views acquired or formed in our own life experience. Furthermore, this information is partial and spotty, just a projection of a world rather than a real object. The conclusion, therefore, may be true within our set of beliefs or it may be contradictory, unresolved, changing, biased and so on.

In a real-life situation, one assumes that, ideally, there are ways of finding evidence and ascertaining what the real state of affairs was (by means of travel, police investigation, newspaper reports, science, etc.), since the referents supposedly do exist "out there." In a literary text, for referents which are unique to its Internal FR (specific fictional characters, meetings, dialogues, lunches, etc.), there are no such ways outside of the given text because those referents did not exist outside of it. We learn about them, however, in much the same way as we learn about any *absent frs* in the real world: by means of further verbal and non-verbal evidence about them, subsuming them under known categories and models and judging the reliability of the informants. Thus, in Gore Vidal's historical novel *Lincoln*, Lincoln and many characters were historical figures, they existed in External Fields of Reference, in the real world, but their food at breakfast and their dialogues as presented in the novel are fictional. Still, we can try to compare those internal *frs* to what we know about the mores of breakfast of that time.

It is often impossible to resolve the various partial and contradictory pieces of evidence and decide what "really" happened in a novel, what "really" the character's motivations were; or figure out the details of an interpersonal situation in a poem, even though the poem may carry an experience of, or a response to, that situation. The author's ideology, his views on any specific issue or the "meaning" of the whole work can often not be reduced to one sentence but must be constructed as a cluster of different, shifting, even contradictory, positions, opinions, observations, possibilities.

10. In the understanding of language in the world, the senses of the words and meanings of sentences are related to specific referents within specific frames of reference and, in turn, are influenced by them. The frame of reference, to which a text or its understander relates the words, provides information both for judging the truth value of any utterance and for specifying, qualifying, metaphorizing or otherwise modifying their meanings.

If I am mistaken or lie or exaggerate, other observations of the *fr* may expose it. If I shout: "close that gate," and the referent in the *present fr*, to which I point, is not a gate but a door, the hearer will reunderstand the word "gate" to mean "door" and then will have to interpret my words to mean: "for me, at this moment, under these circumstances, that door is like a gate"; which may mean: "this door is as wide open as a gate," or: "too many people are flooding in," or "shut the door because of the noise." In the case of the rain outside, if the frame of reference is in the tropics, we may assume that the rain is strong; if it is during a drought, the utterance will convey relief and hope; if we know that there is no rain, we may understand it as a metaphorical expression, etc. When the Israeli poet Yehuda Amichai starts a poem with the words: "Do not accept these rains that come too late," we have a background of a dry country, unanswered prayers for rain, etc. Indeed, the poem enlarges this *fr* into a desert ("Make your pain an image of the desert"), i.e., the poet is fully committed to the rain and its importance in his constructed *fr*. And then he turns the whole *fr* "desert" into a metaphor for another *fr*: the pain or human suffering or resistance to the evils of history. A person cannot really accept or not accept the rain—which forces the reader to see it as a metaphor for human defiance. Thus, the precise meaning of the words is dependent on the *frs* to which they refer.

Yehuda Amichai

Do Not Accept

Do not accept these rains that come too late.
Better to linger. Make your pain
An image of the desert. Say it's said
And do not look to the west.[5] Refuse

To surrender. Try this year too
To live alone in the long summer,
Eat your drying bread, refrain
From tears. And do not learn from

Experience. Take as an example my youth,
My return late at night, what has been written
In the rain of yesteryear. It makes no difference
Now. See your events as my events.
Everything will be as before: Abraham will again
Be Abram. Sarah will be Sarai.

(Amichai, p. 59)

11. From the opposite direction, the meaning of utterances is influenced by the *Regulating Principles* that dominate a text or parts of it. The meanings of words and sentences are influenced by the tone of voice, point of view, genre, political propaganda, circumstances of utterance, stance toward an audience, etc. The authority behind the text—i.e., the speaker or position from which the text is presented, the attitude and kind of text chosen—guides our understanding, tells us "in what sense" (serious, ironic, etc.) to take the senses of the words.

---

5   In Israel, the rain comes from the West, the Mediterranean.

Combining this with the previous point, we conclude that the meaning of utterances is a result of a three-tier construct:

where RP means Regulating Principles; sense—senses of words and syntactic operations of meaning; and *fr*—frames of reference to which the words refer. There is reciprocity between the three levels.

12. In real life situations, when isolated sentences rather than long texts are uttered, often only the middle level is provided in language, whereas the rest is given in "reality." We hear a speaker's ironic intonation, observe the circumstances of her life (mother died, all the neighbors left . . .) and understand the utterance in the light of those. We also observe the real or social situation to which the words apply. In short, the *fr* is supplied by reality, the RP by the speaker, and both interact with the level of language. This has allowed linguists to discuss the middle level alone, language itself, as it were.

Language, however, is not an independent tool for conveying information through the senses of its words and the structures of its sentences alone, but rather a powerful device to operate on our knowledge of the "World" (*Network of Information*): to recall, evoke, name, select from it and manipulate it in order to convey "meaning" (in the widest sense of this word, including information, signification, emotive attitudes, opinions, etc.).

Though only the middle level is given in actual language, the reader of a text has to construct the other two levels from the same text. In a newspaper account we may be given the name of the author and genre but may have to reconstruct ironic RPs as well as the relevant *fr*s. In a scientific theory, we must construct or zoom in into the Field of that theory and its concepts, in order to understand the descriptions relating to it.

In a literary text we don't have the luxury of analyzing language alone: we must reconstruct all three levels. In such a reconstruction there may be several alternatives, thus encouraging multiple interpretations. For example, if a character says something, we can reconstruct her own position or point of view from which the utterance was made; and then, above her, the position of the narrator who introduced this character, and perhaps, above him, the author's position. Similarly, we may be able to apply the same expression (e.g., "Everything changes") to several different *frs* resulting in different, alternative or complementary, interpretations. For example, Eveline's growing up, the leaving and death of people close to her, Dublin, the old world. A similar case is the metaphor of illness ("a patient etherized upon a table") applied to multiple *frs* in interpretations of T. S. Eliot's "Prufrock": the evening, the city dwellers, the salon women, the speaker's "I," the sick Modern world (see in Chapter 2).

This is the basic apparatus, underlying all language use, with which we construct the fictional world and interpret its language simultaneously. How is this world constructed? And how does it relate to the real world, history, beliefs and knowledge outside?

THE INTERNAL FIELD OF REFERENCE

13. A work of literature can be defined as a verbal text which projects at least one Internal Field of Reference (IFR) to which meanings in the text are related. At least some of the referents—personal names, times, places, scenes and episodes—are "fictional," unique to this text, and make no claim for external, factual existence. When I say: "at least one IFR," I indicate that there may be several discontinuous IFRs, as in the opening of Dos Passos's *USA*, before they are integrated in one whole, the USA. And I allow for many additional references—by the text and by the reader—to External Fields of Reference.

This is not a sufficient but a necessary definition of literature, which separates literary from other texts. In my view, it is the only one possible definition; all typical "literary" devices—metaphor, narrative, characters, dialogues, etc.—appear in other texts as well. To the description of literature, however, one may add a number of additional typical features, fluctuating in history (see below, #21).

It is important to note that the text is not identical to the IFR. This can be seen in two respects: Firstly, an essential feature of literary texts is that some of their meanings may, or may at the same time, be related to Fields external to the IFR and existing independently (see next section). Secondly, networks of non-semantic patterns, too (sound patterns, rhythm, key words, repetitions, etc.) profusely appear in literary texts and interact with the semantic patterns organized in the IFR.

It would be hard to overestimate the importance of the IFR in forming the nature and the substance of a work of literature. It is responsible for the so-called "uniqueness" of a work of literature, based on unique proper names of the characters and on the merging of all formal, conventional and thematic aspects in one individualized combination of patterns (the "fictional world" of the text). It is also the carrier of the representational mode: the expressive, symbolic or modeling value of a literary text vis-à-vis the external world and vis-à-vis the author. Furthermore, any interpretation of the "meaning" of a work of literature cannot simply assess the meanings of sentences but must also consider them as stemming from or being related to the individualized fictional constructs.

14. Works of literature have several additional characteristics, concomitant with the IFR, some of them fluctuating but typical. The most important ones are:

(a) The IFR is modeled upon (a selection from) the "real," physical and social human world. That includes objects, types of persons, situations, relations and hierarchies. It typically projects the seemingly accidental, unpredictable and "alogical" heterogeneity of elements linked in one concrete episode, in all its situational details. Of course, the selection from that social world may be highly one-sided and slanted; it does not have to be "realistic" at all, and may use different *reality-keys*. And it may appear in a great variety of alternative forms.

In this respect, the IFR differs from any autonomous FR created in a philosophy or a science, which strives to be systematic and abstracts one aspect under observation. The IFR—by its very existence—represents the concreteness and complexity of the world.

(b) An IFR is a multidimensional semiotic object rather than a linear message. In other words, it does not present one linear unfolding of a narrative or one logical argument or one systematic description of anybody or anything, but a bundle of heterogeneous and co-textual patterns: events, characters, settings, ideas, time and space, social and political situations, etc., interacting with each other as well as with other, non-semantic text-patterns (of style, parallelism, segmentation, sound-patterns, composition of the text, etc.).

(c) The primacy which structural narratology conferred on narrative in fiction is unjustified and misleading for literature as a whole. There are no "narrative texts," but only texts which have narrative structures in them— along with structures of physical space, social stratification, characters, unfolding of ideas, atmosphere, etc. Some of the narrative patterns have been used for the composition of a text—and are traditionally important for "telling a story"—but that does not necessarily make them the dominant aspect of the story. Furthermore, in "non-narrative" stories or "non-narrative" episodes within a narrative novel, other semantic aspects may be used for composition as well (characterization of persons, ideological arguments, elaboration of fantastic fictional worlds, etc.).

(d) In addition to the unique, "fictional" persons and other referents, IFRs often use referents and/or frames of reference from Fields external to them, including the "real," historical world and various "secondary modeling systems" (as the Soviet Semioticians called it): beliefs, religion, historiography, ideologies, scientific views, stereotypical situations, modes of dialogue, etc., and, in turn, reflect upon them.

(e) Even when removed from realism, as in Kafka or in Surrealist poetry, such external references are indispensable. And on the other hand, even when relying heavily on the external world, imitating it or using its referents, the literary text selects elements and reshuffles their hierarchies while creating its own autonomous Field.

(f) Structural narratology chose the event as its key unit. Indeed, events can be seen as discrete points in time, concatenated in a plot. Yet if we observe all quasi-realistic objects in the literary world, it is clear that the richest units are characters: while an event is a point in time in the chain of plot, characters are endowed with an individualized, complex heterogeneity. They are involved in actions and influenced by them. They raise a host of sensibilities, relationships, behaviors, experiences. Moreover, they compose the discontinuous fictional world, because they can move from one *fr* to another in time and space—either physically or in their memory and consciousness. Indeed, in any scene in the present, characters represent the past and the future. They observe the world from their different points of view and conduct dialogues about it. In a capsule, they represent style, action, time, space, biography, psychology, social conditions, beliefs, and so on. The network of characters presents the wide net cast by a fictional world. Characters have minds, through which we observe the projected reality. The name of a person is an *accumulation* of knowledge, gossip, information, ideas, relations, collected throughout the text. It is an *abbreviation* of a wealth of heterogeneous information. Writers are not obliged to unfold a philosophical argument in a technical and precise philosophical language; it is enough to show such a philosophical position through the dialogues and minds of the fictional persons, and in their mundane, non-philosophical language. One can hardly imagine a work of literature without people or observations of the physical world and of mental experiences from the point of view of people; or without concrete, scenic episodes involving persons. George Perec (*La vie: mode d'emploi*) used another complex semiotic object—a building in Paris with all its accidental dwellers, but that building is complex because it presents a conglomerate of persons, their market fairs of details, and their destinies. Vassily Grosman's title for a novel, *Life and Destiny*, could be the title of many classical novels.

15. This description includes poetry, drama and prose, written as well as oral works of literature and folklore, or stories that children tell. It also holds for non-verbal or not purely fictional modes, such as film or figurative painting. As Emil Staiger argued, even lyrical poems that seem to be objective descriptions of objects without a speaker or a "lyrical I" are presented from a person's point of view. The lyric is an *Er-innerung*, an internalized objectivity (as well as a memory). A poem or a story can live without a plot but not without persons and their mediation of the "world."

A single dream, too, may be seen as having its own IFR (somewhat similar to a disjointed poetic vision or an absurd narrative in images). Psychoanalysis, however, projects all individual dreams onto a Field external to them, the person's subconscious.

In defining a work of literature through its Internal Field of Reference, rather than as a fixed language text, we may consider a work of literature which has several versions, or a folktale with a variable text, changing in various performances—as one work.

16. Hence, fictionality is not necessarily a matter of invention. "Fiction" is not opposed to "fact." Fictional works may be based in great detail on the author's actual experiences or observations; on the other hand, works claiming to describe the truth (autobiographies, journalistic reports) may carry a great deal of biased reporting. The issue is not in the amount of demonstrable truthfulness but rather that the former establish their own IFR while the latter claim to describe the "real" world. Here lies the cardinal difference between a biography (or autobiography) on the one hand and an autobiographical novel on the other. In the second case, we are not supposed to bring counter-evidence from the author's life or argue that the writer has distorted specific facts.

Of course, we can transfer descriptions from the IFR to the real world, read the story as a clue to actual events and argue that the author of a novel was true or false to his childhood experiences or has an axe to grind. In this case, however, we read the text as a document for something else rather than as an autonomous work of fiction.

17. An Internal FR is established even in historical novels or in novels including historical figures. Often, secondary historical or fictional persons became the main characters in a historical novel, while the historical figures, e.g., Napoleon in Tolstoy's *War and Peace*, became marginal in the IFR. Even when historically known persons appear in individualized situations (a lunch, a dialogue, etc.), either no claim can be made that those actually happened or such a claim is irrelevant. Usually, the time of such situations is also somewhat detached from real chronological time or is "floating" (see #26 below). Thus, in Doctorow's *Ragtime*, a historical figure, Emma Goldman, appears; she even has some of her known historical characteristics; we are not, however, expected to believe that her lesbian encounter with Eleanor Nesbitt in the IFR actually occurred in the ExFR as well. (Even if such an episode is based on real facts uncovered by the author and documented in archives or private letters, it is outside the scope of that person's historical "image" or contradictory to it.) Furthermore, the historical events and persons are selected in a way functional for this particular IFR rather than for a scientific description of history. Tolstoy knew that his Napoleon is merely a caricature of the historical conqueror of Europe, but needed this image for his IFR.

18. On the other hand, many non-literary texts have so-called "literary" properties: style, metaphors, sound-patterns and parallelism, interesting narrative structures and plot-like "tensions," etc. Such properties are not unique to literature, though they are typically required of works of literature in varying forms in different genres and periods. They enhance the readability of non-literary texts as well, their rhetorical efficacy, even their relative independence from what may be demonstrably true. But such texts do not thereby become works of literary art in the strict sense.

Thus, Roman Jakobson analyzed an American election slogan, "I like Ike," as an example of what he called the "poetic function," defined as a "set towards the message" (i.e., orientation towards the language itself of a work of art or towards formation of the text). Sound patterns are the obvious example. Phonologically, "I" am included in "Ike" and "Ike" is included in "like," yet this is clearly not a poem but a very pragmatic rhetorical device. Indeed, according to Jakobson, the poetic function is not exclusive to poetry at all, though it is, in some way, "dominant" in works of verbal art. How do we establish this dominance? Isn't this election slogan entirely involved in the sound pattern? Without denying the important role of the ubiquitous "poetic function" in works of literature, I think it is not a distinguishing criterion for their definition. "I like Ike" is not a poem. Literature is not simply art in language but, first of all, art in fictionality.

19. Naturally, border cases exist in which internal evidence for the establishment of a text as fictional must be supplemented by external markers or decisions. Dostoevsky's *Notes from the Underground* is a story because it is included in his fictional works and has a fictional character. Its basic FR is internal: a fictional person behaves, thinks, argues, talks within an Internal FR. Much of the semantic substance of the story, however, is projected onto an External Field of Reference: philosophy or meditations on the human condition.

On the other hand, Plato's dialogues, intended primarily as a form for presenting philosophical arguments, can be disconnected from the Field of philosophy and its truth values and read as mere dramatic stories presenting fictional, or fictionalized characters interested in ideas. In that case, the philosophical argument itself is seen primarily in terms of the characterization of the interlocutors or as an object of "aesthetic" observation rather than as a challenge for counterarguments, acceptance, etc. Thus, the decision to read a text for its fictionality or for its "meaning" in the External FR will determine its literary or non-literary nature. An actual reading may use both attitudes interchangeably.

Some books of reportage, travel or history (such as Gibbon's famous *Decline and Fall of the Roman Empire*) may be read as works of "literature," in which case they seem to be divorced by the reader from direct reference to specific facts in the External FRs (both the historical Rome and the academic study of history). In this reading, the truth values of their specific propositions outside of the IFR become immaterial or suspended and they are read primarily for their internal structure and coherence and their impressive power as narrative models of historical events. Actually, however, the issue is more complicated, since works of fiction, too, have an important relation to the external world (see below). Like works of fiction, such books are read for their representative value, as "models" for certain perceptions of the external world. In a sense, Gibbon's vision of Rome or of history is akin to Stendhal's or Tolstoy's images of Europe and history: it erects one version or model of what it was like, though the specific truth-values of individual propositions may be in question. In other words, an autonomous IFR is established, independent of any further historical research, and then its constructs may be seen to have relations of representation to the external world.

Likewise, journalistic reporting often describes individual characters in concrete scenes. We may enjoy such episodes as pieces of literature ("stories," "images," anecdotes); i.e., we read them as autonomous *fr*s, regardless of the questions of their factual truth or just representation. Such reports have "literary" properties: narrative, characterization, scenic presentation, anecdotal wit. Those are used, however, for the description of an External Field of Reference, i.e., with a claim to direct, referential truth value.

Needless to say, in the prevalent cultural tradition, even when read for pure enjoyment, as descriptive and narrative fictional works, the status of such texts as "literature" remains marginal because they do not fit the mainstream literary genres.

ON "WHAT IS A LITERARY TEXT?"

20. It is almost generally accepted today that no distinguishing features separate literary from non-literary texts. "Poetic language," rhythm, metaphor, narrative, structure, etc., can be observed in historical, philosophical, and scientific writings, as well as in journalism, politics and daily life situations. Methods of analysis and insights into the nature of language, texts and interpretations, developed in the analysis of literature, have been successfully employed for the study of those other areas and are far from being fully explored.

Intuitively, however, it seems that a rich variety of works of literature are still different from other texts. The *semiotic reduction* of the study of literature to the general study of texts overlooks something central to human culture, which we are accustomed to call "literature." Rather than dissolve itself in a general theory of texts, it is the task of poetics to formulate descriptions that would satisfy this intuition.

This can be done in several ways.

(a) Let us take "metaphor," "narrative," "semantic density," and other features which have been considered essential to literature: if we observe them not as abstract entities but in their precise functions in specific works of literature, we can see how different their use is from ordinary use elsewhere. I.e., what counts is not the mere presence of metaphors, etc.—which, indeed, is not uniquely literary—but their specific role in the organization, integration, semantic functions and social perceptions of specific texts. This is true even if no general definition for such functions (e.g., of metaphor in poetry) can be formulated.

(b) We should give up any claims that such traditionally perceived categories define the "essence" of literature. Clearly, for any such property— metaphor, narrative, concreteness, intuition, significant form, etc.—cogent examples can be found where it is absent or marginal. However, categories of this kind—offered in theories of aesthetics, poetics, rhetoric, criticism or literary manifestos—focus our attention on crucial aspects of at least some works of art. Hence, we can turn these categories from answers into questions: Where, to what extent, in what forms do they appear? Instead of a misguided essentialist definition, we can use them as a program for research. Features that do not define all of literature but are nevertheless typical and essential to many individual texts are central to the study of literature. I emphasize this because we may be in danger of neglecting the existing thinking and research of such aspects for the sake of one reductionist problem: interpretation.

(c) True, no single property (except for the projected IFR, as described above) will separate all literary from all non-literary texts, or cover all texts that have been called "literature" by one group of people or another. It is not even a case of literature being an ill-defined class of texts with fuzzy margins; there would be no stable core for such a class. A crucial feature of literary history has been precisely the recurrent reshuffling of literary kinds, norms and conventions. Nevertheless, we can observe in history a number of alternative clusters of features which have characterized specific groups of literary texts. In other words, though an intensional definition may be impossible, we may still describe the generically and historically dependent bundles of alternative norms and tendencies which made literature (both when the category and the term "literature" were known and unknown).

21. Having said all this, I would still venture a definition of literary texts— albeit a complex one and open to variants.

Requirements in three domains are essential to a work of literature: an Internal Field of Reference; the autonomy and closure of the individual text; and changing literary norms and conventions. Let us look at them closely.

(a) The establishment of an Internal Field of Reference and a number of properties concomitant with it (see above, #14). The IFR is an absolute requirement, an essential property of literary texts; whereas the additional traits, though necessary, are not exclusive and highly variable.

(b) The autonomy of the text from any transient speech situation and from direct reference, its relative fixity and transferability from one situation to another, from one century to another. The importance of this feature for the internal formation of literary texts cannot be overestimated. It supports various tendencies of "framing" and internal cohesion and structuration of all elements of a text. It reinforces the unity and autonomy of the IFR and its intimate relations with the non-semantic patterning of the text. It foregrounds the many manifestations of equivalence patterns (Jakobson's "poetic function"), both in formal (rhyme and meter) and in free, contextually determined modes (sound patterns). All patterning, rather than being a mere embellishment, becomes part of a move toward the unifying of the text, toward promoting all crisscrossing relations, toward heightening textual density and highlighting the importance of the "language" or texture of a work of art.

If the "poetic function" can be said to be indispensable to literary texts, this can be tested: any changes of the surface of a literary text are not permissible since they would distort the "language" of the text, its meter, style, etc., whereas philosophical or scientific texts, as well as news reports, can, in principle, be paraphrased, because they refer to External FRs.

True, ritual formulaic texts are also fixed and unchangeable, but there the institutionalized, magical or holy qualities are emphasized (an aspect not wholly foreign to poetry). On the other hand, in literature, the surface structures per se or the restless tensions between cotextual patterns are of primary importance.

One might argue that masterpieces of philosophy are also isolated and canonized texts. Here, too, the autonomy of such a text enhances the intensive unification of the presented Field. Because of the differences in the other aspects, however, the result is different. In philosophy, what is decisive is the system of ideas, the dense interdependence of all their details; they all relate to an external FR in aesthetics, metaphysics, Existentialism, etc., to which more texts may refer. In literature, what is special is the unique IFR, its "constructed reality" and unique proper names and situations, as well as the network of language patterns and equivalence structures of each individual text.

(c) The use of a variety of historically and socially changing conventions and tendencies in the fields of language, genre structures, themes and aesthetic norms, as described in literary history and criticism. Such norms inform all aspects of language and of anything that may be represented through language in a text. The specific norms are constantly changing and being reshuffled and recombined; we cannot define or describe them for all literature. But their very existence in a literary text is indispensable. Individually, any of them may appear outside literary texts as well.

The last two categories are not unique to literature and have a wealth of fluctuating manifestations in various cultures, but their appearance is nevertheless essential to works of literature, good or bad. Therefore, we may, for heuristic purposes, start with one, normative theory of literature or its genres and then try to describe the alternative patterns employed in texts where the first requirements fail (e.g., what are the substitutes for narrative in modern non-narrative prose or for metaphor in non-metaphoric poetry).

22. A further complication of this problem is the aesthetic aspect, the variety of aesthetic norms and requirements. Admittedly, often fuzzy and changing in history and society, even from text to text, their appearance, too, is indispensable to the description of literature. In most cultures, what is not "good" literature (or whatever name it had) is not literature at all; though the separation between good and bad is not an absolute one. Intuitively, it seems that there is a continuum between the norms for literary texts and such aesthetic norms, i.e., even badly performed literary texts will try to implement to some degree some of the valued devices. In any case, aesthetic norms, too, are based on preferences and selections of alternatives within the three domains described above (see #21). In different theories, the Internal Field of Reference may be favored when it is both markedly different and separated from external fields and, at the same time, in some sense representative of them.

23. We need not limit the theory to a dichotomy: Internal ("fictional") vs. External ("objective"). There may be intermediate Fields created in any field of knowledge. A historian writing about a movement in history creates an abstracted Field, a model of history, not identical with the individual facts and documents. Myths, philosophies, scientific theories, etc., create their own autonomous Fields of Reference with unique referents (terms, characters, concepts, reified entities, narratives, laws) that may not directly refer to observable referents in the world but are theoretical abstractions to describe it. They are created somewhere between the theory and the hard facts. They are different from Internal Fields in literature in that respect, that in these areas, an unlimited number of texts will refer to the same Field as if assuming its existence outside of the single text to which many texts may refer. Even when a new theory is introduced (Psychoanalysis, Existentialism or nuclear physics), further texts dealing with this theory will refer to the same constructed

Field and its referents as did the first text, although constantly developing and reshuffling it.

In addition, science and philosophy lack the concomitant properties of the literary IFR, being modeled as it is upon the "real" world, its "concrete" aspects and multidimensionality (in the sense of #14). Myth and historiography may share some of these features with literature, without, however, surrendering the claim for a Field outside of the single text.

24. The issue becomes more complicated when writers use the same characters or events in several works of literature, as if mapping them on one hypothetical continuum, a "super-Field" (e.g., Balzac's *Human Comedy*). But this is not an open-ended series of texts, to which anyone can add, as a science may be.

25. The advantage of using the theory of the Internal FR rather than such terms as "World" ("fictional world" or "possible world"), with "objects," "characters" and "events" existing in it, is twofold: a) A direct link is created between the projected "world" and linguistic reference, hence between the ontology of literature and the analysis of language. b) No definite existing objects, characters, events, ideas or attitudes are assumed, merely frames of reference of such kinds, to which language in the text relates or may be related, by various speakers and from various positions. These *frs* are not necessarily stable, may be constructed and reconstructed, the linguistic evidence may be complementary or contradictory, incomplete or false, uncertain or disjointed, etc. Hence, the current debates on interpretation and deconstruction are not foreclosed by this theory. The theory does not separate fictional projection and readers' imagination from the nature of language mediating it. Neither does it forsake the first for the second.

EXTERNAL FIELDS OF REFERENCE

26. If literary texts simply constituted Internal Fields of Reference, separated from the world and from other texts, we could call them "fictions" and limit our analysis to their internal structure. This, however, is only half the story. Works of literature are usually not pure "fictional worlds," their texts are not made of mere "fictional" propositions or of a pure "fictional" language. Meanings in literary texts are related not only to the Internal FR (which, indeed, is unique to it) but to External FRs as well. This double-layered nature of literary reference is an essential feature of literature.

External Fields of Reference (ExFR) are any FRs outside of a given text: the real world in time and space, history, a philosophy, ideologies, views of human nature, other texts. A literary text may either refer directly to or invoke *frs* from such External FRs. This category includes not only such obvious external referents as names of places and streets, historical events and dates, or actual historical figures, but also various statements about human nature, society, technology, national character, psychology, religion, etc.

27. An example from a realistic novel can be seen in the opening of Balzac's *Le cousin Pons*:

> Vers trois heures de l'après-midi, dans le mois d'octobre de l'année 1844, un homme âgé d'une soixantaine d'années, mais à qui tout le monde eut donné plus que cet âge, allait le long du boulevard des Italiens, le nez à la piste, les lèvres papelardes, comme un négociant qui vient de conclure une excellente affaire, ou comme un garçon content de lui-même au sortir d'un boudoir.
>
> C'est à Paris la plus grande expression connue de la satisfaction personnelle chez l'homme.

> [Around three o'clock in the afternoon, in the month of October in the year 1844, a man of about sixty, but who looked older, was walking along the Boulevard des Italiens sniffling and muttering like a merchant who has just closed a good deal or a self-satisfied bachelor emerging from a boudoir.
>
> In Paris, that is the greatest known expression of personal satisfaction in man.]

Granted, the convention of fiction prevents us from seriously claiming that this particular man actually walked in Paris on that day (which day?). However, the year, month, Boulevard des Italiens, Paris are all referents in the real world as well as in the fictional space. If the text does not refer to them directly, it, at least, *evokes* them, presents them to the reader's imagination.

To separate the text from a description of the External FR (Paris), a typical signal of fictionality is used: though the month and the hour are mentioned precisely, one specific indicator, the day, is *floated*. This device indicates that the fictional time and space, however closely located in relation to the real world, is somehow suspended above it, has its own, "floating" coordinates. Such floating may take on a variety of forms: "on one July evening of 1805," "in the year 183*," "the city N.," "he woke up in the morning," or may not appear at all, depending on various and changing conventions.

28. The establishment of the first set of referents in a novel—or any other IFR—may be called *referential grounding.* Unlike the traditional term, "exposition," which is limited to the antecedents in time of the Reconstructed World of the novel, referential grounding deals with the opening of the *Text Continuum* and allows for any kind of referents to be used.

The opening of a text must introduce several specific and concrete referents, from which the other referents in the IFR are developed by extension. The early referents are often "minor" from the point of view of the hierarchy as developed in the text as a whole. This is due to the need to establish some coordinates as soon as possible for an acceptable fictional world in which the story unfolds. For this purpose, "minor" referents are plausible: they can be convincingly accounted for in a limited space. When more important referents are eventually introduced, they appear in the text not out of the blue ("*deus ex machina*"), but as extensions of already established *frs.*

This tendency may be observed on all levels of the presented world. Thus, secondary characters often precede the introduction of more central characters, who are then presented in the context of persons familiar to the reader. Similarly, a setting may precede the unfolding of persons, who then are placed in it. In Tolstoy's *War and Peace*, the text opens *in medias res* with a concrete dialogue from which the persons of the two interlocutors are then built up; these interlocutors themselves are minor characters in the novel, their circle is enlarged in a party, where some of the major characters of the novel (Pierre, Andrei) are eventually introduced: though presented in the party on an equal footing with the others, they are soon promoted to center stage, to be developed independently later; the party itself is a minor scene in comparison with the more central scenes of the novel, both in respect to history and to the more intense personal relationships. Yet it establishes the referential grounding for the whole novel.

A similar device (in a nutshell) is used in Joyce's "Eveline": the most detailed object in the physical world presented in the two opening paragraphs is the new "houses"; they are not even mentioned in the story after that, but as soon as their identity is established, Eveline's "home" is introduced in opposition to these "houses"; and this *home*, of which almost no physical details are given, becomes the symbolic space of the story.

A text may also open with a generalization, a general description or an essay—usually on matters in an External FR—from which more concrete or individual—Internal—examples are then deduced. Another typical opening is a schematic presentation of the *contours* of an IFR or a central aspect of it (its physical space, a basic tension), which is then elaborated and filled with details as the text unfolds. Often, a relatively general yet specific view (e.g., of a landscape) is presented, within which a close-up will zoom in to a more detailed scene. Thus, Joyce's short story "Two Gallants" opens with a description of a warm Sunday evening with crowds strolling in the streets; and the second paragraph zooms in to observe a detail: two particular individuals walking on a specific street, who then become the main characters of the story.

In many cases, both directions, though seemingly contradictory, are combined: an opening with a wider framework, establishing some general contours of the IFR to be detailed later, on the one hand; and the introduction of relatively minor referents, to be extended to more important ones (in the hierarchy of the final text), on the other.

29. A widespread technique of referential grounding is the *anchoring* of a new constructed IFR in some accepted external frame of reference, such as Paris in Balzac's example above. This may be used for the opening, as well as for the text as a whole.

Works of fiction are often anchored in:

– a historical time and place (in novels and short stories by Balzac, Stendhal, Tolstoy);

– the weather, season or time of day (in Turgenev's novels, Joyce's short stories or Japanese Haiku);

– a mythology or national perception of history (in Greek tragedy, Biblical stories, Russian bylinas);

– a combination of these (in T.S. Eliot's *The Waste Land*).

In lyrical poetry a new poem may be anchored in the *persona* of the poet as established in other poems.

The author's newly introduced fictional referents, then, are presented as extensions of referents known outside the fiction; together, they constitute one new internally coherent Field.

30. While using referents from known External FRs, the Internal FR can draw freely on information about such ExFRs. In the Balzac example: Paris, its social structure and urban nature; the street mentioned, its environment and extensions; the period and political regime, etc.—all are available for

the reader's construction of the IFR. To what extent the External field will be used for specific knowledge or merely for background and atmosphere depends on the particular text and may be open to the dialectics of a negotiated interpretation.

31. John Searle cites an example from a novel by Iris Murdoch entitled *The Red and the Green*, which begins:

> Ten more glorious days without horses! So thought Second Lieutenant Andrew Chase-White recently commissioned in the distinguished regiment of King Edward's Horse, as he pottered contentedly in a garden on the outskirts of Dublin on a sunny Sunday afternoon in April nineteen-sixteen.

Searle argues rightly that the author "is not held to be insincere if in fact she does not believe for one moment that there actually was such a character thinking about horses that day in Dublin." The other side of the coin, however, is that this opening is well anchored in the External FR, it actually constructs the first image of its fictional world (in our terms: the referential grounding of the Internal FR) on the basis of the readers' knowledge of such external frames. The year nineteen-sixteen (during World War One), Dublin and on the other hand the British army in Ireland before independence—these are indispensable stores of background information opened by the author. They are referents in both the Internal and External FRs. Though no proposition is explicitly made about them in the External FR, they are evoked and thus presented to the reader's imagination. We may not know whether there actually was such a regiment of "King Edward's Horse"; if yes, it may add to the characteristics of the Second Lieutenant; if not, it may be relevant to find out whether the name is coined from similar names or conveys a parodic stance. Even the garden on the outskirts of Dublin and the sunny Sunday afternoon, though clearly not related to any specific referents in Dublin, draw upon the ExFR (compare, for example, such settings in New Delhi).

The last sentence in the Balzac example ("In Paris, that is the greatest known expression of personal satisfaction in man") is a typical *double-directed statement*. It refers at the same time both to the real Paris in the External FR and to the selection from Paris presented in the IFR. If we accept it as true for the External FR, we draw from this Paris a whole aura and social myth for the IFR. But even if we do not accept it as true, it may not disturb the coherence of the Internal FR. Furthermore, we reflect back on the speaker (or the narrator) and from such a "one-sided" statement construct his attitudes or the attitudes of the figures thus characterized or of society as represented in the novel. We then see it as part of Balzac's (or some character's) view of Paris.

32. A statement about the External FR may be slanted or false; we do not judge the aesthetic value of the novel by the truth value of such statements. But its external truth value is not immaterial for an interpretation. If it clearly deviates from some normal view of the given External FR but is coherent with the Internal FR, it may then expose the particular view of the world it represents.

Thus, Dostoevsky tells us that, when old Fyodor Karamazov learned of his wife's death, according to some sources he rejoiced and according to others he sobbed like a child; according to the narrator himself:

> Quite likely both versions are true, that is to say, that he rejoiced at his release and wept for her who had given him his freedom—at one and the same time. In the majority of cases, people, even evil-doers, are much more naïve and artless than we generally assume. As, indeed, we are ourselves (p. 6).

It is not hard to imagine readers who would object to being included in such a generalization. For the Internal world, however, it demonstrates the basic love-hate psychology which explains the behavior of Dostoevsky's characters. Indeed, when Tolstoy was invited to see a dramatized novel of Dostoevsky, he refused, claiming that Dostoevsky's characters always behave precisely as they are not expected to behave. That is, for Tolstoy, Dostoevsky's statements on human nature are false in the External FR. This deviation, however, from an accepted view of human nature is one of the reasons for Dostoevsky's impact as a writer. It cannot be accounted for without the tension between the two referential directions.

33. Similarly, the description of Napoleon in Tolstoy's *War and Peace* is a biased selection from what was known to Tolstoy about Napoleon, made for purposes of structure (as Shklovsky has shown) as well as of Tolstoy's historiosophic ideology. No doubt, in many places of the novel the text is unclear unless the reader supplements it with outside knowledge about figures and events in history. (Annotations serve this purpose for the modern reader.) However, to what extent Napoleon, as presented in the IFR, should be taken within the presented limits and to what extent the reader may, or should, draw on the Field of outside knowledge cannot be decided in advance, but has to be negotiated in an interpretation. The important thing is that the store of historical knowledge was opened for the reader. In any case, the juxtaposition between the two Napoleon constructs—the "historical" and the fictional—

tells us a great deal about Tolstoy's Russian point of view or about his questioning of the role of leaders in history.

34. A text does not always rely on the reader's knowledge of external *frs*. In the continuation of Balzac's chapter, we read:

> Ce vieillard, sec et maigre, portait un spencer couleur noisette sur un habit verdâtre à boutons de metal blanc!...

> [This thin dry old man wore a nut-colored spencer over a greenish coat with white metal buttons!...]

Balzac finds it necessary to explain the nature and history of this external referent:

> Un homme en spencer, en 1844, voyez-vous, comme si Napoléon eut daigné ressusciter pour deux heures. Le spencer fut inventé, comme son nom l'indique, par un lord sans doute vain de sa jolie taille.

> [A man in a spencer in 1844, you see, is as if Napoleon had deigned to come back to life for two hours. The spencer, as its name indicates, was invented by a lord who was doubtless vain about his handsome build.] (And a long explanation follows.)

In the twentieth century, writers tend to rely more on the reader for such information. (Though Balzac obviously does not merely explain the term but uses the excursus for characterization, creation of historical perspective, etc.)

35. We may now return to the theoretical model. An Internal Field of Reference is constructed as a plane parallel to the real world. In realistic fiction, its events take place in known history and geography, sometimes with precisely specified names of places and dates, sometimes using various signals of fictionality through floating some of the specific indicators, sometimes merely suspended "somewhere" in history: nineteenth-century Russia, in the Middle Ages, in a modern city, etc.; situations and behavior resemble (or are different from or otherwise related to) those in the real world. Thus, the Internal FR is projected as parallel to an External FR. But parallel planes never meet. A character cannot walk out of a fictional house and show up in a real café.

These, however, are "non-Euclidean" parallel planes: though they never merge, they may overlap at several (or many) points: many individual referents and even whole frames of reference are *shared* by both the Internal and

External FRs. Such shared *frs* may include historical figures, descriptions of a city, discussions of psychoanalysis, the modes of American advertising or the description of D-Day. Indeed, many popular novels, though featuring invented characters, quite openly propose to teach the reader about various aspects of the world.

36. Thus, we have two separate but parallel planes, intersecting at several points. Each of these planes has its own continuation outside of the shared referents; for each, the shared elements are merely points in a consistent continuity. For the External FRs, we have more information outside of the given text: Paris continues beyond the streets mentioned; the philosophy of history has examples and arguments beyond those presented in *War and Peace*. On the other hand, the Internal FR includes the shared points in its own proportions and extends them by adding unique referents: even if all the streets named in a novel are real streets, their selection creates an isolated cluster and there will be indoor settings unique to the IFR. Though modeled upon external examples, the Internal Field is unique and internally coherent.

37. We may represent the relationship in the following diagram:

"Double-Decker" Model of Reference in Literature

N – Narrator, S – Speaker, *r* – referent, *fr* – frame of reference,
IFR – Internal Fields of Reference, ExFR – External Fields of Reference.

The arrows between the level of "Speakers and Positions" (N, S) and the constructed Fields indicate that the Narrator and all other Speakers in the text are sources of information about the IFR and about the ExFRs and, at the same time, are constructed from the IFR. The Text and the IFR have boundaries, while the ExFRs are open and "limitless."

38. This model explains the dual referential allegiance of statements as well as of any material that may be referred to or simply located in internal or external FRs. The links between the two parallel planes create *channels* for the possible transfer of additional semantic material from one to the other, and vice versa. This is true for the relations of fiction to the historical world, to nature, to theories, beliefs and ideologies, as well as to other texts. Joyce's allusion in the title of his book, *Ulysses*, opens up Homer's work as a huge store of potential transfers—of character, motifs and composition. What precisely is relevant and legitimate in such transfers must be judged specifically through an argumentative analysis and comparison of the receiving and source FRs.

39. Thus we have in a text direct reference to External FRs as well as to the Internal FR and also sharing of referents and frames of reference. As the diagram shows, there are two additional operations: *modeling* and *representation*. Though not linguistic in nature—we are not limited here to direct statements or propositions—these are powerful devices for relating the Internal plane to External planes of various kinds.

On the one hand, the construction of the Internal FR is *modeled* upon External FRs: we need knowledge of the world to make sense of a work of fiction, construct the frames of reference from scattered material, fill in the gaps, create the necessary hierarchies, even to understand the word "party." On the other hand, there is a relation of *representation* from the IFR to External FRs: certain behavior, scenes, complex meaning constructs may be understood as "typical" (or "atypical" or otherwise representative) when projected upon history, human nature, urban society, or any other generalized FR (in traditional terms: the author has powers of "observation" or conveys a "message"). The specific interaction between relevant patterns in the IFR and constructs in the external world is again a matter of argumentative hypotheses.

40. This model is by no means limited to realistic works of literature. Any kind of deviation from realism can be ascertained only through the juxtaposition of these two planes. The double-decker structure of reference is indispensable for the understanding of Kafka, Gogol, folklore or Surrealism, as

much as for realistic fiction. It is also crucial for the understanding of lyrical poetry, the study of which has centered for too long on questions of poetic language.

41. Literature as a phenomenon in society is a different matter: it is a complex and open-ended conglomerate of genres, norms, trends, writers, institutions, publishing houses, journals, mediating agencies and so on, embedded in the polysystem of a culture (as defined by I. Even-Zohar). The locus, however, of all those phenomena is the individual work of literature.

2 METAPHOR AND FRAMES OF REFERENCE

With Examples from Eliot, Rilke, Mayakovsky,
Mandelshtam, Pound, Creeley, Amichai,
and the *New York Times*

> Metaphor again? This time, an attempt to observe it as part of
> the poetic fiction—rather than as a mere device of language.

1

Metaphor is a curious case. Perhaps it reflects the current state of poetics in relation to other fields of the humanities. On the one hand, there is an endless cross-disciplinary procession of theoretical books and papers on the subject. One wave peaked in the nineteen fifties and sixties, another has developed in recent years. Important contributions have been made to the clarification of the basic notions of a theory of metaphor. Characteristically, many of the significant studies have come from disciplines outside of literary criticism such as philosophy, psychology, linguistics, which are usually better trained in rational theoretical analysis.

However, many of these theoretical writings are interested primarily in a definition, in explaining what "metaphor" *is*, rather than in developing tools for description and research of actual metaphorical texts. With a phenomenon as omnipresent as metaphor (especially metaphor in poetry), a definition will merely provide a label rather than enhance observation of the complex semantic relations or illuminate the differences between various poets and poems.

Furthermore, it is not at all clear that "metaphor" (or "literature" itself) is a well-defined class *sui generis*, with properties all its own. Analogy, similarity, comparison, interaction, etc., appear in metaphors (perhaps not in all of them) and appear elsewhere too. Arguments about their possible inclusion in a definition of metaphor are less crucial than the question of what forms such relations may take if and whenever they appear.

Secondly, many theories of metaphor are based on simple examples, often domesticated and automatized in language (e.g., Max Black's "man is a wolf" or John Searle's "Sally is a block of ice," which, of course, serve their own purposes well). It is not clear that such observations are transferable to more extensive and obscure instances of creative metaphors, either in poetry or in journalism and in everyday speech.

In the following pages, I shall try to approach the problem of metaphor from a different angle. Anyone who has dealt with this subject will understand why I have decided to forgo a preliminary discussion of existing theories: a careful analysis of the major contributions alone would require a whole book, as has been shown so admirably by Paul Ricoeur.[1] I shall analyze some cases of metaphors in Modernist poetry and then observe similar phenomena in non-poetic texts. Rather than isolating the category of metaphor as an independent unit of language, I shall deal with it in the framework of a more general theory of literary texts and text semantics.

2

To begin, we must eliminate a number of preconceived notions which are still implicit in various definitions of metaphor. Metaphor cannot be limited to:

- *one word*, which has changed its meaning or a *name* transferred to a foreign object;

- the boundaries of a *sentence*, which has a metaphorical "focus" within a "frame" (in Max Black's terms);

- a *discrete*, static, prefabricated *"unit"* with limited boundaries, like a morpheme or a word;

- the level of *"language"* or "meaning units" as separate from the level of "represented objects" and the "World" of a poem (in the sense of Roman Ingarden's separate strata).

---

1   In 1964, at the Hebrew University, Jerusalem, I edited an in-house anthology of major theories of metaphor, which is quite similar in scope to the studies surveyed in Ricoeur's book.

As we shall see in the following examples, metaphors may be any of these but are not usually so. If a metaphor is a two-term relation, any of its terms may cover much more than a word in a text. It is often an open-ended relation rather than a fixed unit. A whole sentence may be literal when read independently and become metaphorical in its wider context. A metaphor in poetry may begin with a connotation of a word and grow into a central object in the fictional situation of a poem; i.e., it may stretch between the "style" and the "World" of a poem (see Rilke's "God in the Middle Ages," below).

The point is that metaphor is not a linguistic unit but a text-semantic pattern, and semantic patterns in texts are not segments of the linear text and cannot be identified with units of syntax. Isolating metaphor as a linguistic unit would mean separating the processing of language from a reader's processing of texts, including the construction of fictional (or, in Husserl's terms, "intentional") characters, settings and "worlds," as projected in works of literature. It would also mean isolating the theory of metaphor from the problems of contemporary theories of literary texts, their interpretations, constructions, and deconstructions.

In short, we must observe metaphors in literature not as static, discrete units, but as context-sensitive, dynamic patterns, changing in the text continuum, relating to specific (fictional or real) frames of reference and dependent on interpretations. The study of metaphor is thus lifted out of Stylistics or Rhetoric and located in the study of what I propose to call "Integrational Semantics" (see Chapter 3), which occupies part of the traditional broad field of "Pragmatics."

3

Let us first observe a rather simple example. In his book, *A Study of Metaphor*, J. J. A. Mooij quotes a passage from W. H. Auden's poem on the Portuguese colony "Macao":

(16) A weed from Catholic Europe, it *took root*
Between the yellow mountains and the sea,
And *bore* these gay stone houses like a fruit,
And *grew on* China imperceptibly.

The scholar underlines his metaphors and observes:

> As to (16), the metaphorical character of "weed" and "took root" is consider-
> ably clearer than that of "grew on"—therefore it was not without some hesita-
> tion that I italicized "grew on" (Mooij 1976:2, 6).

This hesitation can be cleared up if we approach metaphor from a different perspective. A metaphor exists only if two domains exist vividly in a
text; the metaphorical expressions belong literally to one and metaphorically
to the other. The words "bore" and "grew on" may not be metaphors at all,
as so many "dead metaphors" codified in language. They are rather semes
of polysemic words, which have one seme for the designation of a concrete
object and another for some abstract relation or psychological state (often
considered "metaphorical," e.g., "a gray life" or "a warm person"). However,
unlike diachronically metaphorical words (such as "window" originating
from the equivalent of "wind's eye"), in which metaphor was merely the process by which a new word was created, "dead metaphors" are still living in the
language as dead *metaphors* and can be revived. For the same words preserve
their concrete ("literal") meaning in another context in the same synchronic
stage of the language (e.g., "bore a grudge" or "bore a burden" vs. "bore a
child" or "bore fruit"). In order to deautomatize the dead metaphor, such a
context must be provided.

Indeed, in Auden's poem, two *frames of reference* are established: one is the
Catholic city of Macao with its stone houses growing on the side of continen-
tal China; the other is a weed, taking root, growing, bearing fruit, etc. The
first frame of reference, "Macao" (fr_1), is presented as *existing* in the world
of the poem (it is further enriched from what we know about the external
world indicated by the real geographical names). The second frame of reference (fr_2), "the weed," is introduced as *non-existing* in the fictional world of
the poem, as brought in for the sake of comparison. It is not even referred to
directly, merely provided with scattered semantic material. As such, however,
it is presented to the imagination of the reader for the sake of metaphorical
transfers. The text exploits the frame of reference of a plant (fr_2) for several
possible connotations, moreover: it develops the weed image in additional directions. These include the "fruit" (not essential to a weed) as well as aspects
not mentioned directly, such as the continuity of an enormous growth, stub-
bornly spreading "between the yellow mountains and the sea."

We could filter out the two frames of reference in the language of this text in the following manner:

fr_1 "Macao"	fr_2 "the weed"
A ... [transplant] ... from Catholic Europe, it took root	A weed ... took root
Between the yellow mountains and the sea,	Between the yellow mountains and the sea,
And bore these gay stone houses ...	And bore ... a fruit
And grew on China imperceptibly.	And grew ... imperceptibly.

As we see, a considerable part of the language may be applied, without change, in either direction.

In this poem, two independent frames of reference are developed, entering mutual relationships in several forms: an identity metaphor (Macao = "weed"); revived linguistic dead metaphors ("took root," "bore," "grew"); a simile ("like a fruit"). Such relations may involve either a whole *fr* or its parts or aspects; e.g., "a fruit" is related directly only to the houses, though it is open for a metaphorical transfer to the whole colony and its culture.

The juxtaposition of the two *fr*s may serve not only for similarity transfers but for any other relations between the thematics and the language representing either. Thus, a "weed" has negative connotations, representing the point of view of China; and it clashes with the positive connotations of "fruit" and the perhaps naïve illusion of "gay" stone houses, representing the internal point of view of Macao. A shift of point of view within what may be called one metaphor—akin to Picasso's wish to see the feminine face simultaneously from two perspectives—is not uncommon in metaphorical patterns.

Under the circumstances, there should be no hesitation as to the metaphoricity of "grew on." Why should we separate the several language metaphors in this strophe, and how can we disregard their continuity? "Grew on" becomes *metaphorical* in relation to Macao precisely because it is related *literally* to the weed, it is part of a concrete image for the reader to visualize. In other words, it is metaphorical for fr_1, because it is literal in fr_2.

As we see here, there is a textual interpenetration between fr_1 (Macao) and fr_2 (plant). Not only is fr_1 described in terms of fr_2, but fr_2 is reinforced in the imagination from the description of fr_1: Macao is like a weed, but it is a stranded weed, far from its source and also enormous and vital, like Macao clinging to the shore of China. In other words, we observe a two-way process: the image of the weed is magnified by the description (and geography) of Macao and then, in turn, as a huge, city-size weed, it reinforces the description of the city.

Metaphor:

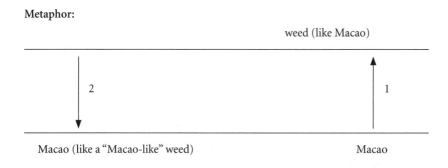

Figure 1

This is precisely the process observed elsewhere (Chapter 6) in sound-meaning interactions: sounds obtain their meaning-tone from some of the co-textual meanings in order then to imbue the text with this tone, reinforce it. E.g., when a critic feels that the many sibilants in Shakespeare's sonnet ("When to the sessions of sweet silent thought / I summon up remembrance of things past," etc.) express a "hushing quality" (Kreuzer 1955), he is transferring a connotation of the meaning in "sweet silent thought" to the sound-pattern, then uses this sound pattern, as colored by such a meaning-tone, to return and suffuse with it the meaning of the whole strophe.

In short, the sibilants absorbed the tone of "sweet, silent thought," and as such colored the whole text. The diagrammatic structure is the same (Figure 2).

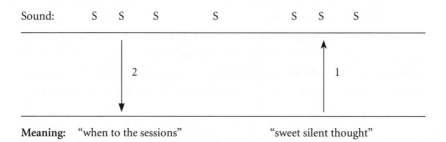

Figure 2

The interpenetration of the two domains is reinforced by the interchange-ability of words: the verbs "took root," "bore," "grew on"—which display a literal-metaphoric tension in their polysemic structure—serve in one lexical capacity in fr_1 and in another in fr_2. As a matter of fact, in this text, "bore" shifts metaphorically from a seme meaning carrying, bearing a burden, in the beginning of the line ("and bore these gay stone houses") to a seme implying fruit-bearing, when the reader is surprised by the simile "like a fruit" (the first seme cannot be "like" a fruit at all).

4

Since metaphors involve relations of meaning—though their import is not of meaning alone—their understanding must rely on a theory of meaning as established in texts. We cannot be satisfied, for example, with a classification of metaphors by parts of speech.[2] Neither can a theory of metaphor be based on syntax. A sentence is not the actual semantic "frame" to which the meta-phorical "focus" relates (as proposed in Max Black's landmark paper, 1962); the alignment of semes on both sides of a metaphor is not necessarily bound to syntactic frames.

Paul Ricoeur has argued for the preservation of two complementary theo-ries of metaphor, using the distinction between "semiotics" and "semantics" as defined by Emile Benveniste, the first based on the word as a sign, the sec-ond on the sentence. "The sentence is the unit of discourse," says Benveniste (as quoted by Ricoeur 1997:68). I would suggest that there is another unit of discourse: the *frame of reference (fr)*, to be constructed by the reader, provid-ing the base for a third, complementary and encompassing, theory of met-aphor. Though not recognized by linguists (because it is not a segment of language and has no grammatically formalized properties), no text coherence can be understood without it.

Both the sentence and the *fr* combine words in a text; but the *fr* goes off, as it were, on a tangent: it selects some parts of a sentence and adds them to (parts of) other sentences, using "reality-like" models. A sentence is a linear unit occupying a stretch of the text; whereas an *fr* is a construct based on dis-

---

2   Such a classification was explored by Christine Brooke-Rose in her *Grammar of Metaphor* (1958), a book full of excellent observations, which does show the relevance of grammatical categories as one important parameter forming metaphor.

continuous elements in a text, which are linked to each other by some kind of a flexible but necessary "semantic syntax."

According to Benveniste, "propositions can be set one after the other in a consecutive relationship, but they cannot be integrated in a higher level," as phonemes are integrated in morphemes and morphemes in a sentence. For this reason, though containing signs, a sentence is not a sign (since a sign requires such a hierarchical relation) (see Ricoeur 1977:68). Yet a sentence, we may add, is the first, linear level of linking signs (words and morphemes) into a text and, as such, is indispensable for text formation. A string of sentences forms a text. But this is only the "floor" upon which all meaning constructs are built. Text formation is not equivalent with meaning formation and text integration.

Frames of reference, on the other hand, can be integrated on a higher level: in higher *frs* and, ultimately, in a Field of Reference (FR). The FR, in turn, can be integrated in the "World" and serve so-called "symbolic" or "modeling," i.e., signifying functions. Granted, both *fr* and FR are flexible units, they allow for a free play of constructs (within the limits provided by the text), whereas sentences have fixed forms. For that, however, the former preserve sign characteristics.

The network of *frs* presents what the text is *about*. They provide the bridge between words of a natural language and the representation of the ever-changing "World." They serve, too, for the transition from the lower, formalized levels of language to the open, individually contextualized, thematic bodies of communication. By means of *frs*, we speak with "world-experience" rather than with codified categories—words of a limited language. We send the reader to an ever-changing, open *Network of Information* and manipulate his knowledge of it, rather than convey all we want to say merely by the words used.

Therefore, a theory of metaphor would benefit from being based on frames of reference as the real units of a semantically integrated text. Within this framework, we may preserve whatever contributions to metaphor are made on the lower levels: syntactic deviance, morphological tropes, sound patterns, neologisms, etc.; all may *signal* a metaphor or provide it with additional formal parameters, on condition that they are accepted by the decisive, semantic factor.

Before attending to concrete analyses of poetic metaphors, I shall characterize in segment 5 the general traits of the main concept I use to describe them: "frames of reference."

5

The basic unit of semantic integration is not a sentence but a *frame of reference* (*fr*). An *fr* is any continuum of two or more referents to which parts of a text or its interpretations may relate: either referring directly and describing or simply mentioning, implying, or evoking. It may indicate an object, a scene, a situation, a person, a state of affairs, a mental state, a history, a theory; it may be real, hypothetical, or fictional. It may appear in reality or in the reader's network of knowledge, or projected uniquely in a given text. Its ontological status is immaterial to semantics: it is anything we can talk about, no matter whether and how it exists.

We may use any object that we know about (from direct experience or mediated via models, pictures, or texts) as a frame of reference: a pillow, a house, a city, a philosophy, a love story, the state of the economy, the haze in autumn trees. We may also refer to *fr*s which we cannot observe directly. We may distinguish between a *present* and an *absent fr*, the latter not directly present in the speech situation; a *known* or an *unknown fr*, of which the hearer may have no previous knowledge; an *existing* or *fictional* (imaginary) *fr*, invented by the speaker.

The amount of information about an *fr* given in a text or available outside of the text may be detailed or partial or spotty: it is not a complete object, merely a frame of reference to which we can refer, in which we can indicate specific referents. Thus, material objects or scenes in fiction, as well as characters, ideas, or experiences, do not have to be defined or presented in full in a text; they may simply be named, referred to, hinted at, or evoked through some of their details. Their existence in the "real" world or in the "fictional world" of a poem or a novel may not be certain at all, their details or forms questionable, depending: (a) on possible knowledge about them from outside the given text; (b) on the speakers and positions ("Points of View") through which information about the *fr* was presented in the text; and (c) on readers' temporary or conclusive, changing or recurring, semantic constructs ("readings" and "interpretations").

Semantic elements in discourse are linked to each other by means of syntax as well as by various devices described in theories of discourse. One of these is "*coreferentiality*," linking two discontinuous words by means of a common referent (the "Morning Star" and the "Evening Star" refer to the same object). The concept of *fr* widens this relation: *co-relatedness in one fr (co-fr)* is a major tool for integrating discourse. If one sentence has a door opened and the next talks about clothing "strewn about," they are linked by a hypothetical *fr*—"room"—as much as if they were linked by syntax.[3] When an *fr* is established—in a text or in an interpretation—semantic elements relating to it will be brought together, integrated with each other. For example, a Freudian hypothesis on a character's Oedipus complex, even if never mentioned in the text, will select and relate such elements of the text which may support this hypothesis (see Ernest Jones's psychoanalytic reading of *Hamlet*).

Such an integration may fill in complementary details, create mutually specified and individualized properties, or—on the contrary—create tensions and contradictions between mutually exclusive positions. This integration works on all levels. For example, when one sentence has "new red houses" and a later sentence has "bright brick houses," the redness becomes redness of bricks, the brightness brightness of red bricks, and the houses become "red-brick housing," a social concept much wider than the separate adjectives may suggest (see my analysis of Joyce's "Eveline" in Chapter 3).

Within any possible *fr* there must be indeterminacies (as suggested by Roman Ingarden), spots not specified in the text, many of which remain indeterminate: no piece of "reality" can be represented in language in all its detail. However, only some of those indeterminacies become *gaps*—as required by the structure of the text or the demands of a reading—to be filled in by the reader. Naturally, such gap-filling encourages reconsideration or enables the formulation of several competing solutions as the text unfolds or as reading history develops.

An actual reading does not usually exhaust all possible relationships in a text or the integration of all elements which may be brought together in one *fr*. Actual readings are selections from, or approximations in various degrees to, a fully integrated meaning-complex of a text. Readers may be encouraged in their semantic integration by various devices of the text or by traditions of reading and genre or by the nature of a *known fr* or by the need to explain or to justify intuitions (e.g., in a written interpretation). An important guide is the global semantic organization of a text.

*fr*s are built of two strains: they are modeled upon *typical* "frames" external to the text (e.g., a room, a hospital, paranoia) and simultaneously *individualized*, provided with atypical referents, specific to a given *fr* (including

---

3   Here, and below, I refer briefly to examples analyzed in Chapter 3.

proper names). In the unfolding of a text, any subsequent material related to an established *fr* must be constrained by the individual features (and, in turn, constrain or revise them).

The boundaries of *fr*s are not fixed, they depend on any possible way of organizing the "World" of comprehension. Two continuous *fr*s (e.g., a person and a street) may merge into one ("person in the street") or be separated for separate attention. *fr*s, or information obtaining in them, may be constructed and deconstructed as a reading unfolds, or in consecutive readings.

An *fr* is not identical with a segment of a text. Indeed, a segment may often be *constituted* by one *fr* (a description of a room, historiosophical considerations, a portrait of a character, etc.). But the same *fr* may receive additional material in other segments or outside the text. Thus, a passage describing a character or an event may be supplemented or contradicted in later passages of the same text. Or a newspaper passage referring to a blast in Beirut may be supplemented, modified, or contradicted by previous, later, or outside information. On the other hand, in any segment of a text constituted by one *fr*, there is also material for the potential construction of other, intersecting *fr*s, e.g., a description of a party includes topics of discourse, which may become central *fr*s in the novel. It includes also people, each of whom may become an *fr* in his or her own right, subsequently unfolded in other parts of the text. The theory of "motifs" as the smallest thematic segments of a text (and Barthes's structuralist "functions" and "indices") collapsed and confused the two (*fr* and segment—basic units of the World and of the Text, respectively).

A number of *fr*s are related to each other in a larger whole: a *Field of Reference* (FR), a hypothetical, discontinuous universe (such as the USA, World War II, Philosophy). A literary text creates an *Internal Field of Reference* (IFR), containing a set of referents exclusive to this text (the so-called "fictional world" of the novel), though it may at the same time refer to *External* FRs as well.

To sum up, *fr*s are not necessarily full-fledged "represented objects" (Ingarden's "Gegenständlichkeiten") but frames that the text, its voices, or its readers may relate to. They are not stable. Their ontology is irrelevant to their textual (and experiential) existence. Using this concept for the description of metaphors, we are not bound by the stability of "objects" or their fixed "associated commonplaces" (Black), but rather depend on the individual features of a specific *fr* and its possible gap-filling. Moreover, we do not limit metaphor to relations between real objects, but use the same terminology if one term of the metaphor is a state of affairs, an abstract concept ("love"), a mood, a religion, an idea.

Here, however, one must stress the crucial role played by the textual mediation of frames of reference. Since *frs* are presented to us in a text not as discrete objects but as patterns of language, usually linking a number of elements (words or sentences or subpatterns), each of those elements, or any combination of them, can have autonomous relations of their own to their immediate or wider context, within this *fr* or outside it. Therefore there may be simultaneously a global relation between two *frs* (two brothers in a novel or two terms of a metaphor) as well as local relations between their parts in different contexts as well as any other kind of patterning: of stylistic, semantic, syntactic, morphological, or sound aspects of the language used. Such relations may include metaphorical transfers as well as other kinds of semantic and non-semantic interactions. And they may include a "dynamic" aspect, employing the sequential nature of a text for the sake of changing relations (and changing the reader's experience and expectations), in metaphor as in any other respect.

6

T. S. Eliot opened his first collection of poems with an "image" (as the New Critics called it) that was still sufficiently shocking in 1939 for Cleanth Brooks to include it in his defense of Modernist poetry ("Metaphor and the Tradition," Brooks 1965). Indeed, it became a marker of "Modernism" for the whole poem, though most of its language was not as strikingly Modernist at all.

> Let us go then, you and I,
> When the evening is spread out against the sky
> Like a patient etherised upon a table;
>
> (The Love Song of J. Alfred Prufrock)

As often in Modernist poetry, we have here—syntactically and rhetorically—a *simile*, rather than a formal metaphor. The simile links the basic situation of the poem (fr_1) with the "image" of a patient (fr_2). The simile, however, is—as often in Modernist poetry—a mere excuse, a patterning device, linking the two objects through one common property: the *tertium comparationis* of "spread out." As any interpretation will show, the trait of being spread out is in itself neither central to the meaning of the poem nor important for the perception of the evening or the speaker. There is, however, in the compared clause, *redundant information.* A man lying on the floor would be enough to illustrate the idea of being "spread out"; the additional specifications ("patient" rather than man, "etherised" rather than lying, "upon a table" rather than floor) require naturalization, or functional integration in the basic situation of the poem.

The compared scene ("a hospital situation") is *denied existence* in the fictional situation of the poem, it can only be integrated through *metaphorical transfers.* Thus, from the point of view of a reader-oriented text theory, or of Integrational Semantics, it is structurally a metaphor indeed; more precisely: a relation with a *metaphorical function.* Instead of metaphor being a channel for similarity relationships, here the simile becomes a channel for *metaphorical transfers.*

The metaphorical transfers, however, do not simply metaphorize individual words: it would be stretching the meaning of the poem to see the evening as someone's patient or to identify in the realistic city scene the equivalents of "ether" or "table." We are encouraged to construct a hypothetical scene (fr_2) of a patient in a hospital waiting for an operation, and see this whole scene in a metaphorical relation to the *basic frame of reference* of the poem. Any property of the secondary *fr* can be transferred to the basic situation except one: its existence. There is no hospital in the streets where Prufrock is walking.

Here a terminological remark is due. I suggest abandoning I. A. Richards's pair of terms, "vehicle" and "tenor," because it implies a limitation of metaphor to a one-directional substitution theory. It seems to assume that the "vehicle" (in the text) stands for some "tenor" and that the "tenor" is absent from the text. This may be true for "A *weed* from Catholic Europe" in the Auden poem. In other cases, however, both domains (*frs*) may be represented in the text. Black's alternative pair, "focus" and "frame," is formulated in syntactic terms, limited to a sentence. In my view, any metaphor, whether presented formally as such or not, requires a metaphorical *transfer* from one *fr* to another. The *fr* to which the transfer is made may be called *base*, and the other one a *secondary fr*, yet the two *frs* may change their functions in the unfolding of the text. We may still keep Black's term, "frame," for that specific part of the *base* to which a part of the secondary *fr*, as a "focus," is related.

As we shall see, however, it is not always clear which is the *base* and which is the secondary *fr* in a poem; it is, however, always clear for a particular metaphorical transfer: semantic material from one ("secondary") *fr* must be naturalized in another (its *base*), "translated" into its language; whereupon the relations may be reversed and the *base* may become a *secondary fr* to its counterpart or to yet another *fr*. I would like to keep the term *base* for the sake of any specific metaphor, as distinguished from the "basic *fr*" of a poem, or of its part.

To return to our example: the word "hospital" does not appear in the text, it is merely the best hypothetical frame of reference which would make sense of all words in line 3 and specify (or "disambiguate") them. Thus, the "table" becomes an operating table (the only seme of this polysemic word that makes sense in conjunction with "ether"); the neologism, "etherised" for "anesthetized," makes the smell concrete, refreshes the whole scene, and adds to the shock value. Thus, just three words map a new *fr* and open up a store of information (hospital, operation, anxiety) available for metaphorical transfer. When we claim that the evening (and further, its metonymies: the city, and the person speaking) attains such qualities as: helpless, passive, semi-conscious, hovering between life and death (of the day? of the person? of his certainties? of love?), we transfer properties of *gaps* in fr_2 ("hospital") not given directly in words of the text.

Thus the metaphor does not simply activate connotations of given words, but also *gaps* in a constructed *fr*. In other words, the evening is compared to "what it feels like" to be a patient etherised upon a table. Indeed, it is not the evening itself, but "what it feels like" to be in such an evening, that is compared to what it feels like to be etherised upon a table; and the first "what it feels like" is further influenced by who it is that feels, as most interpreters queried, which can be reconstructed only from the poem as a whole, perhaps with additional clues from the outside, from T. S. Eliot's attitudes, writings, biography, or the ideas and attitudes of the period.

Therefore, one cannot really speak about precise and specific, discrete meanings that are transferred in this metaphor; the hesitant and hedging language of our interpretation, as of most interpretations of the poem, depends on this need to circumscribe a situation or, better, to name the mutual filtering and mutual fermenting of two unrelated situations. This vagueness or freedom and imprecision in the language of interpretations, accompanied by a profusion of words and circumscriptions, is due to the fact that they interpret not words but readers' reconstructed, though diffuse, empathies with situations (*frs*).

It is one of the praised qualities of poetry that it creates something unavailable in, and irreducible to, codified language (a poem is like a new "word," revealing an insight which has no name in the natural language, as Heidegger described it). There is something radically undecidable, where all solutions are guesses which have to be suggested and taken back at the same time because they were not really expressed "in so many words" and because contradictory solutions hover simultaneously and contribute to the rich, seemingly inexhaustible quality of poetic fiction. This imprecise, inexhaustible, demanding quality of unresolved poetic tensions has a powerful impact on the trained reader, quite unlike direct statements or explicit lexical (or transferred) meanings. What is certain here is not the solution to a relationship but the relationship itself between several frames of reference (as open constructs, to be filled from our world-experience); the material presented to the reader's imagination; as well as the possibilities for several specific, though undecided, solutions. Poetic texts provide us not definite meanings but approximations and open situations.

The secondary *fr* of a metaphor, denied existence in the fictional world of the poem (this is what metaphors do) does not state a belief but sets the reader's imagination in a new situation. It forces on the readers some kind of accommodation between the two, either in metaphoric transfers and semantic resolutions or, at least, in the tension perceived.

Metaphor is one of various modes of speaking about the world not by means of natural language but by using the "language" of the "World," i.e., using fragments of world-experience to convey other experiences. In metaphor, words send the reader to recover such world-cognitions in order to turn them into "world-language" (e.g., the "language" of an operating room—used for the perception of a city scene). It is a language unlimited in scope, full of potential actualizations and rich in reverberations, because it is speaking with *situations* not with concepts, with "world-language" rather than with ready-made signs.

Metaphors are also "concrete universals" (to use Wimsatt's term) in that they present concrete, usually sensuous elements which represent something beyond them. This presentation is extremely abbreviated: no direct description of a hospital scene would be acceptable in three words. *Abbreviation* works in metaphor as it does in flashes of recollection or stream of consciousness—all are forms of secondary *frs*. Furthermore, metaphors are one form of *diverted concreteness*: instead of giving the reader concrete details of what it means to feel in an evening like that, the poem strikes the reader with concrete, sensuous details, but in a secondary domain. Their concreteness is effective, has sharper impact on the reader, precisely because these details are taken out of a continuous, plausible, reality-like context and are not automatized as details of a continuous description may be.

In a standard hospital scene, there are many aspects irrelevant to a possible transfer to the city evening (doctors, nurses, the corridors, white sheets, surgical instruments). Thus it is the basic fr_1, which activates or encourages certain gap-fillings in fr_2, even those that we would not have thought of when first mentioning a hospital scene, and excludes or suppresses others. Such activated gap-fillings (or connotations of a scene) become non-verbal metaphors for fr_1, made explicit in various interpretations. It is, again, a two-way interaction of the type discussed above: the basic scene influences our reading of the secondary situation, which, in turn, illuminates the first. This interdependence of two open frs activates the reader's sensibilities and the interpreters' dialectical negotiating.

Needless to say, the metaphorical transfer described here works only in a certain cultural tradition of "close reading" of poetry which assumes that all elements in a text, as well as the order of all elements, are *functional* to its meaning—an attitude shared by traditional Bible-exegesis, Hermeneutics, Structuralism, the heritage of New Criticism, and Deconstruction. A less functionalist (or a less semantic) view would merely accept the clash, or the juxtaposition, as a rhetorical or poetic effect.

However, even in the framework of such a "maximal meaning" hypothesis, it would be wrong to limit metaphor to its contribution to meaning alone, as some theories seem to suggest. The clash between two frs and their respective language elements, and the various effects this may have on readers, is one of the major non-semantic functions of metaphor. In our case, the metaphorization itself may have been enhanced by the drastic clash between thematically and historically strange materials, included in the two frs. Furthermore, while isolating the simile proper (lines 2–3), only the clash is available; the specifics of transferred meanings are still unclear, their purpose unrevealed. This *clash quality* rather than the specific semantic transfers—even more so, appearing *before* any such semantic naturalization is possible—is what made the poem famous, striking, and Modernist.

Now, because of the two-way interaction, the semantic unit is not closed in lines 2–3 (though the simile is). Indeed, fr_2 ("hospital") seems to be exhausted in line 3, since it receives no further semantic stuff in the immediate continuation: no additional words qualify the hospital scene. But the *base* of the metaphor, fr_1—"the evening"—changes its form as the text unfolds. In lines 2–3, it is still much like a Romantic image of the dying day compared to a human situation, as in Wordsworth's image "The holy time is quiet as a Nun/Breathless with adoration" (quoted by Cleanth Brooks for the purpose of contrast), though, as Brooks points out, Modernist poets introduce "the unpleasant and the obscure" (Brooks 1965:3, 4).

Let us observe: the language of the two *frs* is not separated. "Spread out" is language from the secondary fr_2 (hospital) which penetrated the first fr_1(evening): only metaphorically can an evening be said to be "spread out" like a patient. Furthermore, in order to accept this metaphorical predicate, the evening must become a concrete body occupying only part of visible space (rather than a relational time concept or a quality describing the whole space), which is further underlined by its separation from the sky. Thus, semantic integration requires either metaphorization of "spread out" or concretization of the abstract notion "evening" and counter-intuitive limitation of its scope.

Subsequently, this image of the evening as a concrete spatial body, spread out against the sky (i.e., close to earth), encourages the metonymic transfer from the evening to the evening city. Only the evening city can be seen as a dark body spread out against the sky. Indeed, in the context of the culture of the period in which the poem was published, it is easier to relate sickness to the city rather than to the evening *per se*; the city, in turn, easily becomes a metonymy for its inhabitants, for urban society, or even humanity or the "world" as a whole. A metonymic chain is constructed: the "world" is like humanity is like the people in this city is like the evening city is like the evening is like (by metaphor) an etherised patient.

The New Critics Cleanth Brooks and Robert Penn Warren, who promoted T. S. Eliot and his kind of poetry, in their influential textbook *Understanding Poetry*, did not hesitate to read the evening metonymically and speak of an "evening world," which "becomes more and more important as the poem proceeds." "It is a world of neither night nor day. Twilight is the atmosphere of the poem" (where, clearly, the atmospheric expressions are meant symbolically). With the image of the patient in line 3, "the twilight world becomes also the world of twilight in another way, the realm between life and death." Here, "the notion of a sick world" enters the poem (Brooks and Warren 1960:391).

The image in lines 2–3 can hardly justify such generalizations (which typically represent the contemporary reception of T. S. Eliot's poetry). The interpretation is, rather, based on a reading of the poem as a whole. The point is that, though the second term of the relation was given in full in these lines, the *base* of the metaphor—the first term—is constantly shifting. In lines 2–3, it may still be an evening in nature, in the countryside, in the tradition of Romantic poetry; the following lines make us reunderstand the evening as a metonymy for the evening city (fr_3):

> Let us go, through certain half-deserted streets,
> The muttering retreats
> Of restless nights in one-night cheap hotels
> And sawdust restaurants with oyster-shells:

This description of the street scene may reinforce such additional connotations of the hospital scene as: dim light, drugged, smelling, etc. It also evokes new candidates for the sickness image.

Here, however, a fourth *fr* is introduced: the lyrical narrator. It was from his point of view that the evening was seen as an etherised patient. Was it a projection, an externalized emotion? Is he himself like a patient? Does he feel "etherised"? Line 1, though not a part of the "image" proper, and so playfully unpoetic, is crucial for our perception; it presents a stronger candidate for metonymic transfer: the person walking through this evening (fr_4). This possibility is resumed in the immediate continuation, which presents the city as not only metonymic but also metaphoric to (possibly) his mind:

> Streets that follow like a tedious argument
> Of insidious intent
> To lead you to an overwhelming question . . .

The metaphor is again bi-directional: the streets are personified, i.e., like men; hence we are encouraged to see men as being like these streets that are like men. The explicit metaphor is inverted. The personification leads to *a reciprocal metaphor,* as in Romantic nature imagery: Nature is like Man; Man is like Nature, that is like Man. In our case, the streets are like the speaker's mind—which leads us to an inversion: mind like streets. We entered the metaphor from a description of the streets and exited into a new topic altogether: the speaker's mind. The *base* and the secondary *fr* have changed places. Vehicle and tenor changed roles.

When Brooks and Warren say that "twilight is the atmosphere of the poem," do they mean the city or the narrator or both? The metaphor of the patient may easily be transferred through the evening to its extensions (metonymies), among them the city and Prufrock. Both are developed and changing throughout the poem and therefore leave the hospital scene, too, open for possible reunderstanding. The question is to what extent "Prufrock's world" (a further metonymic chain) is analogous to the slum scene or is its opposite—

both relations can be found in the text. Or is it analogous to the opposite of the slum, the drawing room, thus making both the high and the low meaningless? Both the man and the city, may be read as representing "a world" (in the sense of the ethos of humanity in a certain period, such as "the Modern world"). Interpreters felt that it was a "sick world," thus relating the metaphor further away from its immediate *base*, to generalizations about the poem as a whole or some of its frames of reference (the city, the citizens, the bored women in the drawing room, Prufrock, Humanity). The chain of linkings which enables such interpretative transfers may be represented schematically as shown in Figure 3.

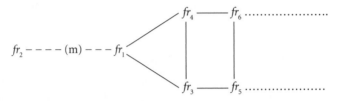

Figure 3

The chain represents: [2] patient—[1] evening—[3] city—[4] Prufrock; [5] the slum inhabitants—[6] the salon women. Lines represent metonymical transfers; m—metaphorical transfer; dots—further unfolding.

To what extent the metaphoric *base* moves, in the eyes of some readers, and encompasses ever wider ranges can be seen from some further quotes from *Understanding Poetry*:

> After a brief digression (lines 70–74) we return to the drawing room and the etherized, peaceful twilight world in which Prufrock does not have the strength to force the 'crisis,' the overwhelming question.
>
> Further, much is made [in the end of the poem] of Prufrock's world—it is a meaningless world of half-lights and shadows, the world of an ether dream, and it is set in another world, the defeated world of the slum.
>
> [...] he speaks to the you of the poem—the reader—only because he takes the reader to be damned too, to belong to the same world and to share the same disease. It is the disease of loss of conviction, of loss of faith in the meaning of life . . . so the poem, in the end, is not about poor Prufrock. He is merely a symbol for a general disease [...] (Brooks and Warren 1960:392, 396).

What a burden on a poor etherized table!

The whole poem is a chain of intertwined frames of reference, metonymically related to each other, which encourage the establishment of parallels, oppositions, metaphorical transfers, or symbolization. The relations are mostly tacit, not clearly related to specific characters, often contradictory, therefore open to constructions and deconstructions, but constantly enhanced by personified descriptions of nature and leaps from generalizations to concrete details, from descriptions to reflections, from dialogues to allusions, which make almost everything seem representative of and/or opposite to everything else. Metaphoric transfers are part of this network. The first metaphor looms as an undigested menace over it all.

7

The word linking two sides of a simile—the common property or common denominator or similarity feature of the two terms (*tertium comparationis*)—may not be a single property at all but just a verbal connective. Thus when the Russian revolutionary poet Mayakovsky writes: "the sky is red like the Marseillaise," the link is through the polysemy of the word, "red" (Figure 4).

semantic structure of the word "red"

1. color
2. blood
3. radical

Figure 4

While the sunset sky is red in color (Figure 5), the revolutionary song is red only metaphorically, meaning: radical. When "red" is connected to "the sky," the second and third semes are excluded (crossed out); when it is said of the "Marseillaise," the first seme is immaterial (Figure 6).

red sky

1. color
2. ~~blood~~
3. ~~radical~~

Figure 5

red song

1. ~~color~~
2. ~~blood~~
3. radical

Figure 6

2. blood is a connotation of both, color and Revolution, and may be an additional link between the two (Figure 7).

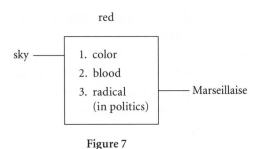

Figure 7

A similar connection through a polysemic word appears in Rilke's poem "Pont du Carrousel":

Der blinde Mann; der auf der Brücke steht,
grau wie ein Markstein namenloser Reiche,
[The blind man, standing on the bridge,
gray as a milestone marking nameless domains][4]

The word, "gray," when used for a person, means "gray-haired, old," and also metaphorically: "colorless, disconsolate, abandoned." On the other hand, the grayness of the stone is a direct description of the color of a milestone and, metaphorically, of colorless vacuity (Figure 8). Since the link between the two is established, further features are transferred from the secondary image, (fr_2: "milestone") to the base: fr, "blind man."

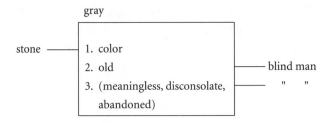

Figure 8

4   The literal translation here and below are mine, intended to be a rendition as close to the original as possible.

For the sake of simile, "gray as a stone" would be enough on both the concrete and metaphorical levels; the additional words provide *redundant* semantic material, they present an *fr* ("nameless domains") with no existential status in the IFR of the poem and hence require a *metaphorical transfer*. Thus the blind man is not merely gray, but lonely as a stone, and he is like a milestone lost in vast nameless spaces, perhaps (by metonymy) nameless and anonymous himself.

Now, when we read the whole poem, the relationship is reversed; we have to reunderstand the metaphor. The blind man becomes the significant, permanent center of an ever-moving, faceless (to him), shallow race. The stone, rather than being gray and lost in space, becomes its point of orientation.

> Der blinde Mann, der auf der Brücke steht,
> grau wie ein Markstein namenloser Reiche,
> er ist vielleicht das Ding, das immer gleiche,
> um das von fern die Sternenstunde geht,
> und der Gestirne stiller Mittelpunkt.
> Denn alles um ihn irrt und rinnt und prunkt.
> Er ist der unbewegliche Gerechte,
> in viele wirre Wege hingestellt;
> der dunkle Eingang in die Unterwelt
> bei einem oberflächlichen Geschlechte.
>
> (Rilke 1:393)

> [The blind man standing on the bridge,
> gray as a milestone of nameless domains,
> he is perhaps the thing, the ever steady thing
> around which, from afar, the lucky star turns,
> the still center of the galaxies.
> For everything around him wanders and flows and shines.
> He is the unmoving Just one,
> set on many wayward paths;
> the dark entrance to the Underworld
> for a shallow race.]

In this poem, too, the compared term (fr_2) was completed in the second line; but the basic term (fr_1)—the blind man on the bridge—is unfolded through the whole poem and endowed with additional metaphors, which eventually reverse the meanings attributed to the blind man. The word "Markstein," meaning simply "milestone" is etymologized (as so often in Rilke), the function of "marking" becomes prominent. His blindness underscores the faceless anonymity of the passers-by (contrasted, paradoxically, by the *named* bridge: Pont du Carrousel). The grayness of the simile (like the "patient" in Eliot) is exposed as a mere linking excuse for a rich metaphorical operation.

Thus, a metaphoric relationship is given in the very opening of the poem; its understanding, however, changes radically as the text unfolds. The first term of the metaphor encompasses the whole poem; whereas the second term, though isolated in one clause, changes its meaning as we read on, due to the interaction with the dynamic first term.

Furthermore, the additional metaphorical images, revealing a parallel structure to fr_2, reinforce this change of concretization and create a transformation in both parts of the relationship. Schematically, the chain may be represented as follows:

fr_1 : blind man	bridge
fr_2 : gray markingstone	nameless domains
fr_3 : ever steady thing	lucky star turning
fr_4 : silent center	galaxies
fr_5 : the unmoving Just one	wayward paths
fr_6 : dark entrance to Hades	shallow race

He started as blind and grey and lost and turned into a marker, the center of orientation for a shallow race.

8

Much more complex are poems building up the secondary fr as a discontinuous pattern throughout a part of the poem. A rather simple example may be seen in another part of T. S. Eliot's "Prufrock":

> The yellow fog that rubs its back upon the window-panes,
> The yellow smoke that rubs its muzzle on the window-panes,
> Licked its tongue into the corners of the evening,
> Lingered upon the pools that stand in drains,

Let fall upon its back the soot that falls from chimneys,
Slipped by the terrace, made a sudden leap,
And seeing that it was a soft October night,
Curled once about the house, and fell asleep.

("The Love Song of J. Alfred Prufrock")

As in the Auden poem ("Macao"), a formal analysis would find in every line a separate metaphor. It is clear, however, that all secondary terms of these metaphors join in building up one *fr*. T. S. Eliot himself emphasizes the near-identity of the first two lines through their anaphoric and parallel structure ("fog" and "smoke" are synonymous, hence "back" and "muzzle" fulfill a synonymous function). In the first lines, one could, perhaps, argue that there is a mere metaphorical usage of certain words. But a fog can hardly have the form of a muzzle; this is the untransferable detail of a more generalized comparison, fog = animal, with the rubbing of a muzzle underlining the wet proximity of the fog. If a "back" may still be a mere metaphorical transfer of one word, rubbing its back is certainly an action of an animal, even though the animal was not named (here, it could still be a pig). Through the use of the text-continuum, more and more animal features are amassed, until the unspecified animal becomes a cat.

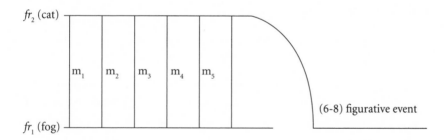

m$_{1-5}$ are local metaphors.

Figure 9

Here a typical transformation occurs. At first the fr_2 = "animal" served merely as a store of metaphors for fr_1 = fog. Metaphors or metaphorical transfers may use all features and connotations of a secondary *fr* except for one: the property of its existence. There is no hospital in the fictional world of the poem, only some of its properties are relevant to that world. While the animal is a metaphor, it does not exist as animal in the IFR of the poem. Toward the end, however, the fog *becomes* a cat (a humanized creature at that) and the cat as such lands on the scene, becomes real, entirely disregarding the realistic possibilities of a fog. Thus an image (animal), once presented to the reader's consciousness (not even in words, but through gap-filling of a metaphor), becomes "real," enters the fictional world of the text. The Russian Formalists called this phenomenon "realization of a metaphor." It may, however, appear in a great variety of forms, not only as metaphor. Graphically, we may represent this strophe as in Figure 9.

The animal descriptions are continuous with each other, the leaping cat is a logical extension of fr_2. The clash (and its functions: irony, absurd, defiance of realism, etc.—depending on the poem) is due to an ontological shift. And it, in turn, is enabled by the fact that the metaphor does not appear in one point but rather as a pattern in which each individual occasion may relate to its counterpart in a different way.

The principle of metaphor requires two *fr*s related like parallel lines that never meet; the two "realities" are not continuous with each other in the fictional world of the poem. In this poem, however, the parallel lines meet "irrationally," the two *fr*s eventually collapse into one: the cat—a logical continuation of fr_2—appears as a cat in fr_1, breaking the boundaries between "reality" and "imagination."

9

Placing metaphoric referents in the "real" world of poetic fiction is a central device of Modernist poetry. It may occur in the form of realized metaphors, realized similes, realized idioms, or what we may call *figurative events* and *figurative situations*. The two latter kinds are said to really occur in the world of the poem but are figurative in relation to a realistic norm.

A more striking example of this kind may be found in Rilke's "God in the Middle Ages":

Gott im Mittelalter

Und sie hatten Ihn in sich erspart
und sie wollten, dass er sei und richte
und sie hängten schließlich wie Gewichte
(zu verhindern seine Himmelfahrt)

an ihn ihrer grossen Kathedralen
Last und Masse. Und er sollte nur
über seine grenzenlosen Zahlen
zeigend kreisen und wie eine Uhr
Zeichen geben ihrem Tun und Tagwerk.
Aber plötzlich kam er ganz in Gang,
und die Leute der entsetzten Stadt
liessen ihn, vor seiner Stimme bang,
weitergehn mit ausgehängtem Schlagwerk
und entflohn vor seinem Zifferblatt.

(Rilke I:502)

[And they saved him up inside themselves
and they wanted him to be and to judge,
and finally they hung on him like weights
(to prevent his ascendance to heaven)
the burden and the massive body
of their big Cathedrals. He should merely
circle over his limitless numbers,
pointing and showing, and like a clock
mark their deeds and daily work.
But suddenly all of him moved, got going,
and the people of the flabbergasted city
left him, alarmed by his voice,
running on, the striking mechanism hanging out,
and fled from his (figure-)dial.]

A secondary image of a clock (fr_2) is constructed throughout the poem. It appears explicitly at first in line 8 as a simile, i.e., does not yet exist in the real world of the poem. On second reading we can detect its earlier elements.

"Gewichte" (line 3) are weights, they indicate: a) the heaviness of the massive cathedrals and b) the weight with which the people want to keep God down to earth; they may also connote c) the "weights" set on the scales of justice, thus joining the pattern of measurement and right judgment, enhanced by the rhyme, "richte"—"Gewichte" ("to judge"—"weights"). "Gewichte" in plural, however, may also mean d) "weights," especially of a big hanging clock. Thus, one word, when combined with other words in the text, creates

four different patterns, activating four different meanings. We may schematically represent it as follows (in English):

(a) weights + burden and massive body of cathedrals = heaviness

(b) weights of cathedrals + preventing God's ascendance to heaven =
earthbound

(c) weights + to judge + pointing and showing + mark their daily work =
judgment and regulation

(d) weights + numbers + clock + striking mechanism + dial = clock

The last sense of the word, "weights of a clock," must be excluded in the
context of the first strophe, but is revived by the pattern of the clock. Thus a
"dead" connotation, first crossed out, lives on in the poem as a dead connotation and is revived in the sequel (Figure 10).

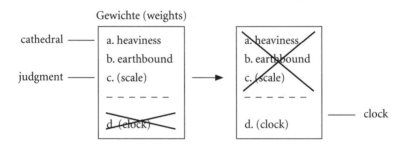

Figure 10

Now that we see the accumulation of meanings into a clock, we can observe further details. In the second strophe, circling over his (limitless) numbers indicates an enormous dial; "Zahlen" (numbers) is patterned with its
synonym, "Ziffer," in line 14 (in the word "Zifferblatt," literally: "numbers
dial"). The word "zeigend" (pointing) evokes the cognate, "Zeiger,"—both
"pointer" and "hand of a clock." In its immediate context, this is at most a
dormant connotation, revived, however, in the sequel. Indeed, the continuation of the sentence (lines 8–9) explains the pointing as giving signs "like a
clock." Thus, when we reach the simile, we already have several referents of
the *fr* "clock": weights, hands, numbers, circling, pointing.

Now the clock, introduced at first through crossed-out connotations of
words, then through a simile—and as such, non-existent in the fictional
world of the poem—becomes real, an object in the fictional world. When ad-

ditional aspects are revealed—the mechanism hanging out and striking, the figure-dial—they are perfectly logical as an unfolding of the fr_2 = clock; they clash, however, with the basic reality. The enormous clock (with cathedrals as pendulae—now the crossed-out connotation [a] is revived), at first erected for the rational ordering of life, reveals its irrational internal mechanism to the people of the Middle Ages. Furthermore, it is God himself who became such a clock, underlined by the Gender-change from the feminine clock (eine Uhr) to the masculine pronouns: *he* became all movement, *his* voice, etc.

The effect of this image is achieved again through building up a secondary, metaphorical pattern and then landing it in the primary *fr*; i.e., suspending the conditional existence of metaphor, collapsing the mere image with the real. This is even further complicated by the introduction of this realized simile (God = clock) into the medieval city (fr_3) from which God was observed, creating the terrifying figurative event, that makes the citizens flee the city. We may summarize this patterning in Figure 11.

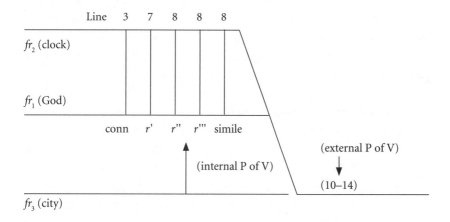

fr_1 – the medieval conception of God; fr_2 – clock; fr_3 – medieval city;
P of V = Point of View.

   line 3: *Gewichte* (weights) – crossed-out connotation
   line 7: *Zahlen* (numbers) – possible referent of fr_2 (r')
   line 8: *kreisen* (to circle) – function of fr_2 (r'')
   line 8: *zeigend* (pointing) – cognate of referent "Zeiger" (hand of clock") (r''')
   line 8: *wie eine Uhr* (like a clock) – simile
   lines 10–14: direct descriptions (action, sound, mechanism, dial)

Figure 11

As we see, not all relations between the two patterns are metaphors. In the first four instances, we have *shared referents*: words that may belong to each of the two *frs* (often, through different semes of the same polysemic root). The fifth instance is a simile. The realization of the simile (in lines 10-14) is accomplished by collapsing its two terms, $fr_1 = fr_2$, and then by making it a direct referent within fr_3, the city. The imaginary clock has landed in the real world. We may call it a *figurative event*, i.e., figurative in comparison with a realistic norm. It created a striking effect, both for the medieval builders of the clock-image and for the modern reader. We may say that instead of using logical argument to prove his thesis about the irrational and terrifying, looming behind the ordered world of medieval religious belief, Rilke used the "irrational" logic of metaphor to make his point.

Are we still dealing with metaphor? Yes, since the image of the clock is metaphorical to those spiritual aspects of the medieval attitude to God and the order of the universe as conceived in the poem. It is a typical metaphorical relationship based not on a transfer of meaning in one word but on an interaction between two (or more) patterns, taking on various forms in the various linking points. Furthermore, the image is not a discrete static unit; various possible aspects of the metaphorical relationship are activated throughout the poem, shifting and even undermining the relation established in the beginning. This is enhanced by a change of point of view: in the eyes of the medieval people, God is like a clock in the sense of giving order to their lives; from an external point of view, however, he turns the tables on them.

Thus the metaphor uses—and exemplifies—the *dynamic aspect* of an unfolding poetic text. In addition, the pattern of the clock shifts from being merely hinted in subtle connotations of words to becoming a central *object* in the World of the poem, thus contradicting Ingarden's separation of "levels" in the literary text.

10

Rilke makes extensive use of such realizations of figures, figurative situations, and figurative events, accomplishing transitions from rhetorical figures and verbal forms to the fictional world of the poem. In other words, for him, words and their meanings, once introduced in a text (literally or through a simile or a figure), may become "existents," beings in a fictional world, concrete objects in space. This tendency is especially strong in "Neue Gedichte" and in abbreviated, often cryptical form in his later poetry, notably the "Duino Elegies" and the posthumous poems.

Rilke's poetics of shifting from language to world is much wider than the phenomenon of metaphor. A key device is the nominalization of adjectives and verbs and the subsequent *spatialization*, enabling figurative events to take place within the space of such concepts. E.g., writing about mirrors: "Und der Lüster geht wie ein Sechzehn-Ender / durch eure *Unbetretbarkeit*" ("and the chandelier goes like a polygon [or a deer] through your *impenetrability*," *Sonnets to Orpheus*, part 2, III. Rilke [1955:752]), where impenetrability itself becomes a penetrable space.

The transition from such spatialization of concepts to the creation of Rilke's mythopoetic space and its imaginary objects is natural. The poem "Der Einsame" ("The Lonely Man") opens thus:

> Nein: ein Turm soll sein aus meinem Herzen
> und ich selbst an seinen Rand gestellt:
> wo sonst nichts mehr ist, noch einmal Schmerzen
> und Unsäglichkeit, noch einmal Welt.
>
> (Rilke I:636)

> [No, my heart should be a tower
> and I myself set on its ledge:
> where nothing more exists, not even pain
> and the unsayable, not even world.]

The "heart," a metonymy for the psyche, becomes a concrete object in space, separated from its owner; and it is a paradoxical space, where emotions and the world itself are banned. As all Rilke readers know, abstract, immaterial concepts, such as the heart, music, decay, etc., receive spatial dimensions, including the famous "Weltinnenraum," the internal space as an externalized world. This spatialized abstract concept can then be furnished with mountains and objects, provided with some concrete details, moved by figurative events.

A striking example is in the first of Rilke's *Sonnets to Orpheus*, which starts with the literal statement: "Da stieg ein Baum" ("A tree grew here"). The tree turns out to be "a high tree in the ear," a complex metaphor for the growth of internal music. Thus, the *base* is turned into a secondary *fr*. But as soon as an *fr* of a tree is introduced, unexpected extensions are developed: a whole forest with "animals of silence," for which Orpheus eventually creates a "temple inside hearing" ("Tempel im Gehör"). The autonomous unfolding of the "tree" *fr* is similar to Mayakovsky's fire below, though with a mythopoeic rather than a grotesque function.

We can place in this perspective another, rather straightforward example of a dynamic use of realization.

Spanische Tänzerin

Wie in der Hand ein Schwefelzündholz, weiß,
eh es zur Flamme kommt, nach allen Seiten
zuckende Zungen streckt -: beginnt im Kreis
naher Beschauer hastig, hell und heiß
ihr runder Tanz sich zuckend auszubreiten.

Und plötzlich ist er Flamme, ganz und gar.

Mit einem Blick entzündet sie ihr Haar
und dreht auf einmal mit gewagter Kunst
ihr ganzes Kleid in diese Feuersbrunst,
aus welcher sich, wie Schlangen die erschrecken,
die nackten Arme wach und klappernd strecken.

Und dann: als würde ihr das Feuer knapp,
nimmt sie es ganz zusamm und wirft es ab
sehr herrisch, mit hochmütiger Gebärde
und schaut: da liegt es rasend auf der Erde
und flammt noch immer und ergiebt sich nicht -.

Doch sieghaft, sicher und mit einem süßen
grüßenden Lächeln hebt sie ihr Gesicht
und stampft es aus mit kleinen festen Füßen.

(Rilke I:531)

[The Spanish Dancer

Like a match in her hand, white
before it leaps into flame, in all directions
stretching flickering tongues—so begins, in the narrow
circle of spectators, bright and hot,
her round dance, widens flickering.

And suddenly it is all flame.

With one glance, she ignites her hair
and in her daring art, turns all-at-once
her whole dress into this blazing fire,
from which, like frightened serpents,
her naked arms, alert and clattering, stretch out.

And then: as if the fire were tight on her,
she gathers it up and hurls it away
imperiously, with an arrogant gesture
and looks: here it lies raging on the ground
still flaming, still unyielding.

But triumphantly, confident, with a sweet
welcoming smile, she lifts her face
and stamps it out with tiny firm feet.]

The fire image is introduced at first within a simile. Even within the simile, it is not a fire but a mere extension of a potential "fire" *fr*: a match, still without fire, white (by metonymy: like her hand holding it). Within the simile, however, connotations of the words contribute to building up the fire semantics by several devices:

(1) A vivid, concrete description of what it is not yet, of a potential flame (lines 2-3).

(2) An etymological morpheme within the German word for "matches." In line 1 he writes: "Schwefel**zünd**holz" (literally "sulfur igniting wood"). Rilke combines two words for "matches" in one: "Schwefelholz" (old) and "Zündholz" (contemporary) and thus foregrounds the morpheme "zünd-" = ignite.

(3) Repetition of "zuckend" (which may be flickering as well as jerky, twitching).

(4) A nervous series of flickering, onomatopoeic alliterations (zünd—zuckende—Zungen—zuckend; Hand—holz—hastig—hell—heiß).

Suddenly, the simile turns into an existent: what was *like* a match that may produce fire becomes real fire. The two *fr*s collapse: the dance *is* a fire, the dancer goes up in the flames. And then, again, the dancer separates the fire from her body, as well as from her dance—and stomps out the fire. Schematically:

1. The dance is *like* (a match before becoming) fire

2. The dance *is* fire

3. The dance is not fire, but the fire exists independently

4. The dance extinguishes the fire

11

A more sophisticated use of a realized fire imagery appears in a fragment of Mayakovsky's long poem, "A Cloud in Trousers." Though built on a tragic-heroic conception of love and language and the individual's fate in history, it may have grotesque overtones in the eyes of today's readers. It would be advisable to place ourselves in the solemn tone of Russian poetry at the time. The literal translation does not convey Mayakovsky's powerful rhythm, oratorical tone, and inventive rhyme-effects, but may serve our purpose here.

> Hello!
> Who is it?
> Mamma?
> Mamma!
> Your son is splendidly ill!
> Mamma!
> His heart caught fire,
> Tell his sisters, Lyuda and Olya,—
> he has no place to hide.
> Every word,
> even a joke,
> which he spews from his scorching mouth,
> leaps like a naked whore
> out of a burning brothel.
>
> People sniff —
> a smell of roasting!
> Some men are rushed in.
> Shining!
> In helmets!

Please, no boots!
Tell the firemen:
On a burning heart one climbs in caresses.
Let me,
My tear-filled eyes I'll roll out like barrels.

Let me lean on my ribs.
I'll jump out! I'll jump out! I'll jump out! I'll jump out!
They've collapsed.
You can't jump out of your own heart!

On a smoldering face,
from the crack of the lips,
a wee cinder kiss rises to spring.

Mamma!
I cannot sing.
In the heart's chapel, the choir loft catches fire!

Scorched figures of words and numbers
from the skull,
like children from a burning building.
Thus fear,
catching at the sky,
lifted
the burning arms of the *Lusitania*.

To people trembling
in apartment's calm
a hundred-eyed blaze bursts from the docks.
My last scream—
at least you
wail into the centuries:
I'm on fire!

The fragment opens with the Russian word, "pozhar," meaning specifically a fire of burning houses or of a city. The poet is ill: he has "fire of the heart." This is obviously a fresh way of using the conventional stock metaphor, "burning love" or "fire of love," through a realization of the semi-dead metaphor of fire. Furthermore, the syntactic form of "his heart caught fire" (literally: "he has fire of the heart") is parallel to expressions for heart diseases, thus the metaphor of fire is crossed with another stock image: love as an illness of the heart. By shifting, however, from the trite (and dead) metaphor, "burning love," to a burning house, a fresh, individualized *fr* is opened up, which may be carried in several directions. A fire in a city brings a noisy brigade of firemen; they, in turn, have bright helmets and dirty boots, they climb upon ladders on the burning building; scorched figures jump out of the flaming house, etc. All these have nothing to do with intensional properties of the concept, "fire," or with the general object, fire, and its connotations; they are rather extensions of a specific description, as chosen and unfolded by the author.

Further branching out occurs when this image is crossed with other Mayakovskian images: additional *fr*s are drawn in, the full understanding of which requires further knowledge about them, provided in Mayakovsky's poems and Futurist manifestos. The bourgeois language is trite, words are worn out like prostitutes, a poet is a source of words, a master of the naked word—hence his heart is a burning brothel. On the other hand, his words are like children in fear trying to grasp at something high, and this evokes the image of useless grasping at the sky by the passengers of the burning and drowning ship *Lusitania*. And, finally, the poet on fire creates a dawn-like torch, blazing into the centuries (alluding to Mayakovsky's prophetic or Christ-like self-image).

In this case, the secondary *fr* ("fire") is coherent and consistently developed, while the basic *fr* ("love story") rambles from one move to another: we imagine the fire developing to its end, but not quite a consistent equivalent of a series of moves in the emotional domain. On the other hand, the individual transfers between the two basic *fr*s are enhanced and branched out into a number of additional *fr*s representing the poet's aesthetics and ideology. In the basic *fr* (abbreviated: "love story"), autonomous sub-scenes are created, not necessarily concatenated in a logical or narrative structure (except for the logic of the realized *fr* of "fire"), representing the autonomous "bricks" of rhymed language which Mayakovsky has later described in his essay, "How to Make Verse."

The Modernist poetic impact—absurd, tragic, or grotesque—occurs when events of fr_2 ("fire") are said to take place in fr_1 ("love"). Normally, in the metaphor, "my heart is on fire," one may transfer any property or connotation of fire to the "heart" (which is a metonymy for the domain of feelings and emotions), except for one, the existence property: the heart is not really burning. In a realization of the metaphor, it is precisely this property which is transferred: the real heart of flesh and blood (rather than its metonymic domain) is really burning. Mayakovsky foregrounds it through a further extension: if a real heart really burns, there must be a smell of burning flesh and people in the street sniff it. Thus Mayakovsky confronts the reader with the results of a collapse of the two disjointed *frs*; he asserts the consistency of metaphoric poetic language over any coherence or plausibility of representation.

In a similar way, a person climbing out of a burning house must lean on some remaining beams; in his chest (like a house) those are his ribs—but then Mayakovsky hits the reader with the truth on the *base* level: you cannot leap out of your own heart! Unlike Eliot's cat or Rilke's "Spanish Dancer," Mayakovsky makes the reader realize the consequences of such a realization of metaphor. Perhaps a fog cannot be reduced to the form of a cat, but a cat can be accommodated in the corner of a house. Rilke's dance *becomes* a real fire, but still the dancer does not actually burn, we do not smell her flesh. The Futurist Mayakovsky provokes by challenging this existential separation, by foregrounding the absurd. However, even with him, the unrealistic clashes are merely individual figurative events, they do not involve the totality of fr_1: the poet still lives, screams, writes.

In other words, *some* predications of existence of referents in fr_2 obtain—counterrealistically—in fr_1, but the merger is not complete. E.g., the heart burns, but not the whole body. The unrealistic effects do not create rules for a new, possible reality. Hence, the strange events remain figurative rather than tragic.

We can describe this phenomenon in another way: the fire is not metaphorical but literal; it *exists* in the basic reality of the poem. When a chain of metaphors is repeated throughout a text, the metaphorical function (the m-sign) can be taken out of the brackets: if "e" is an event, and "me" a metaphorical event, then:

$$me_1 + me_2 + me_3 \rightarrow m\,(e_1 + e_2 + e_3)$$

That is, the events are real, but they occur in a reality (a "possible world") which is itself metaphorical, "unrealistic," contradicting our sense of what is possible in a real world. Thus, metaphoricity, once introduced as a relation between frames of reference within the Internal Field of Reference, now turns into a relation between the IFR and an External Field of Reference, the real world. Metaphoricity is transferred from the *language* of the poem to its fictional *reality-key*. The vividness of this new clash is underlined by the fact that the hero of the poem is Mayakovsky himself addressing his real-life mother and sisters, Lyuda and Olya, i.e., referents shared by both the IFR and the ExFR (Figure 12).

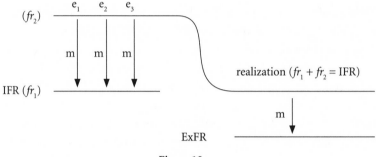

Figure 12

1 2

The ontological status of a secondary *fr* in the Internal Field of Reference of a poem is not always unambiguous or clear. Here is a poem by Robert Creeley:

A Wicker Basket

Comes the time when it's later
and onto your table the headwaiter
puts the bill, and very soon after
rings out the sound of lively laughter—

Picking up change, hands like a walrus,
and a face like a barndoor's,
and a head without any apparent size,
nothing but two eyes—

So that's you, man,
or me. I make it as I can,
I pick up, I go
faster than they know—

Out the door, the street like a night,
any night, and not one in sight,

but then, well, there she is,
old friend Liz—

And she opens the door of her cadillac,
I step in back,
and we're gone.
She turns me on—

There are very huge stars, man, in the sky,
and from somewhere very far off someone hands me a slice of apple pie,
with a gob of white, white ice cream on top of it,
and I eat it—

Slowly. And while certainly
they are laughing at me, and all around is racket
of these cats not making it, I make it
in my wicker basket.

This poem, interesting in its use of the spoken language, was said to be the first American poem on the experience of using marijuana. I shall not analyze it in detail, but merely observe one simile: "the street like a night." Is the street only "like" a night in that it is dark and empty, stressing his isolation or abandonment by those "cats" laughing at him? Or, as in Eliot's simile, is it actually night, and we must disregard the simile marker, "like"? After all, he left the café when the time came and it was "later." Such questions cannot possibly be decided in an interpretation based on the given text. But it does not really matter. Whether the *fr*, "night," is continuous or merely metaphorical with the basic *fr* of the poem, the transferred meanings are similar in both cases.

Furthermore, the night is unfolded and used in several ways in the sequel. The idiom, "pie in the sky," is realized: he sees huge stars in the sky and actually gets apple pie with ice cream, representing the sweetness of "grass" and perhaps suggesting erotic imagery ("I make it"). Whether he was really treated to the sweet things or not, they work as metaphors. He is on a high; he sees stars—real or metaphorical: the effect is the same. In one case, they serve as metonymies: the scene includes a night and huge stars, then the night is separated from the street by an observer, juxtaposed to it as an independent *fr* and opened up for metaphorical transfers. In the other case, they are figments of his imagination or straightforward metaphors of substitution.

In short, whether it is *like* a night or it *is* a night is undecided in the text; in either case a number of referents from the *fr*, "night," are transferred to the speaker's mood, via idioms, metaphors, or rhymes. This undecided ontological state is justified by the presentation of all information through the speaker's point of view and colorful language.

The same holds for the "wicker basket": it may represent a baby's cradle, Liz's car, or allude to baby Moses, who was saved in a wicker basket in the Bible. Its connotations and emotional impact are clear though its reference to the fictional world is blurred.

13

In Ezra Pound's famous "In a Station of the Metro," there is neither a formal metaphor nor an overt simile. Two *fr*s are simply placed next to each other:

> The apparition of these faces in the crowd;
> Petals on a wet, black bough.

We could read the poem without integrating the two lines, as if with the instructions:

> Think: "The apparition of these faces . . . "
> and think: "Petals on a wet, black bough."

The wish (and traditional convention) for integration of a text, however, forces us to turn one of the lines into a metaphor, in order to project it upon the other *fr*. The title decides which is the basic *fr*; it could easily be the opposite: a poem about petals like faces.

Note that here, too, fr_1 has intruded into the language of fr_2: the bough is *black* and wet like a station after a rain.

The famous "thinginess" of the imagists, the Chinese-inspired ideogram, turns out to be quite metaphorical. As Pound himself observed, "The one-image poem is a form of super-position, that is to say, it is one idea set on top of another."

This technique of simply juxtaposing discontinuous *fr*s (even conjoined in one sentence) and forcing metaphorical transfers on the reader is beautifully employed by Osip Mandelshtam (here, a literal, unrhymed translation):

> Sisters—heaviness and tenderness—your signs are the same.
> Bees and wasps suck a heavy rose.

A man dies, warmed sand cools.
And yesterday's sun is carried off on a black stretcher.

Oh, heavy honeycombs and tender nets,
It is easier to lift a stone than to repeat your name!
I have one concern left in the world,
A golden goal, to get rid of the burden of time.

Like dark water I drink the muddied air.
Time has been plowed up, and the rose was earth.
In a slow whirlpool heavy tender roses,
Roses Heaviness and Tenderness she wove into double wreathes!

Mandelshtam was a Russian "Acmeist" poet. The Acmeists, like the English Imagists, extolled poetry that presents the thing itself, names objects, calls a spade a spade, or, as Mandelshtam put it, discovers the identity of A = A—as opposed to the metaphorical principle of the Futurists: any A = B. Indeed, many clauses in the poem are direct descriptions (though sometimes using metaphors to support the description). Mandelshtam, however, transfers the Futurist metaphoric principle from the level of poetic language to the level of composition: the separate descriptions open up many disconnected *frs*. In order to integrate "a man dies" and "warmed sand cools," we must link them metonymically or metaphorically or both: they are not connected syntactically or logically in the text. Either the sand cooled because a man lying there died or because the sun has set (a third independent *fr*); either the sunset is a metaphor of the dying man or the opposite; or they are all metonymic to each other, parts of the same surreal landscape. The same holds for "Sisters—heaviness and tenderness" in relation to "bees and wasps": is the first, the basic *fr* ("heaviness and tenderness"), exemplified by the second, or vice versa?

And what is the poem "about," what is its basic situation, the basic *fr*? Is it about "heaviness and tenderness," represented in bees and wasps, or vice versa? Is it about the sweet and stinging principles of death and love and time? Or are the earlier *frs* later turned into metaphors for a poem about a man's death or about suicide (Ophelia?) or a poem about love (for which all the preceding *frs* represent the heightened emotions)?

As the reader advances, he is repeatedly invited to perform transformations of the *fr* base. Possibly, all of the hierarchical relationships between the different, disconnected *frs* (and "themes" of the poem) are reversible. In any case, metaphorical relations between the segments must be constructed in order to project the disparate *frs* upon the hypothetical basic situation and make sense of this symphonic poem. Another alternative would leave the segments side by side, suggestively unconnected, as a surrealist dream; but even then they must all be projected on a basic *fr*, outside the words of the poem, representing the speaker's "mood" or subconscious. After all, it is only from the position of an associative speaker that such a series of images can be sustained in one short frame.

14

A somewhat different use of interacting *frs* can be seen in the poem of the Israeli poet Yehuda Amichai:

And the Migration of My Parents

And the migration of my parents
Has not subsided in me. My blood goes on sloshing
Between my ribs, long after the vessel has come to rest.
And the migration of my parents has not subsided in me.
Winds of long time over stones. Earth
Forgets the steps of those who trod her.
Terrible fate. Patches of a conversation after midnight.
Win and lose. Night recalls and day forgets.
My eyes looked long into a vast desert
And were calmed a bit. A woman. Rules of a game
I was not taught. Laws of pain and burden.
My heart barely ekes out the bread
Of its daily love. My parents in their migration.
On Mother Earth, I am always an orphan.
Too young to die, too old to play.
The weary hewer and the empty quarry in one body.
Archaeology of the future, repositories
Of what was not. And the migration of my parents
Has not subsided in me. From bitter nations I have learned
Bitter tongues for my silence
Among these houses, always like ships.
And my veins and my sinews, a thicket

Of ropes I cannot unravel. And then
My death and an end to the migration of my parents.

(Amichai, p. 51)

His mode is direct statement, which often may be taken as a literal sentence—as if he were furnishing the described world—but has to be integrated metaphorically in the basic *fr*. The sentence "Rules of a game / I was not taught" has nothing metaphorical about it, but must be projected upon the poet's life and necessarily metaphorized.

Of special interest is the *internalized frame*: the images of the parents' migration (fr_2) by sea, are internalized in the poet's self (fr_1). Hence, "has not subsided in me" is revived into an image of blood "sloshing between my ribs," reconstructed as a *ship* that has not calmed, with his own veins as a tangle of ropes. All other *frs* (mostly descriptions) are projected upon this *fr* of migration (e.g., "winds of long time over stones") which is, in turn, internalized in the figure of the poet, i.e., becomes a metaphor for his being.

1 5

We used examples from Modernist poetry to make a clear case for metaphors that result from the interaction of semantic patterns unfolded in a text, therefore multirelated, changing with the text and employing constructed *frs* rather than mere denotations and connotations of words. The same principles are used profusely in journalism as well as in narrative fiction.

Here is a passage from an editorial in the *New York Times* (1977):

The Right Price of Energy

For all its length, tables, omissions, exhortations and numbing complexity, the Carter administration's energy program proclaimed a single message: the price is wrong. Americans are *energy alcoholics*. For half a century, they have *reveled* on cheap oil, gas and electricity. Not content with one car, they have bought two and three. Not content with toasters, they have generated a whole sub-industry to tantalize them with electric carving knives, crepe pans, cookie shooters. Natural gas is at a premium, home-heating fuel in limited supply; they use it to heat commercial boilers that could readily employ coal instead. But energy is worth more than Americans pay for it—and is rapidly becoming dearer still. If the *revel* continues, *the morning after* will be long and painful, indeed.

(italics mine)

The specific meanings of "revel" in the last sentence and "the morning after" are clearly not isolated metaphors, but depend on a pattern established in line 3: fr_2, "alcoholics," as a metaphor for "energy users." The "morning after" is an unexpected twist similar to the behavior of Rilke's clock, resuming an fr established twelve lines earlier.

Both sides of the metaphorical relationship—oil and alcohol—involve large cultural domains and are a stock metaphor in modern culture. A cover of *The Economist* in 2005 was titled: *Addicted to oil*.

16

Russell Baker is a master of such metaphorical interactions of *fr*s. Here is an opening of an article in the *New York Times* of March 23, 1983:

War and Sweets
by Russell Baker

Disclosure that the Russian army is already equipped with an accurate pie-delivery system is no surprise to those of us in the military-pastry complex.

Two years ago we warned President Reagan that advances in pie-throwing technology already made it possible to hurl a lemon meringue pie with such accuracy that it could hit an enemy in the face at a distance of two miles from the launching site.

This metaphorical relationship is developed throughout the whole article, employing a series of unexpected extensions and allusions: to the military-industrial complex, "a *slice* of the defense budget," slapstick films ("a soldier struck in the face by a lemon meringue pie becomes so angry and embarrassed by his comrades' laughter that he becomes incapable of functioning," as the psychologists found out), and even "a cake just like mother used to make." It is not an allegory with an independent story about a pie, but rather tapping the semantic resources of two parallel *fr*s.

17

In this essay I have discussed primarily metaphors of the "extended" type. The question is to what extent the same approach may work for metaphors with a brief, one-word focus. Without prejudging such a study, I would remark that here, too, an element of a foreign *fr* is projected on a *base*; the secondary *fr*, however, is often not individualized, its features are even less detailed than in the above examples, requiring even stronger activation of gaps in the *base*.

Another point is that the "existence" of the secondary *fr* does not necessarily have to be negated by the *base*. It is sufficient that within one *fr*, that is a building block of the fictional world, two sub-*frs* are isolated, as is often the case in nature poetry: a person is presented as part of a nature scene, but his psyche is also perceived as separate from the nature description; thus we have a metonymic relationship between the two—nature and mind—and metaphorical transfers are encouraged: his or her mood is like aspects of nature and nature is perceived in human terms.

3 AN OUTLINE OF INTEGRATIONAL SEMANTICS

An Understander's Theory of Meaning in Context

1. INTRODUCTION

1.1   The following remarks intend to present an outline and several concrete examples for a new, comprehensive theory of semantics. If semantics is the theory and study of meaning, and if meaning is all the information an understander may obtain while perceiving (reading, or hearing) a text, then it must be clear that semantics cannot be limited to the study of isolated units: words (as "signs"), sentences, speech acts or their combinations. The meanings, meaning-complexes and meaning-chains, which understanders obtain from texts, result from processes of integrating discontinuous semantic materials located in a given text as well as outside of it.

1.11   The *Understander's* point of departure is merely a methodological device, intended at illuminating components of meaning not always accounted for in "objectivist" semantic analyses of texts. Speakers, writers, and other producers of texts are aware of the same mechanisms and invest meanings in the text they produce accordingly (though there may not always be an identity between the speaker's and the understander's meaning).

1.2   Granted, texts are made, on the whole, of words and sentences. Yet the units of meaning are not words and sentences but patterns combining semantic elements, which, indeed, reside in—and are constructed from—these words and sentences. The older stages of semantics: the study of the meaning of words (as summarized, e.g., by Ullman and Weinreich); syntactic semantics; even various new approaches to the theory of texts and discourse—all contributed essential data to the understanding of meaning units and meaning forms. I do not wish to discount the value of such studies, but rather to point out that in actual communication they provide merely potential values in an understander's constructs. I believe that they must all be subsumed within a wider framework which would observe meanings as they really occur: as open-ended networks of constructs, forming bridges between given pieces of language and the world (or language) outside of it.

1.3   The proposed *Integrational Semantics* is the theory of meanings resulting from processes of integration of semantic material, within a text and outside of it. I prefer this name to such more widely accepted titles as "text grammar," "text theory" or "discourse analysis" for two major reasons: (a) If words or sentences are not the ultimate independent units of meaning, neither is a text. A text cannot be produced or "generated" from one "theme" or one core; a text often provides a multitude of "themes," meanings and meaning-patterns; it cannot be exhausted in one summary or even in one interpretation. (b) Elements within a text may be linked semantically not only to their immediate context or not even to other elements in the same text but to relevant elements elsewhere—either verbal or verbalizable. Thus, the fifth sentence in a news item in today's paper may be linked to the third sentence in an item in yesterday's paper more than to its own neighbors.

In short, though a text is the vehicle by which meanings are conveyed, it is both *more* and *less* than any independent complex unit of meaning. A text is not a sign but a network of signification.

1.4   In recent years, a considerable body of work from various directions has confronted the study of discourse and its comprehension.[1] Some contributions are parallel to work done here, or may be accounted for in this framework. Others are more limited or weak for reasons that should become clear from the proposed theory. However, the space of an article does not allow for a proper consideration and critical assessment of the work done in this field. My goal is, rather, to provide an independent general theoretical framework, to propose an outline of a model which may accommodate the disparate concerns in one

1   See, e.g., Reinhart and the survey by Robert de Beaugrand.

perspective. Instead of basing each step on accepted theories and terminologies (which become ambiguous and interpretation-dependent when carried from one theoretical system to another), I shall propose my own terms, explained as simply as possible, and based on the assumption that "in the area of philosophy of language perhaps as much as in any other philosophical field, chaos reigns, little is agreed on, new methods are eagerly seized upon, and we have hardly begun" (Caton 1971).

1.41   In what follows, I shall try to show how the model works and how it can account for various observable phenomena of meaning conveyed by texts.

I shall not propose an abstract framework in its logical order, but rather work up to it, "showing what I mean" through specific examples and particular aspects, combining interpretations with generalizations.

Needless to say, I am indebted to numerous studies carried out in this wide area, as well as in my base, the study of literature and interpretation.

1.5   This approach involves several basic assumptions about language, some of which seem obvious to many contemporaries, but are not fully realized in theory.

a.   The problem of communication is not "how to do things with words" but "*how to convey things with language*": meanings, requests, emotions, attitudes, ambiguities, information, etc. (abbreviated: "*Meaning*").

b.   Language is not an independent vehicle for conveying meaning. It is rather used to (re-)orient the understander in a *network of information* ("World," which includes all previous texts as well).

Utterances often do not carry merely new information, but send the understander to available stores of information (either observable or mediated through language), zeroing in on specific elements and reshuffling, reinterpreting or adding on to them.

In other words, a speaker of language uses language, as well as knowledge of the "World," to convey his intentions, guiding the understander by means of his words (as well as gestures, etc.). This is true even for such highly abstract texts as works of philosophy, which cannot be understood without previous philosophical texts or such notions as "time," "space," etc. And it is certainly true for newspapers, which cannot be understood without newspapers (or newscasts) of previous days.

c.   Semantic theory must overcome the "First-Sentence Fallacy"—the analysis of a sentence as if it stood alone. There are no first sentences in language. The "first sentences" of children are highly embedded in their elementary vocabulary and non-verbal context.

d. We must abandon the inherited notion that sentences are the units of meaning, as expressed, for example, in the following statement: "The logical form of a sentence is identical with its meaning as determined compositionally from the senses of its lexical items and the grammatical relations between its syntactic constituents" (Katz 1972: XXIV). Whether we convey something through combinations of words within a sentence or dispersed in several sentences makes no difference. "I see red brick houses" may be conveyed either in one sentence (as here) or in parts of several, discontinuous sentences: "red houses" in one, "brick houses" in another—to be integrated by an understander (see below, 4.12–4.13). Such dispersed elements are not connected formally in language but are *available* for patterning, in a kind of "semantic syntax" of interpretive constructs, which, in turn, may be analyzed as sentences in a syntactical semantics.

I am stressing this point because even many discourse analysis theories, that declare their wish to go "beyond the sentence," actually see discourse as a combination of sentences rather than a re-structuring of semantic material.

e. This may be generalized: there is a fallacy assuming that semantics lies in discrete, static units, rather than (possible or potential) constructs, sometimes based on diffuse bodies of text.

f. Another limitation lies in the tradition which restricts linguistics to the study of codified forms and expressions. Indeed, "my friend" in English does not indicate my friend's sex, whereas in Russian such information would be codified in grammar. But English can express the same idea lexically: in "boy-friend" and "girl-friend" or in the name of the friend (if the gender is indicated in the name). Similarly, many semantic categories and links may be expressed either in codified or non-codified ways, or both; a semantic integration will decide on the nature of the category (time, embedded speaker, etc.).

Furthermore, even codified forms may be misleading. The third person is presumably indicating a person who is not participating in the dialogue, but it may be used in literature for expressing the first person; and so can the second person in poetry. On the other hand, first person poems may represent a voice different from the author's. A confrontation of such grammatical forms with the contents and genre of the text will provide the correct, "semantic" person.

g. Interpretations of literary texts involve primarily *understanding of language*. A theory of language must be able to account for the modes in which meanings are conveyed in literary texts. This is true not only for "interpretable deviance," for example, metaphor (Weinreich 1980),* but also for the more basic "mimetic" aspect of language, its "world-constructing" capacity.

Applications of linguistics to literary texts were often of limited value not because they did not understand *literature* but because existing linguistic methods do not account for central aspects of *language*. We should reverse the order of investigation: use literary texts for the observation of language phenomena and the construction of a more adequate theory of language.

h. Theory must not shy away from the diffuse, ambivalent, multidirectional, imprecise, potentials-filled nature of language—which is its great strength in interacting with a multifarious and changing "World." One should not confuse method with ontology, the neatness of a theoretical apparatus with a schematic neatness in language. Perhaps not everything may be said precisely or translated into logical formulas; it may be observed nevertheless.

2. A THREE-TIER CONSTRUCT OF MEANING

2.0 Meanings are conveyed in language through texts. To be sure, there are many non-linguistic modes of conveying meaning, either independently or combined with linguistic utterances. I shall not discuss those in the present article though I believe that they, too, can be explained within this general framework.

2.01 However, the structure of meaning and meaning-complexes is not identical with the structure of texts. On the one hand, the establishment of meanings obtained from a text requires the involvement of material outside the given text. And on the other hand, texts often have additional, "superfluous" semantic material, not directly relevant to any given meaning-complex, as well as im-

---

*   U. Weinreich wrote in 1966: "The fresh turn which this work has taken was due, above all, to three stimuli. The first was a realization, stemming from conversations with Benjamin Hrushovski [Harshav] (. . .) that a semantic theory is of marginal interest if it is incapable of dealing with poetic uses of language, and more generally, with interpretable deviance (Weinreich 1980: 188-89).

portant non-semantic devices. The composition of a text is not identical with the composition of its meanings.

For this reason, the description of meaning requires a separate model from the description of texts, though the two are interdependent and intertwined in reality.

2.1   Meaning is a result of a three-tier construction, which may be represented by the following diagram:

RP = Regulating Principles; *fr* = frame of reference

The middle level—the level of "sense"—represents both the senses of words and those aspects of meaning which result from syntactic operations.

2.11   For utterances to become meaningful, they must be applied to specific *frames of reference (fr)*. A frame of reference is any continuum of referents to which utterances, texts or their interpretations may refer.

2.12   *fr*s may be *real*: a certain situation in time and space, for instance, a room, a city, a street, etc.; or *ideal*, for instance, a certain theoretical system, a science, an ideology, etc. Any "theme" or "state of affairs," any abstracted relationship, may constitute an *fr*, for example, the relationship between John and Mary, the war in Vietnam, slaveowner mentality, etc. An *fr* that occupies a specific area in space within the grasp of a human observer and usually tied to a specific point in time is called a *scene*.

2.13   *fr*s may actually exist in the world or be imaginary, fictional, hypothetical. Their ontological status need not concern the semantician; as long as some information about an *fr* is provided, we can adjudge further utterances relating to it.

2.14   *fr*s may be *present* or *absent* in the speech situation. If I say in a classroom: "Please close the door," the *fr* provides information additional to my words, such as, it is noisy outside, the wind is blowing, the door was too heavy for me to move, or somebody just opened it. If, however, I tell a story about an *absent fr*, I cannot simply say that I asked someone to close the door without explaining the reasons or circumstances.

In works of fiction, the characters behave as if they speak in *present fr*s and know all about it, but since the reader is not actually present, the text must provide him with additional information about the fictional *fr*s. When Joyce's Eveline sits at the window and contemplates, she does not need to explain who she is or how old she is. But the reader doesn't know it and the writer has to disperse that information in his text. The problem becomes especially acute in *scenic* fiction, in passages presented from a character's point of view or through his stream of consciousness, since a character would not normally tell or think to himself all the background for his reactions or emotions.

2.15   Absent *fr*s may be *known* to the hearer or *unknown*, in varying degrees. It makes a difference if we say something about an object in the bedroom, known to the hearer, or if we tell him about an object in a foreign city, which he has not seen.

2.16   RP—"Regulating Principles"—derive from the authorities standing behind an utterance: the speaker, the narrator, any represented position of a character or any producer of a text. Point of view, irony, the "tone" of a text, attitudes deriving from the genre of a text—tell us "in what sense" to take the senses of the words.

2.17   The three stories of a meaning construct are much more interdependent than we might assume. In daily life situations, it seems that only the middle story is given in language. Somebody who came running, panting and excited, telling us in confusion of an accident he saw, provides the "Regulating Principles"; we know how to "read" his evidence, his intonations and exaggerations seem to be located not in language but in real life. And so is the frame of reference, the accident, about which he is telling.

In literary texts, on the other hand, all three stories must be present in the text and given in language. Indeed, in non-literary texts, too, important parts of the RP and *fr* are given in language: we do not hear the intonations of a journalist's report, but we have clues to reconstruct them from the text; we do not see the *fr* in Beirut, to which he refers, but some information about it is provided in his text.

2.18 In any case, the competence of using language is based on such an inter-action in a three-tier construct, and even if only the level of senses is provided in words, it cannot be understood properly and precisely without assumptions about the other two levels.

2.2 THE CONSTRUCTION OF AN FR

2.20 The concept of *frame of reference* becomes necessary when we observe the constructs of meaning in interpretations of literary texts. Though less obvious, the concept is needed for the explanation of any understanding of meaning in normal language use.

2.21 This may be demonstrated by the following example:

> (1a) He opened the door. A few pieces of clothing were strewn about. He caught the fish in his net.

The first two sentences are not connected by any syntactic or logical means. There is no relation of co-reference between them. They talk about different referents: door (r_1) and the constructed floor (r_2). Nevertheless, a reader will automatically see the description as coherent. The reader con-structs a hypothetical *fr*: a room, in which both sentences may be accommo-dated (i.e., a hypothetical continuum in which r_1 and r_2 are both located). Thus we obtain a two-story semantic structure:

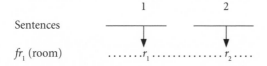

2.22 The concept of *fr* explains how readers perceive or assume things that have not been explicitly stated in language. The room is not mentioned in words. And a normal room must have a floor, walls, windows, furniture and so on. We need not specify all such details when a frame of any "standard" nature is given. The establishment of an *fr* implies the existence of many *indetermina-cies*, which were described in Ingarden's phenomenology but are not taken into account in "objective" theories of linguistics or semantics.

2.23 Thus, two sentences may be connected even if their referents are not co-referential but are "co-*fr*," that is, may be accommodated in one *fr*.

2.24 The third sentence, however, in this example, cannot reasonably be accommodated in the same *fr*. We do not normally catch fish in a net in a room. Indeed, the sentence, though in itself a literal sentence, is automatically perceived by understanders as a metaphor (be it a girl or a culprit in a detective story, according to various readers). The mechanism is simple: since the sentence could not be accommodated in its literal meaning within the constructed *fr*, and "he" in the third sentence may be co-referential with "he" in the first, we must transform the new sentence in order to make the text coherent. In this case, the transformation was metaphorical, based on a conventional male-chauvinist idiom. Without the notion of *fr* and the two-story structure of meaning, we could not account for this metaphor. (To be sure, a fuller analysis would account for the third story, of RP, as well. Thus, the third sentence may be seen as presented from "his" point of view, conveying something like: "He thought to himself: *I caught the fish in my net*").

2.25 In another reading, the third sentence may be accepted literally. In that case, however, we must change our "standard" notion of a room and assume some California eccentric who has a pool with fish and a net in his own room or backyard. Such a hypothesis about the *fr* is possible, but will enforce constraints on any unfolding of the story. Since the hypothetical *fr* was a construct, it may have to be changed or reconstructed, as often happens in fiction. In this case, instead of changing the sentence to accommodate it to an assumed *fr*, we changed the *fr* itself.

2.26 Consider now a different version of the same opening:

> (1b) He opened the door. A few pieces of clothing were strewn about. The beach was beautiful in the light of the early morning. To his satisfaction he saw that he caught the fish in his net. She was not to be seen anywhere. He attended to his business of pulling the net out of the water.

We now see that, in our previous reading, the easy assumption of a "room" accommodating the first two sentences, made us assume automatically that he opened the door and looked inside. One can, of course, open a door to the outside and accommodate the fish and the net by placing the house at a sea-shore. In the second version (1b), one *fr* accepts plausibly both the woman and the fishing in their literal meaning.

2.27 In this version, no metaphoric reading is necessary to justify any sentence. However, not only a negation of literal meaning may create metaphors, as many theories of metaphor assume. By placing the description of fish-catching in close proximity with the description of the girl who apparently undressed (and went swimming?), the text encourages a metaphorical transfer between the two. (In this case, the reader is encouraged even more, by the metonymy of the alliterated "beautiful beach": the beach is beautiful, hence the girl is beautiful.) The one *fr*, based on a continuum in space, was split into two thematically distinguished, sub-*frs*: girl and beach, which in turn entered into a metaphorical relationship.

2.28 In this example, in both versions (1a) and (1b), there was no *fr* known in advance, out there in the world, to which the words might refer. The *fr* was constructed by the same sentences that expressed things about it. It is—to use a famous simile—like sailing on a sea while building (and rebuilding) the boat under your own feet. The interdependence between the two levels, of sense and *fr*, is a characteristic feature of literary texts, as seen in the so-called hermeneutic "circularity" of interpretation. It is found, however, in any language use as well. For example, though the war in Lebanon is an objectively given *fr*, opinions about it are interdependent with assertions about various specific "facts" or properties of that *fr*.

2.3 RELATING SENSE TO FRAMES OF REFERENCE

2.30 Consider the following sentence:

(2) This is a filthy hotel.

This sentence has no definite meaning unless it is related to a specific frame of reference. There are several possible cases:
   a. If the sentence is used in a rundown hotel where the floors or furniture are clearly filthy, the literal sense of the words is accepted.
   b. If the floors are clean, the worse for the hotel: To accommodate the word "filthy" for this *fr*, we must turn it into a metaphor for moral behavior.
   c. A hotel may be "filthy" in both the literal and the metaphorical senses. The proper meaning may be ascertained only by checking the actual *fr*, or reporting about it, and may be contested, in whole or in part, by any observer.

2.31 As we can see, it is not only that senses of words are related to referents, but the referents in turn may influence the meaning in which the "senses" are to be perceived. It is a two-way operation. We need a frame of reference to ascertain the truth-value of sentences or the literal value of words.

2.32 d. If, however, the same sentence is used by a man staying in his girlfriend's apartment, neither "filthy" nor "hotel" can preserve their literal meaning. The whole sentence cannot be accepted as such, because the referent "apartment" cannot accept the index "this hotel." The Understander must process the sentence for a possible meaning in the given frame of reference, for example, something like: "To me, this place is filthy: I see it as a hotel, a temporary residence; I am leaving." Instead of saying "I am leaving you" the speaker used the utterance (2) "This is a filthy hotel," which became metaphorical in the given *fr*.

2.33 Literary texts as well as everyday language are replete with such transfers of sentences from their habitual *fr*s, where their literal meanings obtain, to "alien" *fr*s, requiring of the Understanders various kinds of transformations for their acceptance.

2.34 A further point must be made: When speaking of "truth-value" we must not see it narrowly as an either-or question: true or false. Evaluating the truth-status of utterances involves a wide range of possibilities: observations may be true "in a sense," exaggerated, ideologically biased, partial, or may merely map a *horizon* from which the speaker himself dissociates his position:

> (3) I am not going to tell you that actors and directors are crazy, because that would be either libelous or unnecessary (Walter Kerr, "Does the Actor Do Everything—Or Nothing at All?" *New York Times*, Sept. 23, 1979).

The critic did not say that actors are crazy, but placed craziness as a horizon of meaning: "not quite, but perhaps close." Truth-evaluation is made by comparing a given utterance with other sources of information on the same *fr* (and/or by comparing the speaker's position with other speakers' positions).

2.4 Consider another example. Coming home, I said to my wife:

> (4) Why don't you wear your blue dress.

My wife understood what I meant. It was not the color blue I was interested in, but rather the formality of the dress, which fit the party to which we were invited. My wife's understanding was due to her zeroing-in on two *fr*s:

(1) the possible purpose for changing her dress, namely the party to which we were invited (fr_1); (2) her wardrobe, of which her blue dress was part (fr_2). My sentence sent her to these two stores of information, from which she could easily retrieve the property "formal," justifying my request. Though I did not refer directly to the referent "formal," it was retrieved from the store of information (fr_2) as a possible bridge between the two *frs*.

2.41 My wife, however, answered: "It is not cold." This means that, from all the available information about her blue dress, she selected another property: its being warm, and related it not to the party but to another *fr*: the cold evening (fr_3).

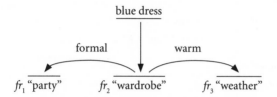

2.42 Of course, such misunderstandings which arise constantly in human communication may be corrected—either immediately or at a later time.

The distinction between the meaning of a given sentence and the speaker's intended meaning is usually described as "utterance meaning" versus "speaker's meaning." It is important to note, however, that such "speaker's meaning," as well as the not necessarily equivalent "Understander's meaning," can be obtained by specifically relating the utterance to concrete *frs* and to available information about them.

2.43 Speakers do not usually convey new information in their utterances, but rather manipulate information known beforehand. Instead of saying to my wife: "Turn back, move three steps to the right, open a door, go to the left wall, there is a closet, open the door, you'll see dresses hanging, . . . " etc., and then explaining exactly where we are going, what is the character of our hosts and why I suggest that she wear her blue dress, I merely used the last clause. One might say that one advantage of a marriage is the acquisition of a common store of information which enables humanly possible brevity of speech.

2.44 One might argue that, in this analysis, I have gone beyond language. But we cannot understand language unless we recognize that it always goes "beyond language," that is, sentences rely on previous information, whether obtained through language or otherwise.

2.45 There seems to be a difference between brief utterances, connected directly to situations in reality on the one hand, and long texts, especially in literature, which first create such situations by means of language. In both cases, however, a sentence will draw upon what is assumed to be "known" about a given situation, whether provided in the language of the "same" text or other texts.

In other words, in daily usage, between one utterance and another there are pieces of a "real" world, creating an illusion that individual utterances may be independent, that language is separate from reality; whereas in literature there is no such excuse: the "real" world is given in a verbalized form, and the mechanism is easily observable.

2.5   One day I opened the French newspaper, *Le Monde*. The first sentences of the newspaper, opening the front page lead article were:

(5) *Une nouvelle Allemagne*

La brutalité avec laquelle le chancelier allemand cherche à "mettre au pas" ses partenaires européens annonce-t-elle que la "nouvelle Allemagne" retrouve par une pente naturelle, certains caractères de la "mauvaise Allemagne" de naguère? M. Schmidt se veut-il un nouveau "chancelier de fer"? (*Le Monde*, Sept. 27, 1974).

[*A New Germany*

Does the brutality with which the German chancellor seeks to put his European partners "in their places" indicate that the "New Germany," in a natural tendency, is regaining certain characteristics of the "Bad Germany" of yesteryear? Does Mr. Schmidt want to be a new "Iron Chancellor"?]

2.51 The language of this article sends the reader to retrieve information from several frames of reference of European history. To understand the sentences, the reader has to know, or find out, about the European partnership to which the German chancellor belongs; the arguments after World War II as to whether a "New Germany" was possible; the dictatorial tendencies of the "Iron Chancellor," Bismarck. Then, the reader has to know the circumstances of the present *fr* to which the sentences refer. Clearly, *Le Monde* could not have meant that Germany returned literally to Nazi tactics or even to Bismarck's rule. (After all, the German Chancellor Helmut Schmidt ruled at the time by a shaky majority of one vote.)

2.52 Indeed, from other articles in the same issue of *Le Monde*, from other news media of the day, and from the history of the problem, it turned out that

Germany vetoed a rise of 5% in agricultural products suggested by other members of the European Common Market at the Commission in Brussels. Only with that knowledge can we understand the meaning of the word "brutality" in this text. Mr. Schmidt did not punch anybody in the nose, he was not even there when the vote was taken. Brutality here means something like "being inconsiderate, forcing of others' hands."

In communicating through language, what we are interested in are not the general concepts which words cover, but their specific meaning in a given utterance. The meaning of a word such as "brutality" becomes specified from the *fr* to which it is applied.

2.53 The same word, "brutality," is specified in a different direction in the following sentence:

(6) [. . .] will *The Times* now advocate that the U.S. public school textbooks reveal the full brutality of the westward "advance" through North America which swept aside hundreds of American Indian nations? (Letter to the *New York Times*, Sept. 8, 1982).

Here the brutality means something approaching genocide.

2.54 Thus, senses of words are not "given" or fixed, and then applied to specific referents. It is from what we know about the referent, and often from a complex state of affairs in a specific *fr*, that the sense of the word becomes specified in its meaning.

2.6 A telling example of an interpretation of an expression based on this mechanism can be found in the prominent journalist Stewart Alsop's *Newsweek* article "The Serious Man" (January 22, 1973) written after Nixon's second inauguration. Alsop claims that Nixon is "un homme sérieux," something that Nixon felt was lacking in his opponent, George McGovern. The article revolves around an analysis of this French expression:

(7) The literal meaning is, of course, "a serious man." Less literally, but more accurately, it means a man who has to be taken seriously. Less literally still, but more accurately in terms of the President's thinking, it means a tough man, a hard man, a man not to be pushed around.

Alsop distinguishes here three degrees of meaning: the literal, the "more accurate," and the real meaning as defined in terms of the President's position and idiolect. This third meaning is the one that really counts in communication and would be perceived as such by any TV viewer at the time. Understanders may arrive intuitively at such a correct meaning; when they have to account for it, however, they will resort to a technique so clearly demonstrated in Alsop's article:

(8) The President has certainly proved himself "un homme sérieux," in his interpretation of the phrase, since his re-election. Within the executive branch, he has been behaving like the grim reaper—and in plague time, at that. Heads have fallen, not only at the Cabinet level, but down to the level of the Census Bureau and the National Institutes of Health. But those who have survived and those who have been newly appointed now know without any question at all who is boss—that serious man, Richard M. Nixon.

Abroad too, by his own lights, he has shown himself a man to be taken seriously. He decided to break off the Paris talks in December, and to resume the bombing of North Vietnam, when Henry Kissinger reported to him that the North Vietnamese negotiators had begun making "frivolous" proposals. The bombs on Hanoi were Mr. Nixon's way of showing Hanoi—and Peking and Moscow too—that the President of the United States was not to be treated frivolously. He stopped the bombing and sent Kissinger back to Paris when assured that Hanoi was ready to "negotiate seriously."

2.61 The process of accounting for the "accurate" meaning may be described as follows. We first try to apply literally the expression "serious man" to Nixon's personality and activities. This cannot work, especially if we keep in mind that the Democratic Presidential candidate McGovern had a Ph.D. and could be considered more serious in that respect. As in the case of some previous examples (hotel, the fish in the net), we will try to find such a transformation of the expression which would make it acceptable in relevant *frs*.

Indeed, while scanning the field of Nixon's activities, Alsop found a number of *frs* to which the expression could be applied: "[. . .] he has been behaving like the grim reaper," firing officials in his administration; pushing the Europeans around in the economics talks; and resuming the bombing of North Vietnam. The phrase, "The serious man," can apply to these *frs* if we transform it into "a man to be taken seriously"; and even here, the word "seriously" can be accepted only in a special, metaphorical sense.

2.62 Thus Alsop established a *patterned relationship* between the expression and a number of relevant *frs* within a *network of information.*

We do not have a case of a direct reference to a given referent, but rather a matching of certain abstractions from possibly relevant *frs* with a fitting transformation of an expression.

2.63 The interpolated phrase, "a man to be taken seriously," has no direct referent in the *frs* to which it applies (Vietnam, the administration, etc.). It is merely *possible* to apply it, as one possible generalization. We feel that such an expression is true for a given *fr* when we feel that it is plausible to abstract from the mass of information (e.g., about Vietnam) a generalized pattern which would justify the given label.

2.64 To support this hypothesis, Alsop does not stop at the interaction between the two stories, of sense and *fr*, but resorts to the third level of RP as well. He observes Nixon's use of French, though "his French is not even vestigial," and explains it by Nixon's meeting with that aloof loner, DeGaulle, giving an additional twist to the image of "a serious man."

2.65 We may represent this in the following diagram:

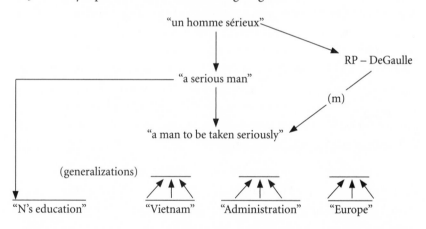

2.66 To sum up: it is not the immediate textual context which specifies the meaning of an expression. It is rather a *patterned relationship* which can be established between an utterance and specific *frs* selected from a wide network of information. An understanding hypothesis will always require: (1) the establishment of such a patterned relationship between an expression and (hypothetically) relevant *frs* to which it may apply; (2) the adjustment (metaphorization, transformation, specification, etc.) of the expression to the assumed *frs*, or interpolation of additional expressions between the two. Clearly, the two activities are simultaneous and interdependent; arguments against the one will usually undermine the other. Such seems to me to be a major point of contention in literary interpretations.

2.7   Consider the following example:

> (9) Raymond Aron says that the French today behave like "the caricature of Europeans." But in fact all parties to the argument are behaving like carica-tures of themselves: the Americans are talking as loudly as the bad Americans of political fiction; the British are trying hard to look as narrow-minded and isolationist as the John Bull of legend; and the French are clamoring about "honor and dignity" as if they still were at the court of Louis XIV (Arrigo Levi, "The Silent Europeans," *Newsweek*, April 15, 1974).

2.71   This example shows that utterances, though referring to a specific *fr*, may not hinge on existing referents in it. Such expressions rather project onto the *fr* new referents (*projected r*s) which serve as generalizations abstracting certain properties from an extremely complex network of information. To arrive from European history to individualized images of the major nations, and from there—to "caricatures of themselves," one would have to undertake a com-plex process of selection and simplification. This arduous road is spared us by the suggestive pseudo-generalizations (often in metaphorical form) which are typical of the language of analytical news articles—as opposed to news items. Though intuition spares us from actually collecting all the facts which would support such claims as Raymond Aron's, we know how to go about finding counter-examples if we wish to contest them.

2.72   Such generalizations ("Americans are talking loudly"; "bad state of the economy"; "the British look narrow-minded and isolationist"; "urban alien-ation") are false summaries of complex states of affairs. We know that other generalizations may be made, probably extracting different sets of facts from the same *fr*. We are not talking about concrete, existing referents, but interpo-lating generalizing referents between us and the world. Sometimes it is done on a level which became an FR in its own right (e.g., economic theory vs. facts of the economy), sometimes it is an *ad hoc* interpolation (as in Raymond Aron's metaphoric expressions). In any case, it refers not to referents in reality but to an Intermediate Field of generalizations or theories about reality.

2.73   Such generalizations take on the form of "*localized universals*." They serve as *semantic abbreviations*. No matter how well we know that "love," "Natasha's love," "Andrej's conversion," "ambivalence," "he is nice," etc., do not convey the complexity and individuality of the situation—and cannot really stand alone, without the detailed information about the given *fr*—we need such *abbreviations* in everyday life as in the reading of novels.

2.74   Another kind of abbreviations are personal names. Though considered semantically empty, in integrational semantics they serve as convenient *accumulators* of masses of heterogeneous meanings. If "Kissinger" or "Haig" said something on the Middle East, their names carry a whole history of negotiations, attitudes, etc. The same holds not only for names of people but of individual situations: "the depression of 1929," "D-day," etc.

2.8   A text is not necessarily a description of a "given" frame. Consider an example:

> (10) Yesterday, at a conference of shop stewards of a teamsters union local representing city employees, Mr. Koch was told that municipal workers expected "real" pay increases beyond cost-of-living adjustments in the round of bargaining talks for new contracts in the first year of the next mayoral term (*New York Times*, Oct. 23, 1977).

In this case, a new *fr* is constructed: a meeting between the mayor of New York, Mr. Koch, and representatives of the Teamsters Union. This passage is an intersection of elements from a number of heterogeneous *frs*. The reader must bring knowledge about those separate *frs* to understand the given passage. The reader must know (or find out) about: the role of labor unions, the special nature of the Teamsters Union, the state of the American economy, as well as the politics of mayoral elections.

The understander, as well as the writer, operates here not only with meanings of words and concepts, but with complex patches of information (*known frs*) which he does not have to detail but merely indicate their availability.

Of course, such disparate *frs* are not merely separate "worlds," but belong together in a wider universe, a Field of Reference (FR): the USA today.

2.9   Another case of intersecting *frs* in the same utterance is their metaphorical use, as in the following opening of an article in the *New York Times* "Week in Review":

> (11) *Administration's Doughboys Draw Fire on the Hill*
> With the President toughing it out in the bully pulpit, the Administration's good soldiers were left to slog up Capitol Hill last week, defending the virtues

of his economic program and explaining the vagaries of the economy (*New York Times*, March 7, 1982).

To the description of President Reagan's defense of his economic program, the author brought allusions to Teddy Roosevelt ("the bully pulpit," "slogging up" San Juan Hill); as well as to the American foot soldiers of World War I (who turned out to be the President's budget director, David Stockman, his chief economic advisor, Murray Weidenbaum, and Federal Reserve Board Chairman, Volcker).

The writer uses such remote *frs* to reflect vividly and succinctly on the given situation as well as to open up a store of possible parallels and contrasts.

3. FRAMES OF REFERENCE AND FIELDS OF REFERENCE

3.1   Frames of reference (*fr*) combine into larger wholes, *Fields of Reference* (FR). An FR is a vast hypothetical "universe" for which a number of (discontinuous) *frs* are given.

3.11   For example, in a novel, a character is presented in certain situations (*frs*) at the ages of two, thirteen, twenty-three, but not during all the years in between. We nevertheless assume that, being a human character in a realistic world, he lived during the non-presented years as well. The FR encompasses the whole span. In the same way, a number of countries mentioned in a newspaper on a given day are perceived as parts of a vaster FR, the globe. Or: the separate *frs*, connected by Mayor Koch's meeting with the teamsters (example [10]) are connected somewhere in one FR: contemporary USA.

3.2   Individual *frs* may intersect and criss-cross an FR in any number of ways. For example, if we conceive of the war in Vietnam as one FR, we can recognize that it is composed in our minds of many *frs*: descriptions of battles, individual human destinies, fictional stories in books and films, political and ideological arguments in the US, the behavior of General Westmoreland, relations between American soldiers and Asian women, etc.

3.3   Individual referents do not "belong" to fixed *frs* (as concepts would belong to a "theme" or a theory), but rather may be organized and reorganized in various *frs*.

This fact is widely used in literary and non-literary texts. For example, the description of a party necessarily includes the appearance of individual persons. The party is an *fr* in one time-continuum and one place. A person appearing within it belongs to another *fr* as well: his own biography, which is not fixed in time and space. Indeed, mention of a character in a party scene serves often as an occasion to move through his biography (or his conscious-ness) to other times and places in the past or in the future (either through the character's recollections or the narrator's remarks).

3.31   The same technique is used in newspapers. Though relying in part on the reader's previous knowledge of any given *fr* to which new information is added, newspapers do not rely on it fully. They tend to use flashbacks or to fill in some of that previous information. Thus, in a description of the death of Haile Se-lassie, the *New York Times*, after first mentioning his name, deviated to tell the biography of the man and his country. In graphic terms, we might say that, within a horizontal fr_1 of the emperor's death and funeral, the article inserted a vertical fr_2 of his life.

Many other *frs*—ideology, opinions, the person's adversaries, questions about the future—may criss-cross the same base.

$$fr_1 \text{ (time = 0) "party"} \quad \frac{\quad fr_2 \Big| \quad fr_3 \Big| \quad fr_4 \Big| \quad fr_5 \Big|}{\Big| \quad \Big| \quad \Big| \quad \Big|}$$

3.32   Indeed, writers as well as journalists favor the establishment of a *basic fr* in the form of a concrete scene, in which other *frs* (characters, political views, ideologies, abstract arguments) are easily embedded.

3.4   Most communication, except for literature, relates to *frs* that exist "out there," either in reality or in a theory. We either had or ideally could have ad-ditional information on the same *fr*, which may qualify, enrich, explain the meanings in the given text or provide a basis for their truth evaluation. This is true not only for things which exist in nature or history, but also for such constructs as myths (to which a number of texts contribute), scientific theories, ideologies, philosophical systems or superstitions.

3.41   A literary text (or as some would prefer to call it, a text of fiction, provided we include drama and poetry in the same category) is a text which creates at least one *Internal Field of Reference* (IFR). That means that at least some of the referents are given only in this text and no outside information may be valid for the truth evaluation of statements about such referents. Fictional characters in a novel as well as many actions and situations in which they appear are of this nature. Furthermore, they must be not just isolated referents but pertain to a coherent continuum, modeled upon some external FR.

3.42   The concept of an *Internal FR* is necessary also to overcome claims such as the argument that statements in literature are "pseudo-statements" (I. A. Richards) or "quasi-judgements" (R. Ingarden) or that "fictional" statements are the opposite of "serious" (J. Searle). *Within* the Internal FR, all statements are "serious" and are processed by the reader as in "real" *frs*: they may be true or false, and variously specified. Of course, with the one limitation: this is done only with available information for the given FR.

3.43   The problem of interpreting literature is largely due to the fact that a literary text both creates its own, unique Field of Reference and at the same time provides semantic material for referring to it. This "circularity," or interdependence, is especially difficult in "obscure" poetry, notably in modernist poetry, where the *fr* is a state of mind rather than an objective scene, and an ambivalent state of mind at that.

3.5   By saying that a literary text creates an Internal FR, I do not imply any absolute separation of a "Fictional World" from reality. Indeed, the reader of a work of fiction must "imagine" an "intentional" field or "imaginary space" into which he projects the reconstructed characters, events, meanings. At the same time, however, semantic material within a literary text may refer or relate to External Fields of Reference (ExFR).

3.51   ExFRs are FRs outside of a given IFR, that is, Fields for which additional information may be obtained outside the given work of fiction, such as names of cities and streets, historical characters, as well as generalizations about human nature, discussions of ideas, existentialism, psychoanalysis, etc. Such means, linking the IFR with the external world, provide channels for the transfer of additional information into the IFR. For example, "Paris" or "1830" open up for the reader a store of information from outside the novel or story. They may also throw light on the status of the internal presentation: whether it is grotesque, ahistorical, socialist, etc.

4. INTEGRATION OF SEMANTIC MATERIAL IN A TEXT

4.0 So far we have analyzed primarily short expressions, discussing the various uses of *fr*s and FRs to which they relate. Speakers, however, tend to develop what they have to say about an *fr* throughout an unfolding text. The integration of material within texts will be demonstrated through some examples, leading up to a discussion of the structure of texts.

4.1 The following passage is the opening of Joyce's story, "Eveline," from *Dubliners*.

(12) She sat at the window watching the evening invade the avenue. Her head was leaned against the window curtains, and in her nostrils was the odour of dusty cretonne. She was tired.

Few people passed. The man out of the last house passed on his way home; she heard his footsteps clacking along the concrete pavement and afterwards crunching on the cinder path before the new red houses. One time there used to be a field there in which they used to play every evening with other people's children. Then a man from Belfast bought the field and built houses in it—not like their little brown houses, but bright brick houses with shining roofs. The children of the avenue used to play together in that field—the Devines, the Waters, the Dunns, little Keogh the cripple, she and her brothers and sisters. Ernest, however, never played; he was too grown up. Her father used often to hunt them in out of the field with his blackthorn stick; but usually little Keogh used to keep *nix* and call out when he saw her father coming. Still they seemed to have been rather happy then. Her father was not so bad then; and besides, her mother was alive. That was a long time ago; she and her brothers and sisters were all grown up; her mother was dead. Tizzie Dunn was dead, too, and the Waters had gone back to England. Everything changes. Now she was going to go away like the others, to leave her home.

Home! She looked round the room, reviewing all its familiar objects which she had dusted once a week for so many years, wondering where on earth all the dust came from.

4.11 In this passage, the writer presents us with a wealth of information and opens up quite a few patterns for possible development in the story: characters, relationships, times, etc.

Let us observe the presentation of one referent: the "new houses." Bits of information about this referent are scattered throughout the passage, both directly and indirectly describing the new houses:

The New Houses

direct information	indirect
the last house	avenue
his home	
the new red houses	cinder path before [them]
	[← → concrete pavement]
	there used to be a field [they played, children]
a man from Belfast built [them]	
bright brick houses with shining roofs	not like their little brown houses

4.12   For a full perception of what the houses are like, the reader has to collect the scattered elements in one pattern and integrate them with one another. The various attributes do not merely specify the house but qualify each other as well. For example, in the expression, "the new red houses," the material of the redness is indeterminate. Later it attains a particular tint and material quality characteristic of bricks, which is quite different, let us say, from the redness of painted wood. Furthermore, it is a bright redness, though both "bright" and "brick" are given in a later sentence (and it is only by a process of inference that we may assume that the "houses" are the same as in that previous sentence.)

In a real life situation, pointing to the "new red houses" would provide the hearer with the additional information, namely that it is the redness of bright bricks. Here the text is presented from the point of view of Eveline, an observer within such a situation for whom it is enough to note something known to her: "*the* new red houses." The reader, however, does not know what Eveline can see and must obtain it from additional information scattered throughout the text.

One cannot convey in language the full particularity of objects. An illusion of particularity and specificity is created through the mutual qualifying of category concepts. All we can say in this text is that "red" is qualified by "brick" and "bright." The integration may be represented thus:

$$red \begin{vmatrix} brick \\ bright \end{vmatrix}$$

Similarly, "new" is qualified in several ways: (1) houses are new as opposed to what was there in the past—a field; (2) they are new houses as opposed to the old type of housing represented by her "little home"; (3) they are very new since only a cinder path rather than the concrete pavement leads to them.

The mutual qualifications of the various properties can be represented in the following diagram:

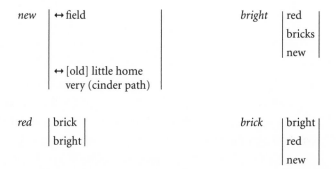

4.13 A further interesting point: "red" and "brick," though scattered in two sentences, when integrated create an image of "redbrick housing." "Redbrick housing" conveys a whole social-cultural concept, reinforced in its "foreign-ness" in Dublin by such remarks in the text as that it was built by a man from Belfast and (in a later passage) is inhabited by Italian workers.

A further interpretation, integrating the redbrick housing with additional elements in the text, will present it as a "new" and "shining" intruder, "in-vading" (a word in the text) Eveline's world and representing her feeling that "everything changes."

4.14 The construct of the houses is, furthermore, used in the text for the con-struction of other semantic materials. Thus, the opposition, "houses" (in the present)—"field" (in the past) provides a motivation for the introduction of two extensions and the resultant opposition between Eveline's own present and the past.

$$\text{house} \rightarrow \text{she, in home, today}$$
$$\updownarrow$$
$$\text{field} \rightarrow \text{she in childhood}$$

4.15 A further opposition is constructed between the "houses" and Eveline's "home." (Only on one occasion is the word "home" used to designate the man's house.) Note the sparing use of attributes: almost no counterparts are given for any attributes, though they are obviously implied:

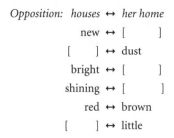

4.16 The carefully constructed house in this passage does not reappear in the story. It merely serves for referential grounding: to make the concept of "home" concrete by opposition. Indeed, "home"—the last word of the long second paragraph and the first word of the third—becomes the locus of the story and its symbolic center, though we get very few physical descriptions of it. The opposition of the "positive" attributes of the "shining" external world to the "negative" attributes of the "little" and dusty home is overturned in the epiphany of the story: "Home" is, after all, a more intimate place than "house."

4.17 In the opening of this story, the house serves a function of *referential grounding*. A secondary referent ("house") is established in the beginning of a text to develop on its basis a more central referent ("home"), continuing in the same *fr*, much as a secondary character is introduced at the beginning of a novel as a basis for the unfolding of the major characters.

4.18 Though some of the specific techniques as observed here may be conventions of literature, and the close and exhaustive attention to the details may be borrowed from literary interpretation, there is nothing literary about the semantic integration itself. We merely attended to a "maximal reading" of the text. The technique of this very elementary example of semantic integration is valid for any text containing scattered elements for the presentation of one referent or one *fr*: be it stories, newspaper articles or conversations into the night.

4.2 A less direct mode of integration may be observed in the pattern of repetition of the word "dust." When it first appears, in the second sentence of the story, it is not part of any statement that the sentence makes; it is merely "irrelevant" semantic material, emphasizing the concreteness of the description.

However, when "dust" here is connected with the repetition of "dust" in the last sentence of the quoted passage, we understand the first "dust," realizing that it expresses Eveline's revolt (apparently, she did not dust the house as she should have) as well as her helplessness vis-à-vis the decaying house: dust is both a symbol of disintegration and a Biblical allusion. The last sentence: "where on *earth* all the dust came from," is an allusion to "from dust you come, and to dust you shall return." Where on earth? Of course, from earth.

4.21   Such reevaluation of former material from later material is well known in the structure of detective stories. It is true, however, for any semantic material dispersed throughout a text. This case is a typical instance of interpretation as practiced in readings of literature. It is however not a *literary* form but a matter of *understanding* literary texts as bodies of language. Such phenomena are to be found in everyday language as well, though perhaps less intensively. Thus, the use (or omission) of expressions in Soviet documents may be interpreted by Sovietologists as indicating shifts in Soviet policies or attitudes, that is, judged in comparison with other texts rather than on its own merits.

4.3   As we see from these examples, elements in a text may be linked discontinuously; this is true for semantic as well as non-semantic (e.g., sound) patterns. Indeed, the patterning of any text is done on two levels: the *Level of the Text-Continuum* and the *Reconstructed Level*. On the latter level we link up and rearrange discontinuous elements in a text, according to their inherent logic: time—in a chronological order, persons—in a psychological structure, and so on.

Reconstructed Level

Binary Oppositions	People
inside—outside	hostile father
dusty—shining	mother dead
home—house	brothers and sisters
present—past	neighborhood children (left)
grown-up—childhood	
staying—leaving	**Points of View**
	Eveline, embedded in Narrator
space	
Dublin—Belfast	**referential grounding**
old homes—red-brick housing	Eveline sitting at window
time past—present—future	
rhetorical oppositions	**sound patterns**

4.31   In this short opening of a story, a very complex state of affairs is conveyed to the reader. On the Reconstructed Level, we obtain a network of relationships, including: relations in space, time, people, binary oppositions, points of view (combining the narrator's and Eveline's positions), as well as such non-semantic aspects as sound patterns.

This network of relationships as presented on the Reconstructed Level will be further filled in and enlarged in the course of the story.

4.4   We may observe that neither the motif of dust nor the house were introduced as subjects or topics of any sentence. They are secondary words, not participating in the explicit proposition of the sentence. They may nevertheless become important, or even merely thematized, on the Reconstructed Level. We may observe how the text continuum led us to the "houses." The first sentence introduces "evening." This becomes a generalization (G_1) for which a detail (D_1) is provided: "Few people passed." Then a detail of this description $(D_1 = G_2)$ is given: one man (D_2).

However, in a concrete description, if Eveline is observing the man, she must see or hear him in some concrete space: she hears his footsteps on the pavement, then on the path. Thus, we are led through a chain of concatenations: evening—few people—one man—walking—path, and the path leads to the houses. Thus, "houses" are introduced not as a theme of any sentence or passage, but as a sixth element in a chain of extensions. In our reconstruction, however, it may become a primary topic.

4.41   Any word or connotation in a text may become thematized in this form in an interpretation and may attain a higher or lower place in an interpretive hierarchy. The word "invade" in the first sentence has nothing to do with the proposition, but may become a key word in the meaning construct of the whole story.

4.42   A further example: the word, "new," is introduced in the same sentence at an even lower level of thematic subordination: as an adjective in "the new red houses."

The next sentence, however, does not develop the theme of Eveline's fatigue or of the evening nor of its subtheme: the passing man. It rather picks up the sub-subordinated word "new," by way of semiotic opposition: "one time there used to be a field there." The word "new," implying "a shift from past to present," is decomposed into its components (past—present), presented in a reverse order. Thus, we moved from an *fr* in the present to an *fr* in the past through the semantic structure of a syntactically subordinated word.

4.43 To be sure, the leap from present to past based on an association from a secondary word is motivated in this text by Eveline's point of view. Eveline's being tired, her inward look (when the outside grew dark) and her stocktaking before leaving her home for good—all motivate the associative composition of this text, moving from present to past, from description to evaluation and vice-versa.

It must be noted that these qualities of Eveline are obtained by the reader as constructs except for the one direct observation, "she was tired."

4.44 Another telling example of the associative composition can be found in the transition from the second to the third paragraph of the story. After listing a number of people who had left her world since childhood (either dead or returned to England), the story tells us that "now she was going to go away like the others, to leave her home." "Home" is introduced as the necessary object of the verb "to leave." The theme was *leaving* rather than *home*. But since all this is presented from within Eveline's consciousness, she responds with an association to the verbal element "home"; the next paragraph begins: "Home! She looked round the room, reviewing all its familiar objects."

From a paragraph centering in the past, we have shifted to a description of the interior of the house in the present. The shift occurred through one word, "home," used in two different senses: the family framework and the physical house.

4.45 As we see, the level of the Text Continuum is organized differently from the Reconstructed Level. The text continuum must provide ways of introducing new sentences and paragraphs, either through syntactic or semantic links. Eventually, all the material necessary for the Reconstructed Level will be provided (and the state of affairs conveyed), but only part of it is given explicitly in direct statements.

4.5 The semantic organization of the text continuum is a highly complex matter, which we cannot discuss here. Many semantic constructs from the reconstructed level are used for linking in the text continuum. We shall give a few examples here.

4.51 The first sentence is linked by the pronoun "she" to the title "Eveline." (It is also linked to the title by the sound cluster: EVEliNe— EVENiNg—INVade—AVENue.)

The second sentence is linked to the first by the pronoun "her"; but also by a double G:D relationship (Generalization: Detail): her leaning head is a detail (D_1) of Eveline's sitting and watching (G_1); the nostrils (D_2) a detail of her head (G_2).

The third sentence, "She was tired," is linked through the pronoun and anaphora. It is also a generalization (G_3) of the previous sentence, though abstracting a different quality (from "the leaning head") than the generalization which preceded the same, second sentence ("she sat at the window"). An interpretation may further generalize from the same second sentence as presenting Eveline in a sensuous rather than a relational mood (G_4).

In a simplified manner, we may represent it thus:

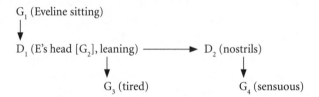

4.52 The next sentence, however, "Few people passed," has no direct link to the sentence preceding it. A reader must construct a link within the given *fr* to connect it with discontinuous elements in the preceding text. Indeed, it is both an example of the evening and the object of Eveline's "watching."

4.53   Here is a schematized diagram of the major links in the text continuum of the whole passage:

Concatenation in text continuum

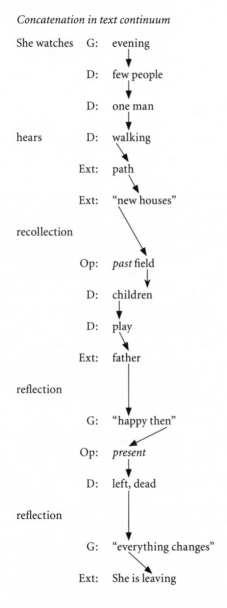

Ext – extension; D – detail; G – generalization; Op – opposition
Slanted arrows represent shifts to other *frs*.

4.54 Though it would seem that the chain of linking in the text continuum is the primary level—indeed, it provides the "floor" from which the *fr* is reconstructed—it in itself cannot be constituted without some material from those constructs. We cannot possibly account for the composition of any discourse on the text continuum level without recourse to patterns which this level uses from the reconstructed level. Such are divisions of texts into thematic subunits, speakers, summary and details, etc. In short, the patterning on both levels must go hand in hand and interact.

4.6   As we see from the "Eveline" example, a sentence cannot be identified with one unit of meaning; almost every word or connotation may be linked with pertinent semantic material elsewhere in the text into patterns, which may then be summarized in sentences on the level of interpretation. Furthermore, texts intend to convey not one theme or idea, but multi-dimensional states of affairs. We cannot possibly decompose them into separate aspects and present each one separately in a text (though we can do it in an analysis). It is impossible to describe an event without providing some semantic material about its participants: chains of event-sentences are made up by narratologists and are not typical for real texts. And so it is impossible to describe a character in action without the space in which it takes place. Thus, any sentence—certainly any *fr*—will provide material for several semantic patterns, in addition to its direct predications.

4.61 Moreover, involving several themes in one sentence is a favorable technique, in journalism as in literature. Here, for example, is a sentence from a news article:

> (13) Miss Schimpf, whose father is a butcher in an A&P store in Lima, Ohio, is in many ways typical of the 12,300,000 undergraduates and graduate students on campuses today ("College Students Squeezed Into Career Paths," *New York Times*, March 7, 1982).

Clearly, Miss S. is not typical in that her father is a butcher. The syntactic structure, if taken as one meaning-unit, would provide an absurdity. To understand properly, we must decompose the sentence and link each thematic element with further relevant material dispersed throughout the article.

5. THE THREE DIMENSIONS OF A TEXT

5.0   Meanings are conveyed through texts. As we noted earlier (2.01), the structure of meanings is not identical with the structure of texts.

We use a three-dimensional model for the description of texts. Since this part of the theory has been explained elsewhere (Chapter 4), I shall merely outline it briefly here.

5.1   As we saw in the "Eveline" example, the perception of a text involves patterning on two levels: the text continuum and the reconstructed level. The patterns on both levels may be separated into three dimensions, three complex constructs abstracted from the same text.

    A. The Dimension of Speech and Position

    B. The Dimension of Meaning and Reference

    C. The Dimension of the Organized Text

The dimensions are intertwined in a text and interdependent and nevertheless they require separate construction and separate methods for their description.

5.11   The Dimension of Meaning and Reference is constructed along the lines discussed above. It is important to note that we do not necessarily have in a text an exhaustive list of definite meanings and references. Even a literary text does not provide a fixed "Possible World." We have rather FRs and *frs* (some—uncertain) in which there is a number of potentially possible and interpretation-dependent references, descriptions and meanings.

5.2   There is, however, no information about real or fictional *frs* which is neutrally available. All information that we have (perhaps with the exception of some immediate sense-data) is mediated through various sources: speakers, creators of texts, ideological or emotive positions, cultural attitudes. This spans all we absorbed about the world—from mother to the latest news report. In literary texts, our information about the "fictional world" (in the IFR) is mediated through the nature of the narrator and the positions of various characters, and is often not resolvable in one definite "meaning." This phenomenon was discussed especially by M. Bakhtin, though his concept of "polyphony" should not be restricted to Dostoevsky.

5.21   The mediation of information through sources is typical of news reports as well. Here are excerpts from a news article in the *New York Times* about the SALT negotiations between the U.S.A. and the Soviet Union:

(14)   **HIGH U.S. AIDES SEE IMPROVED PROSPECTS**
FOR EARLY ARMS PACT
DIFFICULT PROBLEMS REMAIN
But Washington Officials Assert
Remarks by Carter and Brezhnev
Indicate Accord Is Likely Soon
By BERNARD GWERTZMAN
Special to the New York Times

WASHINGTON, Oct. 22—High Administration officials said today that although difficult problems remain to be settled in the intensified negotiations for a new agreement on limitation of strategic arms, optimistic remarks by President Carter and Leonid I. Brezhnev yesterday had underscored the likelihood of an early accord.

The officials, who have long been cautious, said that if Mr. Carter and Mr. Brezhnev, the Soviet Communist Party leader, want an accord soon, they will have it. There have been reports of major progress since last month, when a breakthrough was apparently achieved in the negotiations after three years of stalemate.

Mr. Carter, in a speech in Des Moines last night, went further than any official when he said, "I predict that within a few weeks we will have a SALT agreement that will be the pride of this country."

Afterward Mr. Carter qualified his remarks to say that "I don't know how many weeks it will take." He added: "We have much better prospects than we had a few weeks ago; we are still negotiating with the Soviets and keeping the Senate informed. I think we've got a good prospect, but it's not firmed up yet. That's all I can say."

Brezhnev Cites Progress

A few hours earlier, Mr. Brezhnev said in Moscow that there had been "a definite turn for the better" in the negotiations and that "we would like to bring these negotiations to a successful conclusion without any undue delays." [. . .]

Today, when asked how his comment could be reconciled with those of Mr. Carter and Mr. Brezhnev, the official said, "If the two leaders really believe they can get an accord in a short period of time, they can." The general view among those involved in arms control has been that an accord was probably unlikely before early next year but that it was virtually certain one would be reached.

At first glance, the reader gets an optimistic view. The three stages of the title, however, contradict each other in turn. The reader gets a long series of summarizing remarks and direct quotes in a wavering pattern of optimistic and qualifying or detracting views. These views are further qualified by such hedging expressions as: "a breakthrough was *apparently* achieved," "an accord was *probably unlikely* before early next year, but [...] it was *virtually* certain." The most optimistic direct quote is from President Carter's speech in Des Moines, predicting "that within a few weeks we will have a SALT agreement that will be the pride of this country"; but, as the article tells us, Mr. Carter later qualified his remarks saying that "I don't know how many weeks it will take [...] I think we've got a good prospect, but it's not firmed up yet. That's all I can say."

5.22 The reader got a variety of sources: quotes from Carter's and Brezhnev's statements (however, selected by the author of the article); various sources close to the negotiations, described as "reports of major progress," "details have been circulating in Washington," or, more directly: "High Administration officials" who held a special briefing for reporters. On the other hand, "one official" contradicted the reports.

We have direct quotes and specific details as well as summarizing generalizations such as the author's own statements about "optimistic remarks by President Carter" and "reports of major progress."

The reader will further qualify Carter's remarks by the circumstances in which they were made: in a political speech in a remote place.

5.23 All this contradictory network of concrete details and assumptions is mediated again through three additional positions: that of the journalist, Bernard Gwertzman; the genre of a summarizing news article; the *New York Times*. Readers may be used to this newspaper and accept its reports as the truth, thereby neutralizing the three framing positions; but a comparison with other sources of information may show discrepancies.

5.24 This is by no means an unusual way of telling about a state of affairs. A person describing his or her mother may provide the listener with a similar medley of details, anecdotes and generalizations; understanding involves not taking any single generalization about the mother's character or relationship separately from the other materials relating to the same *fr*. Many things that we want to say we are simply not capable of saying in one, definite statement.

5.3   The truth-value, weight of evidence, irony, exaggerations, circumstantial limitations, ideological bias, etc., of statements must be adjudged by the understander from what he knows about the speaker, the producer of a text or its genre.

The speaker's position, however, is not always given explicitly. Quite often, it must be reconstructed by the understander (using the understander's own limitations of knowledge and ideological bias) from the material at hand as well as from external information. Thus, in the journalist's remarks about the Administration's opinion, the reader has to sort out what elements reflect the journalist's position and which ones reflect the Administration's. A sentence may be judged ironic when compared to external knowledge about the same *fr* or when the speaker's attitude is assessed (e.g., if he is Art Buchwald).

5.4   The meaning of an utterance ("speaker's meaning") is thus a result of processing the level of sense in relation to the *fr* on the one hand and to the constructed speaker's position on the other.

5.41 The speaker himself, however, is a construct from the *fr* in which he is embedded. This is clear especially in fiction. It is not true, as some narratological models would have it, that there is a separate story and a separate narrator outside of it, presenting it. Actually, information about the world of a story is processed not only through a narrator (if he exists) but through the speech and consciousness of all characters and observers in the text. They, in turn, are themselves constructs built from the *fr*s in which they emerge.

Thus, a "circularity" or interdependence occurs: we believe a character's words if he himself is believable; if the words, however, turn out to be partial or manipulative, we are forced to revise our image of the character himself.

5.42 This interdependence can be schematically represented in the following diagram (where S is a speaker and the text may start either with a speaker/narrator or with an "objective" presentation of an *fr*):

Dimension A (S_1) | S_2 | S_3 | S_4 |

Dimension B (fr) | fr' | fr'' | fr''' | fr_{iv}

5.5   Of special interest are dialogues or "talk," in literature as well as in life. The interlocutors talk about things in an external fr_1 (or leap from one fr to another). At the same time, the speech situation itself constitutes an fr_2 which may be different from fr_1. The interlocutors may switch from their topic (fr_1) directly to their speech situation (fr_2). Moreover, their expressions about fr_1 reflect back on their positions within fr_2.

Thus, two Americans arguing in the sixties about the war in Vietnam refer directly to Vietnam but their words "boomerang" and characterize at the same time the speakers themselves, their political and emotional attitudes.

5.51   Indeed, quite often talk "about" things contributes less to those things than to the characteristics and expressions of the speakers themselves. This is certainly true for "small talk."

fr_2 ("talk") S_1 S_2

fr_1 (Vietnam)

This double structure is further complicated by the reflections of talk on the speakers' personalities beyond the given speech situation: $S_1 = fr_3$; $S_2 = fr_4$, with extensions in time.

5.52   The uses of the double level structure of talk are many. One most important use is for the composition of texts. A speaker may leap—in his words, in his consciousness, or in his analogies and generalizations—from one fr in time and space to another, thus spanning a vast field of experience.

5.6   I shall not discuss here the third dimension, the Organization of the Text. The order, rhythm, symmetries and overall structure of any text are of great importance, especially in their rhetorical and aesthetic functions. Sound patterns, repetition, segmentation, breaking up the information in stages, manipulations of the reader's attention, etc., are pertinent to literary and non-literary texts (though essential to and often formalized in the former). Since no complex of meanings can be presented at once, the ordering of information, the shifts in attitude, and the detailing may affect the perception and the meaning of the text itself.

5.7   The organization of the text, in turn, employs patterns from the other two dimensions. There is such formal segmentation as divisions into strophes, chapters, paragraphs, or the use of titles and subtitles. Beyond that, the segmentation of texts may be based on thematic (sub-) divisions, distinctions between speakers (this is the normal technique for separating scenes in a drama), and an editor's (or narrator's) logical or rhetorical structuring of a text (e.g., summarizing an article in the first paragraph or bringing an effective anecdote up front).

6. SUMMARY REMARKS

We may now recapitulate the general framework for Integrational Semantics.

A text (as any other semiotic object) is patterned in three dimensions. Though autonomous, they are interlaced in the text; and they interact in such a way that patterns of one dimension may be used by the other or "translated" onto it.

The second Dimension, of Meaning and Reference, is in turn constituted as a three-tier construct. The elements of each tier rely on outside authorities:

The story of Regulating Principles is constructed from the Dimension of Speakers and Positions.

The story of sense—from the "language."

The story of FR and *frs*—from the "World."

The two schemes—for the Reconstructed World and the Text—are analogous. The third levels, however, are not related to each other. In the domain of Meaning it is a "map" of (a segment from) the "World"; in the domain of the Text it is the structure of the autonomous textual object, on which the whole document is based.

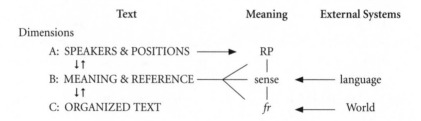

4 THE STRUCTURE OF SEMIOTIC OBJECTS

A Three-Dimensional Model

1. INTRODUCTORY REMARKS

In this essay, I intend to argue that literary texts can be apprehended fully only through a three-dimensional model. For purposes of understanding or analysis we may have to observe one dimension at a time (or certain aspects of it). We cannot, however, disregard its relations with various aspects of the other dimensions. Theories based on properties of one dimension only will remain weak and limited in solving the problems of literary texts in their aesthetic or communicative functions, because bridging between the abstract model and concrete descriptive analysis requires relegating too much to "context," whereas this "context" is merely part of a different kind of organization.

Furthermore, though literary texts—in their wealth of structuration and meaning-relations—most readily display typical properties of sign-complexes, such properties are by no means confined to literature. The three-dimensional model applies actually to all kinds of texts, indeed: to all objects which may be considered "semiotic."

This is a paper on a very general, abstract model, which, I hope, will become clear through a number of concrete examples (however sketchily illustrated). At the same time, it is a simple model, reflecting the simplicity of our basic cognitive operations. Three different kinds of operations—it is argued—combine to grasp any specific complex configuration in language texts or in other objects which convey meanings to us—and this is precisely because meanings are conveyed through objects which possess these three dimensions.

2. SEMIOTIC OBJECTS

Semiotics is said to be the science of systems of signs or of sign-processing. If so, it must recognize that signs rarely appear in isolation. We usually confront sign complexes, to be understood in a variety of ways. Moreover, signs are not floating ideas, they appear in objects in the world, which have their own structure and influence the nature of the sign. They may be either objects made of language, i.e., "texts," or of any other material, such as buildings, nature, colors in painting, etc. Without considering the nature and organization of such objects, we cannot properly understand their signifying functions.

Semiotic objects may originally be intended for sign-functions or not. In the second case, they become "semiotic" if they are interpreted as signs by "understanders." For example, while walking in a city we "read" the forms, sizes or density of buildings to signify: "office buildings," "middle-class homes," "slums," etc., even if such messages were never intended by the producers of those objects. While reading such objects as signs, we select and abstract some parts and aspects of the observed objects, which convey the reconstructed message, disregarding other aspects which serve other, non-signifying functions. For example, a multi-lobed arch signifies Islamic architecture in Spain, while a pointed arch represents Christian Gothic architecture. In both cases, there are of course further qualities symptomatic of their respective "styles," but there are clearly non-stylistic properties as well, such as the existence of walls, the sturdiness of the construction, etc., which make the "coherence" of the object and enable its existence in the world and the performance of its primary, non-semiotic functions. Clearly, structural considerations—in the sense of the material structure of buildings—and its social functions influence the expression of any architectural style. The same, however, holds for semiotic objects originally intended for aesthetic, non-utilitarian purposes. Thus, the conventional length of films will limit and frame the possibilities of cinematic expression (as was pointed out long ago by Eikhenbaum). Or: the constraints of a linear presentation, segmented into parts, dictate a great deal in the nature of the presented "world" in works of fiction.

In recent years, attempts have been made to base literary theories on speech act theory or linguistic functions (in Jakobson's sense); previous theories have discussed literature in terms of a fictional "world" or literary "meaning"; or, on the contrary, reduced everything to "structure." The point of my argument is that it is impossible to account for all aspects and elements in works of literature through any one of those models alone. On the other hand, it seems to me that one can analyze texts exhaustively while organizing their elements into three separate, though interlaced and highly interdependent dimensions:

A. DIMENSION OF SPEECH AND POSITION

B. DIMENSION OF MEANING AND REFERENCE

C. DIMENSION OF THE ORGANIZED TEXT (OR STRUCTURED OBJECT).

In each particular text, patterns of the three dimensions may be intersecting, partly overlapping, embedded in each other, motivated by each other, or even constituted by means of each other. Nevertheless, the dimensions always remain autonomous and are not reducible to any one of them, requiring, therefore, separate and complementary methodologies for their study.

3. ONE EXAMPLE: WORDS IN ARCHITECTURE

Speech and embedded speech surround us wherever we go. Before analyzing the complex phenomena in this dimension, I would like to present one, rather simple, illustration. A building in Berkeley, California, has a number of inscriptions on its walls. Four of them were recorded by my informer (see Table 1). Insofar as the whole building may be considered a semiotic object, it clearly has embedded linguistic texts, which relate variously to the building itself or to related phenomena. "*3a*, Boalt Hall of Law 1911," refers to the building itself and to the date of its construction. On the other hand, "*4*, School of Law," refers to a social institution which is located in that building (and may or may not occupy all of it, or not be located entirely here). Again, "*3b*, McEnerhy Library 1951," clearly refers to only part of the building and presumably does not include the walls of the library, since the date indicates that it was established much later than the building itself. The interpretation made so far is not based on any sign or any syntactic means presented to the viewer. It is a construct which any understander has to make, applying words to specific frames of reference, while using logical argumentation based on knowledge of such social institutions. There may always be knowledge unavailable to the understander which would make his understanding incomplete or approximate. For example, if he is not in the field of law, he may not know whether Boalt or McEnerhy are famous lawyers or donors (both conventions exist in name-giving in American universities).

Table 1. Texts in Architecture

University of California, Berkeley, Law School Building

1. YOU WILL STUDY THE WISDOM OF THE PAST. FOR IN A WILDERNESS OF CONFLICTING COUNSELS, A TRAIL HAS THERE BEEN BLAZED. YOU WILL STUDY THE LIFE OF MANKIND, FOR THIS IS THE LIFE YOU MUST ORDER, AND TO ORDER WITH WISDOM, MUST KNOW. YOU WILL STUDY THE PRECEPTS OF JUSTICE, FOR THESE ARE THE TRUTHS THAT THROUGH YOU SHALL COME TO THEIR HOUR OF TRIUMPH. HERE IS THE HIGH EMPRISE, THE FINE ENDEAVOR, THE SPLENDID POSSIBILITY OF ACHIEVEMENT, TO WHICH I SUMMON YOU AND BID YOU WELCOME.

   Cardozo

2. [In the spring, the trees in full bloom covered up Cardozo's wisdom. The letters are all in caps—in iron on granite.]

3a. BOALT HALL OF LAW 1911

3b. McENERHY LIBRARY 1951

4. SCHOOL OF LAW

A more difficult case is inscription 1. Its second person form of address implies a speech situation, in which a person named Cardozo appeals apparently to students of a law school. It is, however, a speech act within a speech act: the style and the direct solemn message of Cardozo's language cannot possibly be taken without a smile by present-day students. It is as if the heads of the present-day institution were saying to their students: "We would like to tell you something like this if it could be translated into a present-day message." This inscription relates neither to the building nor to the institution within it but to people who attend that institution. Furthermore, it refers to qualities in the minds and behavior of such people. For me, walking by that building has even further embedding because, since I am not a law student, I am not the addressee of that message. I don't even know who Cardozo was, and I don't know whether he addressed students in this law school or elsewhere. Therefore I must further process this message to convey something about the moral purposes which the founders of this school had in mind, possibly as opposed to what lawyers are considered to be in society today.[1]

Inscription 2 was not legible to my informant, because the trees, which seem to be part of the organized architectural space, had grown since the school was built and covered the inscription. What remained was the aesthetic function alone ("iron on granite"), or the "poetic function" in Jakobson's terms: the set toward the text itself.

As this case shows, speech embedded in architecture may be used in a variety of modes. An understander has to construct the intended speech events, relate words to frames of reference and perceive their place in the larger object. In our case, the words are not related directly to their physical "context" and have to be processed in a variety of ways, referring to: the building itself, one part of it, the social institution located in it, people attending that institution, attitudes of such people. Though physically all these inscriptions are embedded within the building, some are meant to be above it, to embed it, naming it or describing it, and some are merely part of it. Only when the building is processed through such verbal material can we abstract further sign aspects from the non-verbal parts of the building. (Even an observation that there are no overt "law-school features" in the architecture may be processed as a sign of modesty, seriousness, etc.). Of course, our analysis is not complete, since

---

1   Further embedding may be imagined if I think of the students and authorities of this school today, who perceive (seriously? solemnly? ironically?) what the message was to the builders of the school, who, in their turn, quoted Cardozo and his immediate audience.

within that building, and within the institutions located in it (School of Law, library) there may be a large amount of archival verbal material pertaining to it, some of which describes the nature of the institution as a whole (programs, schedules, student announcements, textbooks, etc.).

This is an example of how non-verbal and basically non-semiotic objects may use verbal material to guide their understanders' processing of its signification. Verbal intermediaries may be used even where no words are presented overtly, e.g., in medieval paintings representing Biblical stories. On the other hand, verbal texts use our knowledge of non-verbal objects, without which semiotic processing or "understanding" is impossible. Any theory which separates the verbal from non-verbal modes of communication, or overlooks their interaction, is limited in explaining the separate modes as well. Meaning is not simply "given" in objective signs, but depends largely on interactional constructs. Separately studied signs are merely potential units, *assignable sign-forms*, which become meaningful only in larger constructs.

4. THE DIMENSION OF SPEECH AND POSITION

All information conveyed in language is produced and presented, directly or indirectly, by "speakers" and from particular positions. In fact, all knowledge we acquired about the world via language was originally presented to us from specific positions. Our mothers, friends, teachers, mass media, etc., were never entirely neutral sources of information. The same holds for President Carter's opinions about inflation, given to us through a selection of words he chose to use at the particular moment, mediated by a White House spokesman, again excerpted by a specific journalist, printed by the *New York Times*, the position of which we may or may not accept even if we are interested in the factual information. When such a complex series of embedded speech and positions is presented to us, it may be important to know precisely whose position is reflected in specific sentences and it may be quite hard to know it.

Literary texts can be seen as chains of embedded speech. The most general form of speech embedding is:

$$A \; (\underline{S \; (C_1 - C_2) \; D}) \; R$$

A = author, S = speaker, C = character, D = addressee, R = reader.
The underlined symbols represent language in the text: A and R are constructs outside of the text.

In various texts, some elements of this formula may be missing, or may be multiplied and complicated. Since a literary text is usually divorced from a single speech situation, the author (or the so-called "implied author") is a construct to be made by the reader, and may be constructed variably, may be coherent or not, may be identified with the writer (W) or not, etc. On the other hand, there may be a variety of reader constructs; a contemporary reader, a "proper" reader, a present-day reader, an actual reader, etc. In this formula, I used the term "speaker" rather than "narrator" in order to cover poetic as well as narrative texts. In fiction, too, a main speaker is not necessarily a "narrator" in the strict sense: he may present words about a "world" without intending to tell a "story."

It is important to note that such embedding cannot be understood merely through the formal linguistic presentation. Thus, the first person in lyric poetry may represent not the poet but an object or character distinguished from him; and on the other hand, the second person form is often used to express the first person of the lyrical "I"; or: the third person may be identified by the reader as the "poet" himself. The same holds for fiction. Any impersonal narration including language about a character may be reconstructed by the reader to represent that character's speech, thought, feelings, or in general his position. Quite often special linguistic devices are used to indicate this phenomenon (such as "Free Indirect Style") but in many texts or parts of texts this is not the case. In general, any "higher" speaker, while talking about a person embedded in his speech, may represent some of that person's language, thoughts, feelings, and positions. When studied from the speaker's (or narrator's, or author's) side, this phenomenon looks one-directional: simply as "embedding." When seen from the reader's side, however, this is *Combined Discourse*, in which two voices may intermingle. It is not at all true that texts are monolithic in this respect, and are written either from the narrator's point of view or from a character's center of consciousness. Even when one of the two possible voices is dominant, the other voice may occasionally interfere or take over. Where linguistic indicators are lacking, the understander has to separate the two (or more) voices according to general hypothetical constructs which he makes about the possible positions of the intersecting voices. For example, in Joyce's story "Eveline," the reader realizes that most of the text is presented from Eveline's point of view (though she is described in the third person, in an impersonal narration) but a number of generalized sentences betray the narrator's intrusions. The sentence "Everything changes" is suspect due to its generalizing nature. It is only when we finish the story and realize that nothing really changes that we understand that it cannot represent the narrator's position. The sentence is clearly limited to Eveline's position at this particular moment and confined to the particular circumstances. I use the term "position" precisely in order to avoid an assumption that such a sentence must be Eveline's own speech "represented" by the narrator, or even her thought at the moment. The third-person description represents not Eveline's speech—she speaks little—but her mental position, phrased in simple sentences that she would have used had she spoken, but she didn't speak.

The same technique of Combined Discourse is used widely outside of literature; e.g., in a recent historical account of Adolf Hitler's life we find many passages like the following:

> By May 3 Munich was secured but at the cost of sixty-eight Free Corps lives. These, of course, had to be avenged. Thirty Catholic workers of the St. Joseph Society were seized at a tavern while making plans to put on a play (Toland, 1977: 112).

The first two sentences clearly do not represent the author's position, but the point of view of the Nazis (embedded speaker). Nevertheless, the third sentence shifts back easily to an objective historical account.

In Combined Speech, there is no symmetry of represented positions when we move from left to right or from right to left. As we observed, any "higher" speaker, in whose language a person or a position is embedded, may represent parts of the speech and position of the "lower" voice. The reverse is only marginally true, e.g., a newspaper headline "Brezhnev says: Russians Won't Budge." Clearly the language of the higher speaker intruded into Brezhnev's voice since Brezhnev presumably would not have said it so bluntly and would never refer to the Soviet government and people as "Russians." More important, however, is the understanding that we have when encountering a "lower" speaker that his speech may have been selected, misrepresented or even distorted by a higher authority. Often it is not clear how far to the left we must go: if a character is presented in an ironic light, it may be either that the narrator is the source of the irony or that the narrator is a naïve observer and is viewed ironically in his turn by the author of the text. It is a quotation within a quotation: an author presents a narrator who quotes a character (who may quote another character in turn) and a distortion may occur at any stage. For example, in Gogol's "The Overcoat" the opening paragraph makes an elaborate excuse for not mentioning the name of the department in which the story occurred because if it did, all Russia would be offended. This is clearly done tongue-in-cheek, because anonymous presentation would be even more typical. The device has been laid bare, the reader's attention is called to the problem of an intentional criticism of the whole social system. Nevertheless, it is not clear whether the narrator is being ironic or is presented ironically by the author as a simple-minded person who believes anything he hears. The reader's decision on this matter is a very difficult one (if at all possible) and clearly involves an interpretation of the whole story.

I shall not discuss here all possible complex presentations of positions within positions and the reader's reconstructions. In many cases there is no single narrator and (even when there is one) the presentation of the fictional world is divided among a number of characters. The formula I have presented above and a more detailed apparatus derived from it enable us to discuss in one conceptual framework a variety of phenomena which have been dealt with under such headings as "Point of View," "irony," "implied author," "narratee," "implied reader," "clashing norms," etc. Within this framework, and only here, can one apply Speech Act Theory or Jakobson's functions of the speech event. The interpretation of such factors, however, can be made only from the second dimension, the Dimension of Meaning and Reference. For example, when Dmitrii Karamazov threatens to kill his father, we may assume that the "Force" (in the sense of Speech Act Theory) of the Speech Event is a "threat," but towards the end of the novel we realize that there was no such intention and understand his words to represent merely an emotional outburst.

Many semiotic objects are perceived as such without any intentional speech act. The reconstruction that we make from features of period styles, when we say that they are "expressive of," merely uses a *model* of speech events: a period or a culture seems to "talk" to us through some of its creations.

In any case, all voices in a text refer to the same frames of reference and are placed in such frames of reference. In order to understand what a speaker refers to or in order to be able to reconstruct his position, we must construct the Field of Reference to which the words refer and in which the speakers operate.

5. THE DIMENSION OF MEANING AND REFERENCE

Meanings presented in texts cannot simply be considered on a single level. Nor are concepts like "context," and "coherence" sufficient to explain how meanings integrate in texts. Let us define meaning as everything an understander can understand from a text. Meaning so perceived is a result of a three-tier construct.

RP

|

s

|

fr

(RP—Regulating Principles, s—the level of "sense", *fr*—frame of reference.)

The sense of a word, combined into "utterance meanings" is related to specific "frames of reference"; it obtains its truth value or figurative status and is specifically qualified by the frame of reference. Regulating principles, such as point of view, irony, generic mode, derive from the speaker or the maker of the text. They explain in what sense to take the senses of the words (and can be dealt with within the first dimension).

It seems to be less clear how senses of the words depend on the frames of reference they relate to. Let us take an example. The sentence "This is a dirty hotel" when used in a dirty hotel preserves its literal meaning. If, however, the floor is not dirty, the word "dirty" becomes metaphorical (acquires a moral sense). An observation of the referent (within a specific frame of reference), independently of the words and their senses, influences the decision on the meaning to be assigned to this sign. The same sentence when used by a man living with his girl-friend changes its entire meaning. The word "hotel" when referring to an apartment cannot be accepted literally. The sentence then has to be re-understood to imply: "I consider this apartment a temporary place," or "I am not going to stay here any longer." Such processes of re-understanding the words occur constantly in every-day life. It is not only that senses of words add information to known referents, but vice-versa: the information we have about referents qualifies the meanings of words.

Let us define a frame of reference (*fr*) as any semantic continuum, to which signs may refer. There may be *fr*s which are *real* or are *ideal* (e.g., a theory of grammar or an ideology). A frame of reference in space and time will be called a "scene." *fr*s may be fixed in time or extended in time (e.g., the biography of a person). While using language we may refer to *present fr*s or to *absent fr*s, *known* to the listener or *unknown*. If an *fr* is present, simple pointing or labeling of a referent will enable us to obtain further information from the real referent. The same holds for *fr*s known to an understander. Newspaper articles do not provide all the information needed for their understanding since they rely on previous information the readers had about the same *frs*.

A Field of Reference (FR) is a hypothetical continuum of frames of reference, e.g., the world of a novel is a highly complex multidirectional Field of Reference. A character may be presented when he was two years old, and then at the age of 40; the presented *frs* are not directly continuous with each other but are perceived to belong to one wider FR. There may be in a novel *frs* which cannot be integrated as directly continuous with the major FR, e.g., the legend of the Grand Inquisitor in *The Brothers Karamazov*.

The necessity of the level of *frs* can be seen in the following example:

> He opened the door. A few pieces of clothing were strewn about. He caught the fish in his net.

The first two sentences are not connected by any syntactic means. If we want to make a coherent text, we must provide a hypothetical *fr*, e.g., a room. In spite of the fact that many aspects of the room remain indeterminate, the two sentences can easily be accommodated within a normal concept of a room. But the third sentence cannot be accepted. It is normally turned into a metaphor. This sentence has no metaphor when seen separately and becomes metaphoric only when related to such a hypothetical *fr*. It is, however, possible, though less likely, to construct a hypothetical *fr* which would accommodate all three sentences in their literal meanings, e.g., by assuming that it is a backyard with a pool belonging to an eccentric in California. Such an assumption, however, will make the *fr* highly specific and limit any additional information provided by further parts of the text. The interdependence of meanings and *frs* becomes clear.

A further possible understanding construct of the same text can be seen from a slightly different version:

> He opened the door. A few pieces of clothing were strewn about. The beach was beautiful in the light of the early morning. To his satisfaction, he saw he had caught the fish in his net. She was not to be seen anywhere. But he attended to his business of pulling the net out of the water.

Now we realize that in the first example we understood the word "opened" to mean: "opened and entered," but it could just as well mean "opened and went out," especially if the building is placed near a beach. In our second example, metaphorical relationships are still possible, especially in certain genres of

fiction (e.g., the metonymic transfer from the sea-scene to the human relationships) but all literal meanings can be accommodated in one *fr* as well. A
further possible hypothesis: that the door was without a building (like in a
Bergman movie or surrealist painting) would, again, impose global restric-
tions on the whole Field of Reference (or genre of the text).

A work of literature is different from other texts in one respect: it creates
an (at least one) Internal Field of Reference (IFR). There are some referents
such as characters, places, times, for which we have no evidence outside of this
text. We construct the IFR and its specific *frs* using models from the world or
from literary and other conventions and we have access to knowledge about
them only from what is given and what may be constructed in the text. At the
same time, however, many sentences in a literary text may refer to an External
Field of Reference (ExFR). For example, geographical or historical names of
persons, places or events refer both outside and inside the text. Many generalizations about human nature refer to both inside and outside. The reader
judges such statements both from the values of the IFR and from the values of
the ExFRs (the real world).

It must be stressed that the employment of this integrational procedure
does not necessarily imply that a work of literature must have one unified
"meaning" or "message," or even make sense. In any event, the interplay of
elements which have any semantic aspect works through such patterning.

Double (or multiple) referring is a widespread feature in texts. An argument about politics by characters in a novel or in real life presents us with
information both on the political situation discussed and the positions of the
discussants. Nature scenes are conventionally transferred to the moods of
characters in poetry. We may distinguish between direct reference to a specific *fr* and "referability" to other *frs*. We may then analyze the modes, forms
and validity of such transfers (metaphoric, symbolic or other).

6. THE INTERDEPENDENCE OF THE
FIRST TWO DIMENSIONS

The information obtained from texts, which refers directly or is related by an
understander to *frs*, is presented by speakers or from specific positions. Such
positions may be either personal or collective ones, e.g., social and moral
norms or accepted opinions. Therefore an understander constructs his intentional "worlds" of fiction or his understanding of reality by using the positions

of speakers as Regulating Principles. There can be no analysis of meaning or of the information about specific referents and *frs* without considering the dimension of Speech and Position.

The same is true in reverse. In a text, speakers are embedded in frames of reference and in a specific Field of Reference. We do not usually encounter in literature simple quotation within quotation. A speaker presents a piece of the "world" (an *fr*) and within that world he presents another speaker. In order to grasp the position of a speaking character, we must understand his place in the IFR or fictional "World." This relationship may be represented in general in the following diagram (S—symbolizes any speaker):

Dimension A S_1 S_2 S_3 S_4

Dimension B   (*fr*) *fr*   *fr*   *fr*   *fr*

A text may start either presenting "objectively" a world within which speakers are placed or it may start in a speaker's voice ("personal narration"). In both cases, we have to reconstruct each dimension separately. Even in drama, where it seems that we encounter only speech acts, we understand only by integrating words by different speakers relating to the same *frs* outside of their speech and often outside of the stage. The assumption that behind each text there is a creator (or implied author) creates merely an illusion that a text as a whole is an independent speech act. Clearly the author, too, is placed in a world, a tradition of literature, language and culture.

7. THE DIMENSION OF THE ORGANIZED TEXT

The understanding of meanings relating to a Field of Reference involves reorganizing the information in a whole network of heterogeneous patterns, hierarchically related to each other. While reading a novel, we reconstruct from discontinuous elements the characters, plot, the order of time, space, society with its norms, world-views, as well as other relationships. This hierarchical complex, however, must be presented in the medium of each semiotic object, e.g., in linear language in a novel. The organization of the Text Continuum is separated from the reconstructed meanings.

Texts are organized primarily by means of *segmentation*. Segments may be overlapping and variously divided. Segments are not at all parts of "macrostructures" (of meaning, or plot), or "surface" manifestations of "deep" global patterns. They may be constituted by rather "trivial" means. But they are the necessary *floor* from which all constructs are built. To some extent they are constituted by formal devices, such as strophic structure, chapters, paragraphs. To a large extent, however, texts use for their organization the other two dimensions. For example, scenes in a drama are divided by changing the grouping of speakers. A major means for segmenting a text is the use of thematic material, or shifting from one *fr* to another *fr*.

The motivations for introducing segments or discontinuing them, too, are derived from material of the other two dimensions. For example, in *The Brothers Karamazov* Alyosha's curiosity (a character trait) and his mission in the world (a role) are responsible for his going from one place to another to hear what various characters have to say, dividing and linking thereby the chapters of the novel. This cardinal role which thematic material plays in the organization of the structure of a text is responsible for the enormous variety and the individuality of structure of literary texts.

On the other hand, patterns in the Dimension of the Organized Text may be related to the other dimensions. Thus, structural properties are said to participate in the "meaning" of a novel, sound patterns are related to the meanings of words in poetry, etc.

Space does not allow us to discuss here similar phenomena in non-literary or non-linguistic texts. Clearly, newspaper articles must have their own structure in order to be printed on a page and in order to be read, or to be read throughout. Here, too, thematic material is used for segmentation. For example, in a specific news article, the headline summarizes (part, sometimes a sensational part of) the topic; the first paragraph presents a more detailed summary; the second paragraph may summarize background information on the *fr* discussed; the third paragraph may describe in detail one item; the fourth paragraph may quote from one person's views on the issue at hand, etc.

In representative painting, the composition of a picture uses elements of the *fr* for its organization. In cubist painting, on the other hand, relations of forms and colors may intrude into the organization of the *fr*s. In any case, if signs are used, they must be presented in objects, which must have their own conditions for existence and coherence. Even non-material presentations of signs, e.g., in conversation, must have their own coherence. For example, conversations are linear, cannot be held endlessly, must use shifters to move from one part to another, "attentional" devices to focus the listener's interest, etc. This is true even more for objects which are read as signs but were not intended primarily as such. Buildings, cities, cars, clothing have their own structure and functions which can only then accommodate the semiotic aspect.

8. SOME CONCLUDING REMARKS

The three dimensions discussed here are interdependent, in part overlapping; each may use patterns of the others for its own constitution, but must be considered separately in an analysis. They each require a very different methodology, because they have their separate modes of integration, and cannot be reduced to each other.

Where are artistic norms and values located? Aesthetic or other functions of semiotic objects are based on selections of elements and patterns in all three dimensions. Sometimes an aesthetic function may be located primarily in one dimension, e.g., in the dimension of meaning and reference by Marxists or in the dimension of the organized text by structuralists. Separating the patterning in each dimension in an analysis of any semiotic object must be supplemented by an observation of the relations between them. It seems to me that the separate concerns of recent theories (such as fictionality, metaphor, speech act theory, parallelism) must be seen within one overall framework.

5 ON PRESENTATION AND REPRESENTATION IN FICTION

A work of literature is neither a purely fictional text nor purely representational but a more complex relationship between the two. To understand fictionality, we must understand the nature of representation and vice versa, and both depend on the structure of meaning and reference in literary and non-literary texts. This is true for all kinds of literary works, from the most realistic and descriptive prose to the most hermetic or disjointed poetry. The problem of literary science in this field lies in the need to go beyond the general theoretical or philosophical definitions of the concepts involved and develop a descriptive apparatus for concrete research in the enormous range of phenomena. In this brief article I shall merely explain and illustrate some of the basic concepts of my theory of Integrational Semantics as applied to the fiction-representation nexus.

On the face of it, fiction can be described as language offering propositions (or providing a basis for propositions in an interpretation) which make no claim for truth values in the real world. Thus, the philosopher John Searle explains 'fictional' utterances in opposition to 'serious' utterances in a similar way as he deals with the opposition 'metaphorical'—'literal.' According to him, "fictional utterances are 'nonserious.'" "For example, if the author of a novel tells us that it is raining outside he isn't seriously committed to the view that it is at the time of writing actually raining outside. It is in this sense that fiction is nonserious." (Searle, p. 60)

Searle's analysis makes the important link between fictionality and commitment to the truth of a proposition. In this respect, he joins a venerable tradition, including such concepts as I. A. Richards's "pseudo-statements" and Roman Ingarden's "Quasi-Urteile." In the sense of his analysis, he is right: the novelist, indeed, makes no commitment that it is actually raining "outside" (of wherever he is) "at the time of writing." The problem, however, is that the truth value of propositions can be judged only within specific *frames of reference (fr)* to which they are—or should be—related. A person using the expression "it is raining"—in a novel or in a letter—may refer to his immediate surroundings or to any other frame of reference that he recalls or tells about (e.g., on the other side of the globe).

In the case of a work of literature, it is not isolated propositions we are dealing with but an *Internal Field of Reference* (IFR)—a whole network of referents—to the construction of which they contribute and to which they refer at the same time. Within this Internal Field of Reference, we judge the truth values of propositions (given in the text or constructed in readings and interpretations) from whatever other information for the same Field we may have.

The use of language in a literary text is basically the same as in real life situations which are outside of our direct experience: we cannot judge the truth value of utterances about them by means of direct observation but can only compare them with other utterances (or non-verbal evidence) relating to the same frames of reference. We have at our disposal only information mediated through different sources, speakers and points of view as well as views acquired or formed in our own life experience: the conclusions, therefore, may be true within our set of beliefs or contradictory, unresolved, changing, biased and so on. In a life situation, one assumes, ideally, that there are ways of finding evidence and ascertaining what the real state of affairs was (by means of travel, police investigation, science, etc.), since the referents really "existed" "out there." In a literary text, for referents which are unique to its Internal FR, there are no such ways outside of the given text because these referents (specific characters, meetings, lunches, etc.) did not exist outside of it, or not in the same form. We learn about them, however, much in the same way as we learn about *absent* frames of reference in the world: by means of further verbal and non-verbal evidence about them.

In the understanding of language, the senses of the words and syntactic contributions to meaning are both related to specific referents and to specific frames of reference and, in turn, are influenced by them. The frame of reference, to which a text or its understander relate the words, provides information both for judging the truth value of the utterances and for specifying, qualifying, metaphorizing or otherwise modifying their meanings.

Hence, we must go one step beyond Searle. When an author of a novel tells us that it is raining outside, we must assume that he is, indeed, "seriously committed to the view that it is [. . .] actually raining outside" *in the frame of reference he is speaking about* (though he is not committed to the view that this *fr* itself exists in the real world). Thus, in a novel as in the real world, if during that rain a visitor arrives, he or she must be either wet or was not really in the street or we must assume that the narrator was mistaken in his assertion or is lying on purpose or is altogether an "unreliable narrator." Needless to say, an author rarely tells us anything directly, he does it through various speakers and narrators, who are committed to the same truth within the Internal Field of Reference or else are exposed as being ideological, ironical, ignorant or unreliable.

At the same time, the frame of reference serves as a basis for modifying or specifying the meanings of the words. E.g., in our case, if the frame of reference is in the tropics, we may assume that the rain is really strong; if it is during a drought, the utterance will convey relief and hope; if we know there is no rain, we may understand it as a metaphorical expression, etc.

Let us define our terms. A *frame of reference (fr)* is any semantic continuum of two or more referents modeled upon any kind of continuity whatsoever: it may be a scene in time and space, a character, an ideology, a mood, a state of affairs, a plot, a policy, a theory, the wind in autumn trees, the mountains of Corsica, etc. An *fr* may be *present* to the speakers or *absent, known* or *unknown* to the hearer; it can be real, hypothetical or fictional; its ontological status is unimportant for semantics—it is anything that we can speak *about*.

A Field of Reference (FR) is a large universe containing a multitude of crisscrossing and interrelated *fr*s of various kinds. We may isolate such Fields as France, the Napoleonic Wars, Philosophy, the "world" of Tolstoy's *War and Peace*, the world today, etc. When reading a newspaper, we get information about a large number of heterogeneous, disconnected *fr*s: segments in the economy, politics, trade unions, a literary prize, gossip about a personality, a description of an accident, the next day's weather, etc. We do not perceive them as isolated objects, floating in a void; but rather as spots on a vast map, a

Field of Reference (USA or the world today), which has a hypothetical (though fuzzy) scope and coherence.

A similar thing happens in the "world" of a novel: it is not given in language as one fully detailed "reality" but rather projected as a hypothetical continuum, for which only some *frs* are presented or mentioned. Thus, a character may appear at the age of two and at the age of twenty with nothing in between; the reader must assume a hypothetical continuity within the encompassing Field of Reference. Another example: in *War and Peace*, Moscow, Petersburg and some other places are described; they are merely spots in a hypothetical continuous space, modeled on the real geography of Europe. Here, as in any other aspect of meaning, an important distinction must be made between what is *presented* in a text and what is *represented*. The relations between the two—the kinds of selection, proportion and disproportion and representational claims—play a central role in defining the nature of various kinds of literature.

Similarly, an *fr* has only some of its referents presented in the text (e.g., if a person is walking through a city, only some of the street names may be mentioned, a few items about buildings, stores and people introduced), the rest is indeterminate. Various hypothetical constructs in the text (of plot, structure or "meanings") will turn some of these *indeterminacies* (to use Ingarden's term) into *gaps* to be filled by the reader. Thus, an *fr* is an excellent tool for conveying things by means of language precisely because it provides a shortcut, using abbreviated "situations," "states of affairs" or "world experiences" instead of full verbal descriptions or mere concepts, i.e., intentional meanings of words. At the same time, of course, the meaning of a text is not fully given in language but depends heavily on constructs, which may change in different parts of the text or with different readings.

The interesting thing about literary texts is that they construct their own *Internal Field of Reference* while referring to it at the same time; to use a well-known simile: they build the boat under their own feet while rowing in the sea. The "outside" in Searle's example is a referent projected in the novel at the same time as something is being predicated about it (that it rains there). This interdependence between the constructed frames of reference and the meanings and propositions relating to them is at the core of the problem of interpretation.

A literary text, indeed, can be defined as 1) a verbal text which projects at least one Internal Field of Reference (IFR) to which meanings in this text are related (though, as we shall see below, some of them may, or may at the same time, be related to Fields external to it). At least some of the referents—personal names, times, places, scenes and episodes—are unique to this text and make no claim for external, factual existence. This is not a sufficient but a necessary definition of literature. The issue becomes more complicated, of course, when writers use the same characters or events in several works of literature, as if mapping them on one hypothetical continuum (e.g., Balzac's *Human Comedy*).

Other major characteristics include: 2) the autonomy of the text from any direct speech situation as well as its relative fixity which supports various tendencies of "framing" and internal cohesion and structuration; 3) a variety of historically determined conventions of language, genre structures and aesthetic norms—though any of these may appear outside of literary texts as well. This definition includes poetry, drama and prose, written as well as oral works of literature and stories that children tell. It also holds for non-verbal or not purely fictional modes, such as film or figurative painting.

On the other hand, myths, philosophies, scientific theories, too, create their own autonomous Fields of Reference with unique referents (terms, characters, concepts, reified entities, narratives, laws) that may not directly relate to observable referents in the world. But they are different from literature in that respect that in these areas, a theoretically unlimited number of texts will refer to the same Field as if assuming its existence outside of the single text. Even when a new theory is introduced, further texts dealing with this theory will refer to the same constructed Field and its referents as did the first text, developing and reshuffling it (e.g., in Psychoanalysis, Existentialism or nuclear physics). In this respect, a dream may be like a work of literature (like a disjointed poetic vision or narrative); psychoanalysis, however, projects all individual dreams onto a Field external to them, the person's subconscious or the human mind in general.

The advantage of using the theory of the Internal FR rather than such terms as "World" ("fictional world" or "possible world") with "objects," "characters" and "events" existing in it, is twofold: 1) a direct link is created between the projected (or "intentional") "world" and linguistic reference, hence between ontology of literature and the analysis of language; 2) no definite existing objects, characters, events, ideas or attitudes are assumed, merely frames of reference of such kinds, to which language in the text relates or may be related, by various speakers and from various positions. These *frs* are not necessarily stable, may be constructed and reconstructed, the linguistic evidence may be complementary or contradictory, incomplete or false, uncertain or disjointed, etc. Hence, the current debates on interpretation and deconstruction are not foreclosed by the theory. The theory does not separate fictional projection and readers' imagination from the nature of language mediating it. Neither does it forsake the first for the second.

This, however, is only half of the story. The problem is that works of literature are usually not pure fictions, consisting merely of "fictional" propositions or a pure "fictional" language; they are not purely "fictional worlds" with exclusively unique characters and events. The language in a literary text is related not only to the Internal FR (which, indeed, is unique to it) but to External FRs as well.

External Fields of Reference (ExFR) are any FRs outside of a given text: the real world in time and space, history, a philosophy, ideologies, views of human nature, other texts. The literary text may directly refer to or invoke referents from such External FRs: names of places and streets, historical events and dates, actual historical figures, but also various statements about human nature, society, technology, etc.

An obvious example is the opening of Balzac's *Le cousin Pons*:

> Vers trois heures de l'après midi, dans le mois d'octobre de l'année 1844, un homme âgé d'une soixantaine d'années, mais à qui tout le monde eut donné plus que cet âge, allait le long du boulevard des Italiens, le nez à la piste, les lèvres papelardes, comme un négociant qui vient de conclure une excellente affaire, ou comme un garçon content de lui-même au sortir d'un boudoir.
>
> C'est à Paris la plus grande expression connue de la satisfaction personnelle chez l'homme.

Granted, the convention of fiction prevents us from accepting seriously that this particular man actually walked in Paris on that day. However, the year, month, Boulevard des Italiens, Paris—are referents in the real world as well as in the fictional space. A typical signal of fictionality is used: though the month and the hour are mentioned precisely, one specific indicator—the day—is *floated*. This device indicates that the fictional time and space, though quite precisely located in relation to the real world, is somehow suspended above it, has its own, "floating" coordinates. (Such floating may take on a variety of forms or not appear at all, in changing conventions.)

The establishment of the first set of referents in a novel (or any other IFR) may be called *referential grounding*. Unlike the traditional term, exposition, which is limited to the antecedents in time of the reconstructed world of the novel, referential grounding deals with the opening of the text continuum and allows for any kind of referents to be used. The opening of a text must establish several specific and concrete referents, from which the other referents in the IFR are developed by extension. The early referents are often "minor," to be convincingly accounted for in a limited space. This is why secondary characters often precede the introduction of more central characters, which are then presented in the context of persons already known to the reader; or setting precedes the unfolding of characters, who then are placed in it; or a concrete dialogue opens *in medias res*, from which the interlocutors are then built up. A text may also open with a generalization or a general essay (on matters in an external FR), from which more concrete (Internal) examples are deduced.

A widespread technique is the *anchoring* of a new constructed IFR in some accepted external frame of reference. This may be used for referential grounding as well as for the text as a whole. Works of fiction are often anchored in a historical time and place; the weather, season or time of day (in Turgenev's novels, Joyce's stories or Haiku); a myth (in Greek tragedy); or a combination of those (in T. S. Eliot's "The Waste Land"). In lyrical poetry they may be anchored in the "image" of the poet as established in other poems. The author's newly introduced referents, then, are presented as extensions of known referents within one new coherent Field.

While using referents from known External FRs, the Internal FR can freely draw on information about such ExFRs. In our case: Paris, its social structure and urban nature; the street mentioned, its environment and extensions; the period and political regime, etc.—all are available for the reader's construction of the IFR. To what extent this will be used for specific knowledge or merely for background and atmosphere depends on the particular text and may be open to the dialectics of interpretation.

The last sentence in the Balzac example ("In Paris, this is a man's greatest possible expression of personal satisfaction") is a typical double-directed statement. It refers at the same time to the real Paris in the External FR and to the selection from Paris presented in the IFR. If we accept it as true for the External FR, we draw from there a whole aura and social myth. But even if we do not accept it as true, it may not disturb the coherence of the Internal FR:

we reflect back on the speaker (the narrator), construct his attitudes from it, or the attitudes of the figures thus characterized or of society as represented in the novel. We then see it as part of Balzac's (or some character's) view of Paris.

John Searle cites an example from a novel by Iris Murdoch entitled *The Red and the Green*, which begins:

> Ten more glorious days without horses! So thought Second Lieutenant Andrew Chase-White recently commissioned in the distinguished regiment of King Edward's Horse, as he pottered contentedly in a garden on the outskirts of Dublin on a sunny Sunday afternoon in April nineteen sixteen.

Searle argues rightly that the author "is not held to be insincere if in fact she does not believe for one moment that there actually was such a character thinking about horses on that day in Dublin." The other side of the coin, however, is that this opening is well anchored in the External FR, it actually constructs the first image of its fictional world (in our terms: the referential grounding of the Internal FR) on the readers' knowledge of such external frames. The year 1916 (during World War One), Dublin and, on the other hand, the British army in Ireland before independence—these are indispensable stores of background information opened by the author. They are referents in both the Internal and External FRs, though no proposition is explicitly made about them in the imagination. We may not know whether there actually was such a regiment of "King Edward's Horse"; if yes, it may add to the characterization of the Second Lieutenant: if not, it may be relevant to find out whether the name is coined from similar names or conveys a parodic stance. Even the garden on the outskirts of Dublin and the sunny Sunday afternoon, though clearly not related to any specific referents in Dublin, draw upon the ExFR (compare, for example, to such settings in New Delhi).

A statement about the External FR may be slanted or false, we do not judge the aesthetic value of the novel by the truth values of such statements. But its truth value is not immaterial for an interpretation: if it clearly deviates from some normal view of the given External FR but is coherent with the Internal FR, it may then expose the particular view of the world it represents.

Thus, Dostoevsky tells us that, when old Fydor Karamazov learned of his wife's death, according to some sources he rejoiced and according to others he sobbed like a child; according to the narrator himself: "Quite likely both versions are true, that is to say, that he rejoiced at his release and wept for her who had given him his freedom—at one and the same time. In the majority of cases, people, even evil-doers, are much more naïve and artless than we generally assume. As, indeed, we are ourselves."[1] It is not hard to imagine readers who would object to being included in such a generalization; for the Internal world, however, it defines well the basic love-hate psychology which explains the behavior of Dostoevsky's characters. Indeed, Tolstoy, when invited to see a dramatized novel of Dostoevsky, refused, claiming that Dostoevsky's characters always behave precisely as they are not expected to behave. That means that for Tolstoy, Dostoevsky's statements on human nature are false in the External FR. This deviation, however, from an acceptable view of human nature is one of the sources of Dostoevsky's impact as a writer. It cannot be accounted for without the tension between the two referential directions.

Similarly, the description of Napoleon in Tolstoy's own *War and Peace* is a highly biased selection from what was known to Tolstoy about Napoleon, made for purposes of structure (as Shlovsky has shown) as well as of Tolstoy's historiosophic ideology. It can be shown that the reader has to supplement in many places of the novel his knowledge about figures and events in history. To what extent, however, the Napoleon as presented in the IFR should be taken within the presented limits and to what extent one may draw on the field of outside knowledge remains an open question. The important thing is that the store of historical knowledge was opened for the reader. And in any case, the juxtaposition between the two Napoleon constructs tells us a great deal about Tolstoy's Russian point of view or his disregard for the importance of leaders in history.

Not always does a text rely on the reader's knowledge of external *frs*. In the continuation of Balzac's chapter, we read:

> Ce vieillard, sec et maigre, portait un spencer couleur noisette sur un habit verdâtre à boutons de metal blanc! ...

Balzac finds it necessary to explain the nature and history of this external referent.

---

1   Dostoevsky, F. *The Brothers Karamazov*, transl. David Magarshak, Penguin Books, vol. 1.

Un homme en spencer, en 1844, voyez-vous, comme si Napoléon eut daigné ressusciter pour deux heures. Le spencer fut invente, comme son nom l'indique, par un lord sans doute vain de sa jolie taille. (And a long explanation follows.)

In the twentieth century, even writers of popular novels tend to rely more on the reader for such information. (Though Balzac obviously does not merely explain the term but uses the excursus for characterization, creation of historical perspective, etc.)

We may now return to the theoretical model. An Internal Field of Reference is constructed as a plane parallel to the real world. In realistic fiction, its events take place in known history and geography, sometimes with precisely specified names of places and dates, sometimes using various signals of fictionality through *floating* some of the specific indicators, sometimes merely suspended "somewhere": in France, in the Middle Ages, in a modern city, etc.: situations and behavior resemble (or are otherwise related to) those in the real world. In non-realistic texts, the IFR is in various ways evidently dissimilar to the ExFR. It is, clearly, not divorced from it. Thus, the Internal FR is projected as parallel to an External FR. But parallel planes never meet. A character cannot walk out of a fictional house and show up in a real cafe.

In literary texts, however, we have "non-Euclidean" parallel planes: though they never merge, they may overlap in several (or many) points: many individual referents and even whole frames of reference are *shared* by both the Internal and External FRs. Such *shared frs* may include historical figures, descriptions of a city, discussions of psychoanalysis, the modes of American advertising or the description of D-Day. Indeed, many popular novels, though featuring invented characters, quite openly propose to teach the readers about various aspects of the world.

Thus, we have two separate but parallel planes, intersecting at several points: the "shared" referents and frames of reference. Each of these has its own continuation outside of the shared points. For the External FRs, we have more information outside of the given text. The Internal FR develops the shared points in its own descriptive proportions and extends them by adding unique referents. Though modeled upon external examples, its Field is unique and internally coherent. We may represent the relationship in the following diagram:

"Double-Decker" Model of Reference in Literature

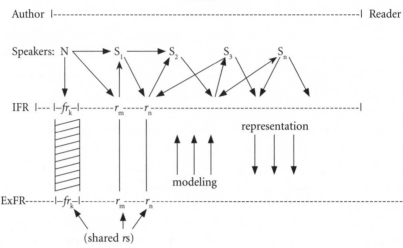

TEXT

Author |--| Reader

N – Narrator, S – Speaker, r – referent, fr – frame of reference,
IFR – Internal Fields of Reference, ExFR – External Fields of Reference.

The arrows between the level of "Speakers and Positions" (N, S) and the other Speakers in the text are sources of information about the IFR and the ExFRs and, at the same time, are constructed from them.

This model explains the dual referential allegiance of statements as well as of any material that may be referred to or simply located in internal or external FRs. The links between the two parallel planes create channels for possible transfer of additional semantic material from one to the other, and vice versa. This is true for the relations of fiction to the historical world, to nature, to theories, beliefs and ideologies, as well as to other texts. Joyce's allusion in the title of his book, *Ulysses*, opens up Homer's work as a huge store of potential transfers—of character, motifs and composition. What precisely is relevant and legitimate in such transfers must be judged specifically through an argumentative analysis and comparison of the receiving and source FRs.

Thus we have in a text direct referring to External FRs as well as to the Internal FR and also plain sharing of referents and frames of reference. As the diagram shows, there are two additional operations: *modeling* and *representa-*

tion. Though not linguistic in nature—we are not limited here to direct statements or propositions—these are powerful devices for relating the Internal plane to External planes of various kinds.

On one hand, the construction of the Internal FR is *modeled* upon External FRs: we need knowledge of the world to make sense of a work of fiction, construct the frames of reference from scattered material, fill in the gaps, create the necessary hierarchies, etc. On the other hand, there is a relation of *representation* from the IFR to External FRs: certain behavior, scenes, complex meaning constructs in the text may be understood as "typical" (or "atypical" or otherwise representative) when projected upon history, human nature, urban society, or any other generalized FR. (In traditional terms: the author has powers of "observation" or conveys a "message.") The specific interaction between relevant patterns in the IFR and constructs in the external world is again a matter of argumentative hypothesis.

One must stress that this model is by no means limited to realistic works of literature. Any kind of deviation from realism can be ascertained only through the juxtaposition of these two planes. The double-decker structure of reference is indispensable for the understanding of Kafka, Gogol, folklore, or Surrealism. It is also crucial for the understanding of lyrical poetry, the study of which centered for too long on questions of poetic language.

6 THE MEANING OF SOUND PATTERNS IN POETRY

An Interaction Theory

For Roman Jakobson who placed all studies
of sound in the perspective of meaning.

1

It is common practice in the interpretation and teaching of poetry that the interpreter "mobilizes" the sound effects of the poetic text to reinforce his argument on the poem's meaning. The insight formulated by I. A. Richards that poems are written with the "full body" of words finds its obvious expression in this domain. Such observations are made not merely by critics interested in the "form" of the poem, but even more so by practical critics preoccupied with the poem's "meaning" or the poet's "message," who feel, perhaps, uneasy about the dense and complex network of sound patterning in verse and try to incorporate it, sometimes sporadically and casually, often ingeniously, in their total interpretation. In the other camp one finds prominent critics and theoreticians who deny altogether any specific meanings inherent in specific sounds. The two extreme positions are well represented by M. Grammont (1967) on one hand, who collected many examples for the classification of "expressive" properties of sounds (esp. in *Le vers français*, which appeared in many editions), and P. Delbouille (1961) on the other hand, who provided a resounding criticism of all "expressive" theories of sound in poetry and saw it as merely a contextual matter.

The problem of the relations (arbitrary or natural) between sounds and the meanings or the reality which language may represent is as old as Plato's "Cratylos," and the literature in the field is enormous. Besides literary critics and theoreticians, the arguments were shared by philosophers, psychologists, linguists, and poets of various persuasions.

Indeed, do sounds have meaning in poetry? And if so, how? As many basic issues of aesthetics, this question cannot be answered in an either-or manner. It all depends on the sense in which the question is understood and what kind of "meaning" we have in mind. Furthermore, one must avoid a confusion, so often encountered, between the nature of a method and the nature of the object this method is supposed to study. Thus, structuralist methods of analysis were often taken—by adherents and by adversaries alike—for ontological assumptions, and seemed therefore to fail (or to be "forced") where such assumptions could not be held in any rigorous sense. In our case it is clear that, for methodological purposes, in order to have a clean discussion, we must abstract the issue of sound-meaning relations and deal with it separately; but we must not overlook the fact that the sounds themselves do not normally exist as separate entities in a text, except for a few poems by Dadaists and the *zaumny yazyk* (trans-sense or translogical language) of the Russian Cubo-Futurists. I believe that this issue—though autonomous—may gain from becoming part of a general theory of literary texts. I shall discuss it in such a framework, and return (in the end of this paper) to parallel phenomena in other aspects of texts.

In what follows I shall proceed from actual examples rather than from existing theories, with the view of proposing a simple model for a general theory of sound-meaning relations in poetry.

2

Let us take an example. A well-known introduction to the study of poetry devotes a chapter to sound. The author claims that:

> in reading poetry, then, it is important to remember that the major importance of sound must always be realized in terms of content. Merely to discover alliteration or assonance, for example, is but a small part of the total process of dealing with sound; the larger part is discovering precisely what the function of the sound pattern is in terms of the poem as a whole. (Kreuzer, 67)

In view of such an approach the author uses an example from a famous Shakespearean sonnet:

[1] When to the sessions of sweet silent thought
I summon up remembrance of things past,
I sigh the lack of many a thing I sought
And with old woes new wail my dear time's waste:

The author analyzes the mood of the poem and argues:

> But sound, too, makes its contributions to the mood of the first twelve lines
> and to the changed mood of the couplet. The sibilants in *sessions, sweet, silent,*
> *summon, remembrance, things, past, sigh, sought, woes, times,* and *waste*—all in
> the first four lines—reinforce with their hushing quality the quiet that is part
> of *sweet silent thought.* (68)

In this time and age, when the reader's response seems to be of primary
importance, we cannot simply dismiss the evidence of such an experienced
reader, especially since it represents a widespread practice.

It would be easy, of course, to bring counter-examples from English and
other languages where repetitions of sibilants—a widespread element of
sound patterning in poetry in many languages—seems to represent quite the
opposite. Here, for example, is a strophe from E. A. Poe's "The Raven":

> [2] And the silken, sad, uncertain rustling of each purple curtain
> Thrilled me—filled me with fantastic terrors never felt before;
> So that now, to still the beating of my heart, I stood repeating,
> "'Tis some visitor entreating entrance at my chamber door—
> Some late visitor entreating entrance at my chamber door;—
>
> This it is and nothing more."

The sibilants clearly represent here not the silence of sweet thought, but the
rustling of silken curtains, muted by overtones of uncertainty, sadness, "fantastic terrors," and expectation.

Indeed, sibilants may represent various kinds of sounds, for example:

> [3] [. . .] the deep sea swell [. . .]
> A current under sea
> Picked his bones in whispers.
>
> (T. S. Eliot, "The Wasteland," IV)

Here the sounds represented are different from [2] in both their sound qualities and in their emotive overtones. Furthermore, there is a transition from
the powerful noise of a sea swell to the sound of whispers (which, therefore, is
overshadowed and brings forth its metaphoric connotations).

> [4] There is not even solitude in the mountains
> But red sullen faces sneer and snarl.
>
> (ibid., V)

Here the strong sound effect of the sibilants in the text hardly represents any real sounds in the description: the mood expressed overshadows them (though in a small part it may lean on the sound of "snarl"—only to use its emotive overtones). In other examples of patterning of sibilants hardly a trace of either sound or silence remains.

[5] And smell renews the salt savour of the sandy earth ("Ash Wednesday")

or:

[6] Blessèd sister, holy mother, spirit of the fountain, spirit of the garden,
Suffer us not to mock ourselves with falsehood.

....

Sister, mother
And spirit of the river, spirit of the sea,
Suffer me not to be separated

(Some readers may transfer effects from other sibilant patterns in their past experience and read, for example, silence into the first lines or the swell of the sea into the last.)

As the examples show, sibilant sounds may represent silence or noise, and, at that, very different kinds of noise that are shaded by different emotive qualities, or have no relation to noise at all. It seems that no meaning can be imputed to the sounds themselves. Therefore they cannot be said to have a "hushing quality." It is rather the meanings of the words that make the sounds carriers of some expressive meaning, or shades of meaning.

We are not concerned here with the question of whether or not this critic describing Shakespeare's sonnet [1] was right, but rather the question: Whenever meanings are imputed to sounds in poetry, how does it occur? What is the structure of such a reading *if* and whenever it happens?

Let us return to example [1]. Clearly, not *all* sounds represent *all* meanings in this quatrain. A pattern of sibilant sounds is established, based on their obviously large number, especially in the first line of the text (the "primacy effect"). This pattern is so strong, it seems to overshadow other groupings of sounds, such as the "m" pattern based in line 2, "w" in line 4, or the S + T pattern, which starts in "SweeT SilenT ThoughT" and covers all four rhyming words (I use a capital S for all sibilants here). Then this pattern intersects with a certain motif or word or semantic element from the cotextual network of meaning, in our case: "sweet silent thought." The semantic element must be sufficiently important for the global construct of meaning of the poem and must be capable of being "expressed" or "reinforced" by the given sounds. In other terms, the semantic element must "motivate" their dense patterning. At this point the reader *transfers* a quality, a tone, a connotation, or the like, from the domain of meaning to the established sound pattern.

From now on the whole sound pattern is perceived as *expressive* of a certain "meaning," tone, or mood. For example, the central theme of the first line, "sweet silent thought," colors the repeated sibilant sounds with the shade of its meaning, and this coloring seems to suffuse the lines dominated by the given sound pattern. So much so, that even the word "sessions"—part of a metaphor from the court of law—is perceived by the reader as contributing to the expression of "sweet silent thought." Indeed, "sessions," as the first important word, is the mover that establishes the whole sound pattern, which has nothing to do with the content of the word itself. A mere alliteration of opening consonants in adjacent words, such as in "sweet silent," is so frequent in English that it may almost be perceived as automatic, until revived by the opening "S"-tripling in "sessions."

In short, we have a two-directional process: first, a sound pattern is established, then, certain meanings in the same text are transferred to the sound pattern, and then the tone of this sound pattern, colored by such meanings, is transferred back to the level of meaning, reinforcing it. The structure of this interaction is similar to many other interactions of heterogeneous patterns in literary texts. For example, in Romantic nature poetry, descriptions of nature are often personified; nature carries a human "mood" because its parts are imbued with metaphors from the human domain in the first place. But then, nature seems to "express" in some way (direct or opposite, allegoric or subtle) the mood of the lyrical "I" or other persons in the poem. It is not simply that a person is like (or unlike) nature, but that man is like nature, which is like man. And in our case, meanings are like sounds, which are like meanings.

These two stages of transfer appear in this necessary order only in a logical sense: the sounds must first be colored by certain meanings before they can return to color the meanings of words. The psychology of perception, however, may see them simultaneously, especially in view of the fact that both sides of the interaction are selected and patterned by the reader for the sake of such an interaction, i.e., when a hypothesis of their mutual dependence becomes plausible.

Literary texts unfold bundles of heterogeneous patterns, which are *cotextual* and interact strongly with each other: Sound patterns, lines of plot, descriptions of nature, various characters, threads of ideas, etc. Such interaction brings about mutual reinforcement and mutual motivation of the patterns involved. This is often, as in our case, a two-directional process.

We are not talking about "given," objective patterns, such as regular meter and rhyme; the process of interaction encourages a selection and reemphasis of textual elements from both sides. For example, in our case, the possibility of transferring meaning to the sounds has brought forth the "sweet silent thoughts," and these, in turn, influenced the selection and foregrounding of several sound patterns (from all available in the given text). A careful interplay of prominence (in various respects: in a statistical sense, in the placing in rhythmically prominent locations, in a thematic sense, or in the sense of stylistic selection) makes certain elements and interactions more conspicuous than others; and this—involving a process of weighing, selecting and hierarchization—depends both on the makeup of the text and on the inclinations and habits of readers and readings.

One must stress an important point, often overlooked in literary theory: the two interacting patterns are not parallel to each other as a whole and do not interact as a whole. The sound pattern is autonomous in this respect: it stretches over parts of the text irrespective of whether the words carry the related meanings or not. On the other hand, the meanings belong to a larger semantic construct, parts of which are not related to these sounds at all. We have an asymmetrical relationship of two autonomous patterns, interacting through certain *points of intersection*. If we represent a sign in a simplified manner as a certain relation between sound and meaning: s/m, poetry dissects this Saussurean tie, separating the sounds and linking them to sounds of other words and the meanings to other meanings. A new relationship between sound and meaning is created, not in one word but in a construct made by readers, not arbitrary but contextual, the meaning of which must be deduced from the particular context.

Graphically, our case may be represented in such a schematic form:

s	s	s	s	s	
		m	m	m	m	m

s = sound, m = meaning.

When a point of intersection is established, the process of bidirectional transfer occurs, which may be represented thus:

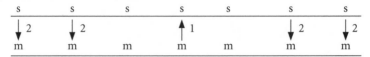

1 – first stage of transfer; 2 – second stage, from the sound pattern to other parts of the text.

There may be more than one point of intersection, and sometimes the effect of the whole sound pattern may be related to the whole mood of a poem ("soft," "harsh," "euphonious," "drastic," etc.).

Now, if this is the case, would not any sound pattern do? Let us try to "rewrite" the Shakespearean lines using words similar in content.

When to the CRuX of CRystal QUiet thought
I CRave and Call RemembRance of things past

We have clearly a very similar network of sounds, this time based on the repetition of the sound K, strengthened by the cluster K + R (involving the original word "remembrance" too). Nevertheless, it seems that this sound pattern cannot possibly express silence, though "quiet thought" starts with K as "silent thought" started with S. It is plausible that a reader will impute to this text something strong and harsh, reinforced by the sound pattern and the cluster KR. The pivotal word may become "crux." One may generalize that, in a part of a text in which a sound pattern coexists with a number of semantic elements, the sound pattern may contribute to shifting the center of gravity from one direction of meaning to another.

It seems now that the critic whose remarks we quoted was not so far off the mark. Indeed, a specific sound does not have one specific meaning. The sound may join various directions of meaning to the point of creating an impression on the reader that the sound itself carries certain meanings. There seem, however, to be various general qualities accompanying at least some sounds, which lend to these sounds *potentials* of meaning impressions. One sound may have several potentials, representing a variety of shades, such as: whisper, whistle, sound of the sea swell, snarl—in sibilants, or even contradictory potentials, such as: noise on one hand and silence on the other, expressed by the same sibilants. Some of the meanings of the words in a specific context may activate such potentials in any specific direction, or not at all. It seems that sounds with potentials *contradictory* to the meanings of the text ("crux" vs. "quiet thought") cannot be harnessed for any meaning, or may even be used as counterpoints to the meanings of the words.

To what extent are such potentials fixed or free? Are all sounds of a language equally endowed, or are there degrees in the ability of sounds to carry meanings? Are such potentials human (psychophysiological) universals or bound to specific languages? Are they historically determined and changing? These are very difficult and complex questions precisely because the sound-meaning relations in this domain are not codified, discrete and "arbitrary" in a Saussurean sense. The main problem, however, is that the contextual nature of any such transfer makes it dependent on the specific combination of sound patterns and sound contexts on one hand, and combinations of meanings and the selection of specific words on the other hand.

The literature in this field is vast. Much of it, however, is biased and presents partial selections of evidence for a certain writer's position. In any case, the effect of sounds in a context is not at all the same as the effect of the same sounds when isolated for experiment or observation. Sounds in a text tend to be subordinated to the meanings of sentences and their potential effects subdued unless they are reactivated through purposeful patterning, supported by the expectations of a genre (especially poetry) and by the conspicuous sound structures of verse.

It is not at all clear to what extent one could codify all the sounds of a language and assign to them fixed (and sufficiently specific) polysemies of such "potentials" (in the form of a dictionary) to be disambiguated in any given context.

Any given sound may be activated through a number of parameters in language: 1) metaphors (or analogues) of its articulatory properties; 2) metaphors (or analogues) of its acoustic properties; or 3) association with specific words or groups of words carrying this sound in a given language. The specific context may activate one direction or another. The third parameter, especially, depends often on sound clusters and on the evocation of specific words or domains of words.

3

In what follows I shall propose a general model for sound-meaning relations in texts. It seems that many controversies on this issue are pseudoquarrels and cannot be resolved simply because they lump together several meanings of the word "meaning" (or of the word "expressive") and regard the whole area as one phenomenon. As a matter of fact, there are various kinds of relations between sounds and meanings in poetic (and other) texts, and in each kind the problem takes on a different aspect. Though the specific configurations may be very complex, it seems to me that they largely fall into four basic categories.

Type I: Onomatopoeia—Mimetic Sound Patterns

The seemingly simplest and most direct relation between sound and meaning obtains in the wide area of onomatopoeia. Onomatopoeia is said to occur when the sounds of a word imitate the sounds of an object which the word denotes. There is, in other words, an iconic relation between the signifier and the signified. In fact, however, there is a whole range of possible relations. In some cases the word is actually denoting a sound ("meow," "moo") or naming a kind of sound ("barking," "rustling," "whistle," "whisper"). In other cases the sounds represent a noise produced by, or connected with, the object denoted by the word. Thus, "cuckoo" is not the name of a sound but the name of a bird producing a "coo-coo" sound. A "sea swell" is the shape of water, and it may suggest the noise of the sea.

Furthermore, not all the sounds of onomatopoeic words participate in the imitation. And, as we said, they do not cover necessarily the whole asymmetry. Therefore, a more correct definition would be: a word (or a group of words) in which a *part* of the sounds is, in some way, equivalent to a *part* (or an aspect, or a metonymy) of the denotation, if that part denotes a sound in nature. There must be an evocation of a sound in nature for the onomatopoeia to exist.

It is, however, not a real imitation of nature. Though some onomatopoeic words are easily recognizable by their phonemic makeup deviating from regular words in the language, still the sounds of nature are filtered through the rather small selection of sounds and sound combinations that are possible in a human phonemic system of any given language (perhaps with some enlargements existing specifically for this purpose). Furthermore, such sound words are codified in each language ("arbitrary" in Saussure's sense, though of course not arbitrary in their iconic features). Thus "whistle" (English), "Pfeife" (German), "fayf" (Yiddish), "svist" (Russian), "shrika" (Hebrew), all designate the same sound produced by the mouth or by a whistle, yet each word foregrounds a different sound as imitating nature. A similar example: "whisper" (English); "shópot," "shépchet" (Russian); "láhash" (Hebrew);

"flüstern" (German). All these words are perceived as imitating the sound denoted by them. They actualize various parts or aspects of the sound or its production. It seems that the speakers of each language actually tend to hear in nature that direction of the sound which is represented in the word.

There is, thus, a reciprocity between language and perception of reality. In human affairs, they may even produce different sounds. A slight but sudden reflex of pain evokes in English an "Ouch," but in other languages: "Ach," "Oy," "Ay," etc. In this case the sound itself is an imitation of a psychological response to a physical cause.

As Grammont pointed out, a cuckoo actually calls "ou-ou" but for phonetic reasons the two syllables are not left without consonants (and Grammont [1933] explains why k is the "natural" consonant in this place). The examples of differences between languages in onomatopoeic words are well-known (e.g., rooster's call: "kukeriku," "kikericki," "coquelico," "cock-a-doodle-doo," etc. in different languages. See Brown, 1958). The different phonetic developments of the languages influenced this area, too. An onomatopoeic word is as arbitrary as the rest of the language, but it still preserves the indication of iconicity.

Furthermore, onomatopoeic words may not represent any additional properties of the signified. Indeed, the word is connected to a represented object through the most direct link: sound properties of the word to sound properties of the object. However, when such a link is established, further properties may be conveyed by the sound combinations of the words in so-called "sound symbolism": sound patterns may be "harsh" or "soft," "pleasant" or "disgusting," "mellifluous" or "cacophonic," conveying specific qualities of, or emotive responses to, the denoted object.

Through the channel of the sound link other connotations are transferred, the sounds themselves become colored by those connotations, and vice versa. Thus, a "shrill" voice has not merely a high-pitched quality, but often something piercing and unpleasant as well. "Crunch" is defined by a contemporary dictionary: "to chew with a crushing noise"; "crush" in the same dictionary is defined not as a noise but a force: "to press with a force that destroys or deforms"; and yet the first definition assigned a noise to it: "crushing noise." In the first word, "crunch," sound is part of the definition; the meaning of the word is conveyed via an onomatopoeia. This onomatopoeia, however, represents not merely a sound; the sound is colored by the quality of crushing, breaking-up (which may be turned in a pleasant direction too, as in potato chips). In the second word, "crush," there is no onomatopoeia in the definition; sound, however, is a concomitant, a connotation of the meaning (much as crushing was a connotation of the sound in the first word).

When T. S. Eliot writes: "red sullen faces sneer and snarl" (in example [4] above), after a buildup of an S-pattern, there is the strong cluster SNR repeated in two words that merge into one: "SNeeR-and-SNaRl." Is it onomatopoeic? Our dictionary has for "snarl": "1. to growl angrily, showing the teeth, as a dog; 2. to speak in a sharp or angry manner." In the first definition the sound is central; in the second it disappears, but is still hovering in the faded metaphor ("speaking in a sharp manner"). In "sneer" ("1. to smile scornfully, as by curling the lip") no sound is indicated, except by metonymy (and in "2, a sneering look or expression" it is further removed metaphorically). It seems that we have here on one hand an onomatopoeic expression heavily colored by an emotive connotation, and on the other hand the reverse. Through the sound structure of the whole pattern, the reader's attention to the sound aspects (and the possibility of onomatopoeia—even the vision of teeth) is sharpened. But then the whole onomatopoeic effect is turned into a metaphor, since sound apparently does not refer in this frame of reference; it is merely a sensuous channel through which the negative effect is conveyed.

As the last example shows, poetry does not merely use onomatopoeic words given in the language (such a use would seem a primitive device, befitting children's literature at the most). As in other aspects of poetic structure (metaphor, stress, parallelism, etc.), poetry employs a principle existing in language, but makes of it quite independent use, notably by creating new sound patterns based on combinations of words, such as "sneer and snarl."

Unlike linguistic onomatopoeia, poetic onomatopoeia is never a feature of a word, but of a pattern, abstracting sounds from several words. Such a newly created sound pattern, always spanning more than one word, enters into onomatopoeic relations with some aspect or connotation of the meaning of one of the words, or of a combined result of meaning or reference relations. Clearly, since such onomatopoeias are not codified, the reader has to decide in each case whether or not an onomatopoeic element is at hand. The possibility of having noise, as part of the denotations of the words or as a connotation or metonymy in the projected frame of reference, is a necessary prerequisite. The relationship, however, usually goes beyond the mere imitative.

As in the case of metaphor, poetry may create new onomatopoeic patterns, modeled upon the structure of onomatopoeic words. At the same time, it may make use of onomatopoeias existing in language. As in metaphor, we must distinguish on one hand between *conventional* and *novel* onomatopoeias, and on the other hand between *dead* and *vivid* ones. A vivid onomatopoeia is a word or a pattern in which the onomatopoeic aspect is still felt beyond the normal word structure. That is, in addition to the "arbitrary" relation between signifier and signified, there is also an iconic one. It is still conventional, if codified in the language. A novel onomatopoeia is created ad hoc and supported by a specific context. Poetry may *activate, deautomatize* any conventional onomatopoeia by involving the relevant sounds in a sound pattern spreading over several words. See, for example, the T. S. Eliot text [4]: "Red Sullen faCeS SneeR and SnaRl (R + S)." Or the activation of the onomatopoeia in "rustling" in Poe's line "And the silken, sad, uncertain rustling of each purple curtain" [2] through a chain of S-sounds strengthened by RP and RT clusters.

One may pronounce the word "wind" in English with such an emphasis on the beginning of the word that it will be felt as imitating the sound of a wind. But normally the "w" in wind is at most a dead onomatopoeia. It may be considered one only in the diachronical view of language. And so is "east wind," "north wind," and "west wind." When Shelley, however, writes "O, wild West Wind," he creates a W-pattern that revives the dead onomatopoeia (and, probably, calls for an emphatic reading), much as dead metaphors come to life in poetry when their dead vehicle is extended in context. The borderline between *dead* and *vivid* onomatopoeias in language may be blurred; the activation of either one depends on the genre and the nature of the context and the activity of the reader. In a dead, or not sufficiently vivid one, the sounds of the word are transparent. By making these sounds valuable again, by pointing the reader's attention to them, by involving them in an autonomous sound pattern, the onomatopoeic relation also comes to life.

Type II: Expressive Sound Patterns

The second type is much more widespread in poetry. Grammont has devoted a very detailed discussion to the possible "expressive" qualities of various sounds in poetry. Others have analyzed it as "sound symbolism" or "sound metaphors." The Shakespearean example above is such a case.

In this category the sounds are perceived as not imitating a real sound but as carrying (or "reinforcing") a certain content quality, tone or mood, usually connected not with the meaning of one word but with a whole situation or frame of reference. Ivan Fonagy, for example, brought much statistical evidence to support the claim that in various unconnected languages "harsh" sounds (such as the plosives: k,p,t) are more prevalent in poems of a drastic or harsh content, and "soft" ones in poems with a "softer" or pleasing content.

The relations established in these two kinds of sound patterns may be graphically represented thus:

Type I: Mimetic	Type II: Expressive
Sound	sound– – – – –→ mood, tone
| |	| |
meaning: "sound"	meaning– – – –→ mood, tone

\| \| indicates equivalence; → indicates disconnect between sound and meaning.

In the second type not the sounds themselves, but rather a certain tone or expressive quality abstracted from the sounds or from the sound combination is perceived to represent a certain mood or tone of content abstracted from the domain of meaning.

In semiotic terms we may see it as follows: Any sound patterning in poetry breaks up the habitual, automatic link of the signifier and signified, undermines the transparency of the sound in referential language, simply by deautonomizing the sound itself and making it conspicuous. However, the human tendency of reading all language elements as signifying, if possible (reinforced in the tradition of close reading of poetry), turns the new sound pattern into a new signifier. The same device, which broke up the regular signifying relation and pointed out the "split" nature of a sign, has created a new, composite signifier. This signifier, even when falling into conventional combinations, is always perceived as creative, as made up *ad hoc*, simply because no lexicalization can happen: it is a partial, selective and discontinuous sound pattern, stretching through several words and not related to the full denotation of these words but only to one part (or aspect).

In type I this composite signifier has a unique signified: usually in the denotation of one word or merely in one connotation of it. Hence the tendency to read a text as if the meaning has spread (as an overtone) through the whole range covered by the signifier (the sound pattern).

In type II we encounter not merely a composite signifier, but a composite signified as well. Here belong Heidegger's *Stimmung* (mood, atmosphere) and the New Critical "tone." Furthermore, its contours and precise meaning remain often vague and open-ended. The reason is obvious: sounds grouping into a pattern are recognized by their identity, while the "meanings" represented (or "reinforced") are made not of identical elements, but of an interacting group of word meanings. It is often an undefined "mood" of a situation or a frame of reference projected by these words.

The new signifying relations are not lexicalized; the meanings are not discrete. In the first type we have at least a specific sound alluded to. Even so, the same S-pattern must be reinterpreted in each case to make it represent a different specific sound, derived from the individual nature of the object (and our extra-linguistic knowledge). In type II, sound groups may be said to represent only very general directions of tone; they gain their specificity from the interaction with the cotextual domain of meanings. And even here we deal with rather vague, composite and not precisely verbalizable feelings—which is why the use of such sound patterns (especially since Symbolism) is considered suggestive and valuable for poetry.

Since the signifier, the sound pattern, stretches over several words, it may enter into several kinds of relationships with the cotextual meanings. In the above-mentioned line from E. A. Poe, both types interact. The opening of the first line, "And the Silken, Sad unCertain," creates a strong sound pattern (S, in combination with several consonants) which is expressive of a certain mood. If we had only "sad, uncertain," the combination of the two meanings would have one direction; when qualified by "silken," it attains a somewhat different tinge, perhaps softened or mysterious. Type II would be preserved if continued: "And the silken, sad, uncertain swerving of the purple curtain." A sound connotation may be felt (activated from the silken curtain), but it is not directly signified. In the actual poem, however, the sound pattern,* already established and imbued with an expressive mood, obtains in "rustling" a link to the first type, onomatopoeia. Schematically, we have two channels:

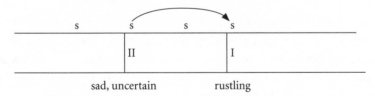

* The actual sound pattern is very complex. It starts with an S-thread, repeated in four consecutive words (at first, in the beginning of the words, which makes it prominent). The S, however, is accompanied by changing clusters of consonants representing two kinds: L,N, and plosives (K,P,T). Into these clusters an R is interwoven; it too is repeated four times. The whole cluster is shifted and transformed towards the end of the line, and the S dropped; the R-thread takes over; more harsh and less imitating sounds come to fore. The relevant consonants are:

ND SLKN SD NSRTN RSTLNG PRPL KRTN.

By the rules of semantic integration, however (see Chapter 3), all adjectives in one *fr* may qualify each other. Thus "silken" qualifies the "rustling." Then the whole expressive pattern (II) seems to color the onomatopoeic one (I), to use it as a channel for conveying the mood. This mood is further colored by the "purple" quality of the curtain, and further, by the magical-irrational mood of the second line (reinforced, in its turn, by the sound pattern based on an F-thread): "Thrilled me—Filled me with Fantastic terrors never Felt beFore." Since we have not one static unit (a word) but two interacting patterns (of sound and meaning), and each is changing and transformed as the text unfolds, the resultant transfer of meaning changes too and obtains further and richer dimensions as the reading advances. The various changing effects themselves interact, support, or cancel each other.

Type III: Focusing Sound Patterns

Quite a different kind of sound-meaning relations may be found in the following passage from T. S. Eliot's "Ash-Wednesday":

> If the lost word is lost, if the spent word is spent
> If the unheard, unspoken
> Word is unspoken, unheard;
> Still is the unspoken word, the Word unheard,
> The Word without a word, the Word within
> The world and for the world;
> And the light shone in darkness and
> Against the Word the unstilled world still whirled
> About the centre of the silent Word.

The passage has a wealth of equivalence patterns of all kinds and allusions to the world of Eliot's imagery and beliefs. We shall analyze here only two sound patterns. An obvious one is "word-Word-world-whirled." This sound cluster appears 14 times in the 9 lines (and is further echoed in the repeated "unheard," rhyming with "word"). Neither the specific quality of these sounds nor any tone or mood associated with them plays any semantic role. Nevertheless, the sound pattern focuses our attention to some key words of the passage. What is equivalent here is not sounds and meanings, but a *relation* between several sound clusters and a *relation* between the meanings of their words. In graphic terms:

$$s_1 \underline{\hspace{3cm}} s_2 \underline{\hspace{3cm}} s_3$$
$$\underline{\hspace{0.5cm}} \quad || \quad \underline{\hspace{0.5cm}} \quad || \quad \underline{\hspace{0.5cm}}$$
$$m \underline{\hspace{3cm}} m_2 \underline{\hspace{3cm}} m_3$$

The keys words: "word," "Word" (in the sense of Logos) and "world" are brought together, and the specific relationship between them is left to the reader's interpretation. The focusing pattern, however, does not create any automatic parallelism between sounds and meanings. Thus, the word "whirled" belongs to the sound pattern (reinforced through the almost tautological double chain of sounds: unSTILLed WORLD/STILL WHIRLED) but is not part of the thematic pair "word-world." "Whirled" is rather connected to a central image, involving different-sounding words: "unstilled," "centre," "light." Perhaps the sound link calls our attention to the essential link between these two patterns of theme and imagery.

Indeed, a new sound pattern of related consonant clusters emerges towards the end of this passage: "unstilled-still-centre-silent." We have here a cluster of 4 consonants, at least 3 of which appear in each word: NSTL—STL—SNT—SLNT. This sound pattern, too, links up central words (perhaps less central thematically, but important for Eliot's imagery). But the sound pattern involves the word "still," which cannot be said to have any thematic importance, though it is as prominent in the sound pattern as any other (even reinforced through the tautological double chain). Furthermore, the same line starts with the word "agaiNST," which leads directly to the opening of the chain in "uNSTilled." "Against," however, may have been overlooked, being peripheral in a semantic and syntactic respect. Upon rereading, we may further add the words "lost," "spent'—LST, SNT, in the first line. An additional consonant P, in the cluster SP, develops an additional thread: LoST-SpeNT_SPeNt-unSPokeN, which, in turn, is taken up by "UNspoken-UNheard," linked to the central sound pattern both by anaphora and by morphological and semantic parallelism, and then, by rhyme: "unhEARD-wORD."

To summarize: simple repetitions of sounds or sound clusters may not be felt by a reader, unless reinforced by syntactic or rhythmical parallelism or semantic and stylistic prominence. In our case, there is mutual reinforcement: central words (in theme or imagery) strengthen the importance of a sound repetition; and the sound pattern, in its turn, focuses attention to the relations between these words (in meaning, or imagery). Eliot, however, does not permit an absolute sound-meaning parallelism. The sound patterning is autonomous, because it involves also words thematically not related to the central group; and vice versa: some words related by meaning, or central to the poem, may not participate in a given sound cluster. Again, asymmetry prevails. This is only natural, if sound patterning (or any poetic form) is not to become an automatic (and therefore redundant) concomitant of meaning.

In other words, a focusing sound pattern is a pattern linking clusters of sounds in several words, some of which are linked thematically; or: *part* of the sound pattern includes a *part* of the key words in a context. Focusing patterns do not merely make important words conspicuous, or link disparate images, they may also reshuffle the emphasis of importance of words in a text, thereby imposing upon the poetic text an additional principle of order: that of sound relations.

In focusing patterns, relations between sounds call the reader's attention to relations between meanings (or other properties of the interrelated words). The specific nature of such relations must be resolved in each case, not as a whim of the reader but supported by a reasoned interpretation of the text and its intertextual adherences. Along with the reinforcement of a link between two related ("word"-"world") or mutually qualifying words ("sad," "uncertain"), totally disparate words may be brought together. For instance, Mandelshtam links wasps ("osy") with the axes of the earth ("osi") through a focusing sound link and makes them the pivotal themes of the poem.

Structurally, too, there is a great variety of possibilities. Many cases of local alliteration and paranomasia belong here. A more complex case is the juxtaposition of several sound groups, like musical "motifs," each carrying a thematically different group of words. Thus, David I. Masson (1967) has observed in the opening of *Paradise Lost* several "themes": Theme A: "The fall and its instruments are connected together by motifs in *f, r, t,* and in *r, s, t*" "First," "Fruit," "Forbidden Tree," etc.); and Theme B: "Man's original disobedience is linked to its results in his expulsion and mortality, by motifs in *b, d, n,* and *i, d, n, t* ("Disobedience," "Forbidden Tree," "Loss of Eden," etc.). It seems to me that in this case, too, there is no one-to-one relationship between sound and theme; and insofar as it is at all possible to disentangle such separate sound chains (perhaps, indeed, with the help of thematic groupings of words), only a *part* of any chain will be reinforced by the respective thematic material, by no means automatically. (For example, how can "First" belong to "the Fall and its instruments," and "Disobedience" to a different theme?)

Type IV: Neutral Sound Patterning

The most widespread use of sound patterning, however, has no direct relation to the meanings of the immediate words, or to the relations between such meanings. These sound patterns are *neutral* in respect to their cotextual meanings. In this case sound patterning contributes to the meaning of a poem in a higher sense: it is part of the *Poetic Function* as defined by Jakobson: "a set towards the message," that is, calling attention to the language and the formation of the text itself. There is both a subversion of the normal sound-meaning relationship and an emphasis on the density of poetic language.

Diagrammatically the four categories[1] of sound-meaning relations may be represented thus:

I. Mimetic	*II. Expressive*	*III. Focusing*	*IV. Neutral*
s	$s_1 \longrightarrow s_2 \longrightarrow$ tone, mood	$s_1 \longrightarrow s_2 \longrightarrow s_3$	$s_1 \longrightarrow s_2 \quad s_3$
| |	| |	$\longrightarrow$ | | $\longrightarrow$ | | $\longrightarrow$	
m: "sound"	$m_1 \longrightarrow m_2 \longrightarrow$ tone, mood	$m_1 \longrightarrow m_2 \longrightarrow m_3$	$m_1 \longrightarrow m_2 \longrightarrow m_3$

In actual poetry we find easy transitions from one type to another. It seems that there is a psychological hierarchy, by which the reader tries first the most direct transfer and only failing that he moves to the next stage. The signifying nature of language, as well as the tradition of poetry explications and of harnessing every poetic device into interpretation, encourage such transfers. The neutral, or "poetic," function operates in all cases, but is not felt as such whenever a "motivated" appearance of sounds may be discovered. On the other hand, within any pattern of the more abstract kinds we may often discern partial relations of the more immediate types. In any text with predominantly neutral sound patterning, an interpretive close-up may detect possibilities for mimetic, or expressive, or focusing local transfers, which make at least parts of the poetic sound patterning directly connected to the poem's meanings.

The density of sound patterning in a text may play a role in guiding the reader. Metrical alliteration that appears regularly (as in Old English or German poetry), or regular rhyming, automatizes the device and attributes it to the general conventional form; an especially strong schematic or stylistic deviation is needed to revive attention to a possible local meaning transfer. The same alliteration or "rhyme," however, when appearing sporadically (as in Modernism), calls for immediate attention to a possible local transfer.

---

1   In semiotic terms one might identify the first three kinds as: iconic, symbolic, indexical, and in the fourth type there is no direct sign relation. I avoided this terminology because, for lack of discrete signifiers and signifieds, the units are more complex. For example, in the second, expressive type, the symbolic relations obtain between the resultant abstractions ("mood"), but each of them is derived metonymically (i.e. "indexically") from the meanings of words.

In any case, when encountering a possible sound pattern, the reader has to decide whether a transfer of meaning is feasible, of what kind that transfer may be, and what its specific content is. All this is not codified in any way but must be worked out from the interactions of cotextual patterns. As we have seen, the very decision about bringing a sound pattern to the center of attention (or even whether it should exist as such)—except for obvious cases of dense and close sound groupings—may depend on such a possibility of interaction. In this respect a variety of factors may play a role, including the generic nature of the text (e.g., sound repetitions in casual texts may be overlooked, as being teleologically unrelated to the chief functions of the genre—informative or phatic).

Though I brought all examples from poetry, it must be clear that prose fiction and drama, too, abound in such patterning. In poetry it may have seemed, historically, more prominent, for lack of such other "essential" genre features as mimesis or plot; and also because such patterns, being made of sounds, are naturally linked with the compositional patterns of the poem, which are also made of sound material: verse and strophic structure. It is, however, as widespread in fiction, the study of which in this respect has hardly begun.

Let us observe one example, from James Joyce's story "Eveline," which we used earlier. The first sentence of the story reads: "She sat at the window watching the evening invade the avenue." The title of the story, "EVEliNe," is strongly connected by a focusing pattern to: "EVENiNg," "INVade," "AVENue." Indeed, thus the basic spatial setting is created. The word "invade," however, falls out of this semantic chain and opens up (by its being a drastic synonym to the expected "falls") a pattern of expectation and a symbolic reading of the story as a whole. The attention to this word is concentrated through the focusing pattern. Thus, in simple language, without verse or meter, a poetic density is achieved.

A similar focusing device is used twice towards the end of the story:

[. . .] she felt him *seize* her hand:
"Come!"
All the *seas* of the world tumbled about her heart. He was *drawing her* into them: he would *drown her.* [italics mine. —B.H.]

In both patterns there seems to be a transformation of meaning (motivated by the presentation through Eveline's mind, which is associative in general, and irrational now): to "seize" her hand is like pulling her into all the "seas"; "drawing" is like "drowning."

In the same story there are other kinds of sound patterns, most of them standing out because the bulk of the text is written in a simple prosaic language (reflecting Eveline's point of view), avoiding obvious embellishments. For example, "OF course, her Father had Found out this aFFair and had Forbidden her . . ." Locally, this can only be a neutral sound pattern. In the larger context, however, it may be linked to the fact that both opposing forces, "Father" and "Frank," start with an F. If this connection is made (in a focusing pattern), it may imply that in the very act of forbidding, the father evokes in her mind Frank's name.

At the same time, Joyce is not shy of simple onomatopoeic effects: "she heard his footsteps CLaCKING aLONG the CONCReTe pavement and afterwards CRuNCHiNG on the cinderpath . . ."

4

The structure of sound-meaning relations, as described above, is similar to other kinds of pattern interactions in the literary text. I shall mention here a few points.

1. A text provides a vast amount of material, only some of which is obviously patterned. Other elements may be patterned by readers under certain conditions.

2. Patterning links up elements into discontinuous chains of heterogeneous nature.

3. Two or more cotextual patterns may enter into relations of hierarchy or interaction. Cotextual patterns may mutually select (or filter) the elements of each other, relevant for interaction.

4. Interactions enable mutual reinforcement, opposition, or transfer of meaning from one pattern to another. Such interactions occur in symbol and metaphor; between two characters; between nature descriptions and human emotions; between plot and ideas, etc.

5. Since interactions are not between two static and discrete units but between patterns, each of which is spread out through several language elements and projected situations, there may be several kinds of transfer at several points of intersection of these patterns. (See my study on "Poetic Metaphor and Frames of Reference," Chapter 2.)

6. In the transfer of meaning from one pattern to another there is a hierarchical scale, from the most immediate iconic and imitating, through the most abstract or interpolated, and up to neutral cotextuality (similar to the four types described here).

7. Two patterns which may be perceived as parallel and expressive of each other are usually autonomous in this respect: only parts of each pattern relate to parts of the other, related one. Thus, two characters in fiction conceived as parallel (or opposite) to each other in some respect are not *all the time* parallel (or opposite) to their counterparts, and sometimes must be unrelated altogether if their autonomous existence is to be justified. Likewise with sounds.

8. Since we deal here with semiosis outside of what is codified in language, and with composite signifiers and signifieds spread through many language elements, there is a necessary process of *construction* by readers. We cannot in advance solve each interpretative case or provide final clues for its solution. But we can describe the parameters influencing such constructions and the structure of such transfers, if and whenever they are made.

·

Personally, I do not believe that a *laissez faire* field, a free for all, should be left to the readers. We can certainly use a great deal of experience: from our own introspection, from the observation of teachers and students, as well as from records of written criticism. We can clearly and precisely describe the *kinds* of arguments that should be made in defense of one interpretation or another, including arguments from genre and history. We cannot decide in advance which of the competing heterogeneous factors working in one context may have the upper hand, but we know how to go about it. In any case, we should not confuse the observation of ambiguous texts (which lend themselves to *several* interpretations), which can be made quite unambiguously, with an inherent and unresolvable ambiguity in the discussion itself.

Be it as it may, the problem of interpretation (or reader's constructs) enters irrevocably in any analysis of literary structure.

7 'LITERARINESS' REVISITED

A Contemporary Manifesto

A. SOME POLEMICAL CLARIFICATIONS

The set toward "*Literariness*," both in the methods and objects of study, was a powerful creative force in Russian Formalism and in the movements of literary theory which, directly or indirectly, it engendered. It was a battle cry for freedom of literary scholarship from the encroaching neighboring disciplines coupled with a battle cry for freedom of literature from being a mere servant or reflector of history, sociology, psychology, and other human concerns. Whether defined directly, as in Jakobson's writings, or tacitly embraced, as in other Formalists, Czech and Polish "Structuralists" and such phenomenologists as Roman Ingarden, it posited a separate object of study: *literature* and, hence, a separate scholarly discipline, the *science of literature.*

Most literary critics today, especially in the Anglo-Saxon world, would dismiss out of hand the notion of "literariness" and the very idea that literary texts can be clearly defined and separated from other texts. Furthermore, it seems that "literary criticism" today is the most open field in the humanities, a free-for-all, where ideologies, terminologies and idols from philosophy, semiotics, linguistics, psychology, anthropology, Marxism, feminism, psychoanalysis, and other human disciplines are vigorously employed, combined, battled and rebutted till all become domesticated as metaphors in a pan-cultural mode of activity, which may be called "critical discourse." Thus literary criticism becomes a kind of "analogue computer," imitating the condition of literature itself as a field open to the intersections of all so-cial and cultural trends.

This kind of literary criticism may be classified as a "contextual disci-pline" investigating the ever changing interactions of heterogeneous forces in specific historical and textual contexts rather than abstracting individual aspects for analytical investigation as the natural and social sciences used to do. The problem itself, of "contextual science," is not limited to the study of literature. Satellites and mathematical models, enhanced by superpower com-petition in space and by television comedy, can investigate and map the dif-ferent parameters that make up the forces of climate; but I still don't know whether to take a raincoat tomorrow morning in New Haven, Connecticut. The local, contextual interaction between such forces that would bring about a particular rain in a particular place and time is beyond precise prediction. The same could be said for economics: all the powerful mathematical models and Nobel prizes cannot tell governments exactly what to do next and indi-vidual investors when to get in or out of the stock market. One reason is the enormous complexity of the interactions of heterogeneous forces that affect such a field; another reason is the impossibility of weighing the constantly changing relative values of different parameters in any specific combination; and yet another reason is the interference of "extrinsic" factors, such as (in the case of economics) mass psychology, propaganda, changing international politics or the personality of an elected leader. The same is basically true for practical literary criticism, biographies of writers and fully contextualized lit-erary history.

The uninterrupted continuity from total predictability to total chaos (or idiosyncratic individuality) was sharply observed by Italo Calvino in a short story, "How Much Shall We Bet?" (*Cosmicomics*). The problem, thus, is in-herent in the nature of the world and poses difficult questions to the system-atic sciences and the traditional philosophy of science. To account for it, we may want to develop a general "theory of contextual sciences." On the other hand, aware of it, we will, surely, bestow more value on an experienced and original critic's insights into the individual case in its accidental and specific complexity—be it an interpretation of a poem or the treatment of a case by a psychiatrist.

But abandoning all systematic study, including abstraction of aspects, trends and problems, is throwing the baby out with the bathwater. We must accept the fact that, in the fields of language, culture and society, there are no pure objects, no demarcated biological species, many forces intersect and interact in any one case, both in rule-governed ways and in random combinations. But saying that they "intersect," influence or deform each other, implies recognizing that such strains exist autonomously, too, and can be investigated in isolation—artificial as it may be. There is no possibility of knowledge—unless by knowledge we mean accounts of individual experiences—without such an assumption that we can isolate for observation one aspect, mode of discourse, source of influence, cluster of cultural forces; or an individual text, period or personality lifted from its existential setting in a universe of texts, producers and consumers.

No doubt, there was a tendency among Russian Formalists and some formulations (notably, by the young Jakobson) implying that the object of literary study is literature *minus* all the other human expressions that occur in literary texts—those are legitimate objects of study in their own right but should be relegated to sociology, psychology, politics, history, philosophy, religion, etc. What makes a work of literature, the argument goes, is the *poetic function* (as formulated by the later Jakobson) being *dominant* in a given text. This dominant function is assumed to be the proper object for the study of poetics.

In my view, this is extreme reductionism, akin to the Futurist separation of the language of poetry from its content (in his Communist stage, Mayakovsky invited the party to provide that content). It is based on an essentialist fallacy, requiring a separate essence or *sui generis* properties for each kind of object and each separate discipline. It fails in not recognizing central areas of literary texts—the very substance of the "fictional worlds" of works of literature—which are typical and central to literature or to various literary genres without being exclusive. It overlooks, on the one hand, the intensive and intimate, local integration of a medley of thematic and linguistic elements in any given work of literature and, on the other hand, the different ways of existence of such "thematic" elements in literature and outside of it. It locates the literary in *language* without the domain of *fictionality* and in speech acts without the autonomous object, separated from the flow of communication, the literary text. It fails even in its essentialist thrust, because all candidates for the title of "literariness" (metaphor, narrative, rhythm, sound orchestration, etc.) turned out to work outside of literature as well, as Jakobson readily admitted, while "dominance" is very hard to prove internally.

The counter-move, however, is reductive, too, and depends on the same essentialist fallacy. Since metaphor, figuration, narrative, readings and mis-readings, etc., can be observed in other domains as well, it is not fashionable anymore to define literature as a separate domain. Since there seems to be no separate essence of literature, or any separate literary property, its boundaries are abolished. Everywhere we find texts and readings, figuration and narrative, dialogue and polyphony, etc. and no distinction is needed between readings of texts in poetry, philosophy, politics, linguistics, Midrash or the unconscious. This is the *semiotic reductionism* of literary studies today, embraced by a whole range of approaches, from Jakobsonian analysis to Deconstruction on the one hand and Neo-Marxism on the other. In this sense, too, Deconstruction is much more rooted in the linguistic-semiotic tradition than it would seem on the surface, though it stands on the opposite pole in its (perhaps half-hearted) mistrust in the possibility of systematic study.

To be sure, a study of any of these aspects or strategies across the field of texts in culture is absolutely legitimate precisely because there are no individual devices essential or exclusive to literature. As one may wish to study social mores or ideologies in literary and non-literary texts alike, so one can do with what were formerly called "literary" devices. Metaphor or narrative appear not only in literature and may be defined in ways that would recognize their omnipresence. But their appearance in literary texts is very different and plays a different function—even though these may take on many manifestations, not reducible to one definition.

More importantly, a work of literature is not simply the result of a specific function in a linear use of language or an application of a narrative scheme to a text, but a complex and individualized semiotic object, in which many such heterogeneous strategies intersect, clash, and intertwine. And so is, on a higher level, literature as a historical body of texts and changing norms. All this is very clear to many practical critics, close readers or historians of literature but became problematic on the level of theory—and a self-defeating theory it is.

The idea of "literariness," thus, turned out wrong either as a delimiting or as an exhaustive definition of literature. But, having failed as a definition, it can serve as a powerful perspective for the study of literary and non-literary texts. Precisely by carving out typically (though not exclusively) literary objects of study, in poetics as in literary history, it enabled the formulation of well-focused questions and analytical methods for the study of those aspects, which—if not exclusive—are certainly central to major bodies of literature.

Furthermore, all those devices had a second life when the isolation of literature from other texts was overcome. A repeated pattern has emerged in the
history of criticism: questions and methods formulated in the well-controlled
domains of literary texts, norms and history, were fruitfully transferred outside
its boundaries. This happened to many schools of literary studies: in the transition from Slavic poetics to modern Semiotics; in Leo Spitzer's investigations
of literary style later transferred to style in general; in the widening of the New-
Critical interest in Metaphor as a central feature in the language of poetry to a
general philosophical and psychological interest in "trans-logical" expression;
in the transfer of New-Critical close readings of poetry to Harold Bloom's or
Paul de Man's close readings of other texts; in the transition from French Narratology in literature to narratology in history, philosophy and daily life; and
in the widening of Russian Formalist models of literary history to the study of
cultural history in general.

The opposite, unfortunately, has not happened. We do not have any proper
theory for the different uses of social, psychological, ideological and thematic
materials in literature (outside of their subordination to form). When such interests are prominent—e.g., as in recent Feminist or Marxist criticism—they
normally see the literary text as yet another document for whatever "non-
literary" tendency is discussed.

Thus, the lack of a recognized literary essence or literary properties *sui
generis* and the omnipresence of "literary" strategies in the universe of texts,
seem to justify the *semiotic or pan-textual reduction*. Intuitively, however, we
must insist that works of literature are different from other texts (and so are
works of philosophy, diaries, private letters, research in psychology, etc.) and
cannot be reduced to the general dichotomy of "texts" and "readings." The
theory and study of literature proper must find a description of literature that
would explain this intuitive separateness. If no essentialist definition of literature is possible, we may be well advised to look for other ways of describing
literature.

One way of circumventing the problem of defining literature is the recourse to social convention: literature is not one class of texts but whatever
was considered literature at one time or another. I do not wish to deny the
value of social institutions in this respect: something called "a poem" and
printed in a book of poetry or something called "art" and placed in a museum
(Duchamp) must be considered as such even if its intrinsic properties do not
fit any preconceptions about poetry or art. Nevertheless, in many periods,

texts were not labeled "literature" and we may still read them as literary texts; and, on the other hand, labels may be misleading: a "diary" may really be a work of fiction, genre-labels may be in need of reinterpretation (Gogol's grotesque novel *Dead Souls* is subtitled: "a poem"). The institutional solution thus cannot cover all cases; it is yet another receding argument which literary critics often take to avoid direct analysis.

The solution lies, rather, in admitting frankly that literature is not a logically well-defined class (nor are other domains of human existence) and we cannot have one meaningful definition in the form of a statement with several precise attributes. But this does not mean at all that literature cannot be recognized as a separate domain; we can—and must—describe it nevertheless in a more complex and open manner.

The present paper will outline some principles of such a new description of "literariness." Of the two major modes of existence—the individual work of literature and literature as a phenomenon in history—we shall focus here on the first.

B. TOWARD A NEW DESCRIPTION OF LITERARINESS

The trouble with many definitions of literariness or aesthetic definitions of art was that they wanted to subsume it all under one principle or in one linear model (the "poetic function" imposed on language or a "narrative" dominating prose fiction) while we are dealing with *multi-dimensional objects with changing and optional forms on all levels and in all aspects*. It is possible to describe literature if we show it not as one monolithic phenomenon but as an *intersection in flux* of several forces, elements and constructs, changing from case to case and regrouping through the dominance of historical trends, genres and individual writers. Instead of one essence, we must consider *alternative clusters*. Whatever norms or devices have developed in literature (meter, rhyme, plot, character, genre) appear only in part of the texts. Such norms may be studied in isolation, provided we understand that on every level and in every aspect we encounter optional and changing forms.

The literary system includes many texts that are not works of literature in the narrow sense. For isolated aspects under observation, those may be as relevant as works of fiction. To reconstruct a writer's ideology, aesthetic taste or biography, we may use his diaries, letters, witness accounts, as well as his poems and novels. But intuitively, and traditionally, the poems and novels are of a different category. Often, the works of literature are those that justify an interest in the writer's life in the first place. Hence, we must distinguish between "works of literature" and other "texts" (within the social system of literature or outside it). Though works of literature and their perceptions have many things in common with other texts, they are also different. Jakobson's claim that the study of literature is merely a matter of linguistics has been recently substituted by the claim that those are merely "texts." However, philosophy, law, science (including the science of language), cannot be reduced to being mere "texts" requiring "readings," as the *semiotic reduction* would have it, any more than they could be reduced to linguistics. Neither can works of literature in the narrow sense.

A work of literature is a relatively open set of constructs arising from a text relatively fixed. Some theoreticians would call the bundle of constructs a "poem" or an "aesthetic object" which is a "concretization" of the text (Ingarden, Duffrenne). Today we must be more careful and assume that there may not be one monolithic, ideal "poem" or "novel," not even several competing concretizations of the whole; that there may be partial constructs which do not account for all aspects of a text as well as competing and contradictory partial constructs. Hence, the above definition.

A work of literature is a three-dimensional semiotic object to which several specific principles are applied, which make it into a work of literature. The three dimensions are interlaced in the text and interdependent. They are:

A. A chain of *Speakers and Positions*, embedded in or otherwise concatenated with each other. That includes the external Speaker (or Author) responsible for the whole text, as well as the Narrator or the "Lyrical I" and other speakers presented in it. "Positions" are not overtly presented as speech or indirect speech, but may nevertheless be constructed from part of a text as representing a limited view (from the point of view of a character, mode of discourse, or perspective of observation) of whatever is presented in the text.

B. A complex of *Meanings and References*. All meanings, definite or fuzzy, presented in sentences or constructed by readers, can be fully understood only when related to specific *frames of reference (fr)* which may be projected or evoked in this text or existing outside it. The same words may refer simultaneously to two different *fr*s and create different meanings.

C. *Text Formation.* Here we may include the framing of a text, its opening and closure, its composition and segmentation, such devices as meter, sound patterning and strophic structure, as well as the nature of language and discourse selected in a given text or its parts.

All three dimensions arise from the same verbal material. In various genres, any of the dimensions may be more important for the composition of the text (e.g., speakers in drama, versification in poetry). Any dimension may use material from the other dimensions for its constructs. Thus, the composition of a text may rest on formal structures (chapters or strophes) as well as on constructs of meanings and frames of reference (e.g., parts of the text are constituted by themes or scenes in space and time) or groups of speakers (notably, in drama). The dimension of meanings may subordinate constructs of form (sound patterns, plot) to its interpretations. Furthermore, all meanings and frames of reference are not objectively stated but are presented by speakers and from certain positions; while those speakers and positions, in turn, are constructed from the frames of reference presented in a text. This is a typical case of "circularity" or interdependence which marks literary texts as different from, let us say, philosophical texts.

Thus a model emerges which looks more like a multifaceted cube than a linear chain of discourse. Such a three-dimensional structure exists in other texts and other semiotic objects as well. But in literature, the relative importance of all three dimensions and the circularity of their relationships are essential. The dimension of "text formation" can be found in works of philosophy or in Freud's writings as well. Those may be extremely important rhetorical tools responsible for bringing the text to the attention of readers, but are not essential aspects of the theory, which constitutes the central function of the text. Similarly, poems and novels may be important carriers of ideology, but here the ideological positions are presented through particular points of view, domesticated in the psychology and life-circumstances of the speakers, hence convincing in their situatedness in a concrete "fictional world" rather than through a sustained logical argument; such ideas must not necessarily be accepted or rejected by the reader but rather perceived as parts of a circular *social space* of the novel. In poetry, typically, such ideas are not logically unfolded but situated in the poem's frames of reference (often, fleetingly changing) and molded by the patterns of text formation of sound, verse and discourse.

For this "cube" to be a work of literature, it has to fulfill several specific principles, all combined together:

(1) It is a text that projects an *Internal Field of Reference* (in the sense described below) while simultaneously relating to *External Fields of Reference* as well;

(2) It is a fixed text, isolated from a speech act and transferable to other reading situations;

(3) It employs a variety of historically changing norms, conventions and devices in all domains of the text.

Only the first of these principles is exclusive to literature. All three have large areas of optional manifestations. But all are necessary for a text to be a work of literature. Deriving from these principles governing a text, there are further, concomitant features, typical to all or some literary texts. We shall describe the main principles one by one:

1. A literary text is a text which projects an *Internal Field of Reference*. At the same time, the text or the readers' constructs from it may refer to *External Fields of Reference* as well; indeed, the interaction between the Internal Field and External Fields of Reference is essential to the meaning of the text.

The projection of an Internal Field of Reference (IFR) is a unique and necessary though not sufficient condition for a text to be a work of literature. In spite of the general skepticism as to the possibility of isolating any exclusive feature of literature, I believe that this property is unique to literary texts and to them only (these include stories and anecdotes that may be embedded in oral discourse). Of course, some clarifications are in order.

An Internal Field of Reference is a field projected uniquely in this text, to which both the sentences of the text and the readers' constructs may refer. It has two major characteristics: 1) the projection of unique referents, for which no external information may be valid; 2) a specific *selection* of referents and frames of reference, closed off in the given text. The first condition is obvious in most works of prose fiction, where we find unique persons, marked by individual personal names, as well as unique scenes in time and place. Even in "factual" or historical novels in which most or all persons existed in the external field of history, there are specific frames of reference, scenes, dialogues behavior unique to this text, for which we can bring no counter-evidence from outside.

In some poems, however, it seems that no unique ("fictional") referents appear; in that case the second characteristic takes over. Thus, the description of Autumn as "Season of mist and mellow fruitfulness" in itself refers to an External Field of Reference: autumn as a season of the year. When referring to such an External FR, we may argue with this statement, e.g., claim that the fruitfulness is not "mellow" at all or that the speaker's point of view is limited to certain geographical areas. However, when embedded in Keats's poem "To Autumn," we are presented with an Internal FR and cannot ask whether it is true or false outside of it. The selection of referents in this poem, making up the presentation of "Autumn," is unique and not arguable. Furthermore, it is "circular," being presented from a specific observer's point of view, and is reinforced by the sound-structure and discourse-formation of the text. Even in a historical novel, such as Gore Vidal's *Lincoln*, the concreteness of presentation makes the arbitrary selection a given and tilts the perception of historical figures and events in the direction chosen by the author. Both the truth values of propositions (in the text or constructed by readers) and the specific, individualized nature of various descriptions are judged from the limited information presented in the IFR.

An IFR, however, is not a fixed "fictional world" but a field to which language refers, assuming such a "world." The language may be ambiguous, contradictory and construct-dependent. Furthermore, it is not a closed-off object or "world." It is in the nature of reference in works of literature (and in reading works of literature) that reference is double-directed: to the Internal and simultaneously to various External FRs as described in my "double-decker model" of literary reference (see Chapter 1). This is done both in using External referents (names of places, dates, names of philosophical schools, etc.) and in direct referring to ExFRs in the text (by describing historical events, cities, the nature of man, etc.). It is also done by the readers' *secondary referring* of constructs in the IFR to External FRs. A historical novel is perceived by readers as grotesque, realistic, idolatory, etc. through keeping the Internal constructs in a comparative perspective with accepted perceptions of the External FR. The works of Kafka, encouraged by their non-realistic features, were related in various interpretations to a variety of extrinsic fields: Austro-Hungarian bureaucracy, Jewish alienation, the impossibilies of interpretation, totalitarian social systems, etc. Though, evidently, no such single interpretation can be uniquely valid, the very nature of the text invites such optional and competing constructs as part of this "work of literature."

This "double-level" nature of literary reference supports the focus on the contributions of literary texts to external reference: ideology, thematics, representation of historical situations, as is again fashionable in literary criticism today. One must not forget, however, that the external reference of the text as a whole is made possible through the establishment of an Internal FR first.

In very few texts, notably in some "Concrete" poems, based on letters and graphic elements organized on a page, no Internal Field of Reference may be detected. But in those cases there is no reference of the text as a whole. To cover such cases, we might rephrase the definition and say that a literary text is a text which, if any fields of reference are evoked in it, at least one of them is "Internal." But the phenomenon is so specific to "Concrete" poetry that, instead of slipping into a cumbersome general formulation, we may account for it as a marginal and special phenomenon.

In some texts, there is a historical ambivalence between an External and Internal FR. Those are simply ambivalent texts and become works of literature only to the extent that we autonomize the presented field from its external reference. Thus, a book of history may be read as a book of literature but then the evidence of other historical studies contradicting some of its claims becomes irrelevant. The same holds for a case study written by Freud: when read as literature, we internalize Freud as a narrator within the fictional world, which is presented from his point of view, and we do not bring counter-evidence about the character or about the psychoanalytic theory itself. Such *literary readings* of not intentionally literary texts are further enhanced by the use of literary devices (principle 3).

2. A literary text is a fixed and isolated textual object, cut off from both the flow of discourse and its original act of communication and transferable to many new reading occasions in other times, places and reading contexts. Coupled with the IFR, this creates : a) a *framing effect*, calling attention to the formation of the text and to possible equivalences between its sounds, language, characteristics, etc. Here, Jakobson's "poetic function" is activated and plays a major role; b) *a symbolizing effect*, encouraging to see in the presented text something more than a one time "message," as representing a wider phenomenon.

This feature per se is not unique to literature. A classical text of philosophy is an isolated textual object in the same sense. But the philosophical text refers to an External FR, a domain in philosophy to which other texts refer too. And its composition is based on a logical argumentation rather than on an individual IFR and text formation.

In short, it is a necessary but not exclusive principle of literary texts.

3. The use of a variety of specific—but historically changing—norms, conventions and devices in all domains of form, theme and language. These may be required, accepted or favored in literary texts of certain periods or kinds and may be specifically literary or drawn from other domains (of language, ideology, social perceptions, etc.). No such norms are used in all literary texts, they are changing from one group of texts to another; they do not have to be fixed and formalized but may shift constantly and may be formed in this very text and be valid for only a small group of texts. In any text we encounter various kinds of full or *partial systematicity* (representing genres, trends and other groupings of texts). But the very use of some such norms in a given text is absolutely necessary and helps domesticate that text in the polysystems of literature and culture.

This feature, too, is common to all texts in culture. But the specific clusters of norms used in literary texts of specific groupings are typical of literature and its various genres and trends.

Concomitant to the three major principles, there are several more specific principles resulting from combinations of the above and typical of literary texts:

4. *Concreteness.* This is a very fuzzy and changing concept and requires more detailed discussion. Basically, the literary IFR must have some kinds and levels of "concreteness," in which any abstract ideas or concepts are anchored. This includes *presentation*, i.e., scenes in time and space; information through *persons*; contextually relative concrete items or properties; and, above all, *contextual clusters*, combining a number of heterogeneous patterns—such as: characters, psychology, speech, social setting, ideas, events, space, time—in "reality-like" frames of reference. Literary cognition is *situational cognition*.

Concreteness and presentation may be used in other texts as well (notably, in journalistic reportage) but in literature they are indispensable and make up the basic body of the IFR (while in reportage they, at least, claim to refer to external FRs).

5. *Individuation.* The combination of the first two principles, the Internal FR and the isolated text, enhanced by the principle of concreteness, creates an individualized object both on the level of the text organization and of the IFR. Any modes of discourse, ideas, norms, or semantic "frames" brought in from the outside are individualized and framed in this particular work of literature. On the secondary level, of course, this individualized text and

individualized Field of Reference may be projected onto External Fields and perceived as "symbolic" or "representative."

6. *Density*. The fact that the text is closed-off from the flow of language, that it constitutes a unique and individualized object, coupled with the tradition of reading literature, calls attention to the density of internal relationships in the text (semantic and non-semantic). One major tradition, from Biblical Hermeneutics to New Criticism and Deconstruction, assumes a maximal functionality of all elements and all orders of elements in a text.

Interpretations assume usually such a maximal functionality, even though they may select only some close-ups from it. Historically, this is certainly not a fixed but a changing feature of literary texts.

One major aspect of density is the principle of mutually reinforcing co-textual patterns. In fiction, the characters are reinforced by the ideas they express and the ideas, in turn, are reinforced by being carried by those specific characters, from their specific situation and psychology. In poetry, the interactions between meaning and sound patterning may fulfill a similar role.

Though most of those principles, when formulated on an abstract level, may be observed in other kinds of texts as well, their function there is secondary. While in combination and located in the three-dimensional textual object, they make up the very nature of works of literature.

8 THE STRUCTURE OF NON-NARRATIVE FICTION

The First Episode of *War and Peace*

1. PRINCIPLES OF A UNIFIED THEORY OF THE LITERARY TEXT

1.1. The Text and the Reader

1.1.1. Everything we experience in literature or say about it is based on texts. A work of literature, however, is not to be identified with a text as a fixed object. As we know, primarily from Roman Ingarden and from the practice of endless interpretations of texts, there are many things readers have to add to the actual language presented on the pages of a book. A work of literature is a text to be read by a reader. The reader "realizes" the text, links up things which are not explicitly connected, makes guesses, fills in gaps, constructs generalizations and points of view, creates tensions, etc.

1.1.2. When speaking about the reader we should not give up the study of literature for a subjectivist anarchy. We can certainly discuss what should be a "proper" reading of a certain work of literature—whether we can settle on one such reading or not,—what additions and interpolations the text itself requires, what norms are imposed upon us by the language of the period, the author's possible intentions, the tendencies of his time and genre, etc.; or what kind of different reading hypotheses may be posited in a given case.

1.1.3. In the "realization" of a text by a reader there are two major aspects: *understanding* of the "meanings" presented in the text and *experience* of the non-semantic, rhetorical, or poetic effects of the text. In both respects a realization of the text as an aesthetic object involves the linking of numerous elements within the text: sounds which are repeated and make alliterations or rhyme patterns, repetitions of words or scenes, events in a chain of plot, behavior incidents of characters, comic or tragic qualities, etc.

1.1.4.   The linking made by a reader is based either on specific "instructions" of the text, such as rhymes in a regular pattern or on various principles of "understanding," for example the construction of a hypothesis that a character is afraid based on an interpretation of a certain situation in which the character is presented.

   To any linking made by a reader in the process of realization there must be an equivalent in the text which we may call a *pattern*. Patterns may be stable or ambiguous, formalized or free. If we want to talk about observable facts rather than about the psyche of the reader, we have to discuss such possible or plausible patterns, rather than the individual reader's linkings.

1.1.5.   We must distinguish between the cognitive act of actual understanding or experiencing literature, which may be largely intuitive, and the reasoned *accounting for* and justification of specific structures and meanings understood and realized in a text. Actual understanding usually proceeds through guesses and approximations rather than listing all the details supporting a hypothesis. It is not a final act and does not usually exhaust all possible meanings and effects of a work of literature. Even well trained readers are not immediately aware of all the meanings and poetic patterns they perceived in the text.

   If we want, however, to account for a certain impression, we must link up all those elements scattered in the text, which are relevant to support the impression-hypothesis. The analysis of a literary text by literary critics is, in a sense, an interference. They make explicit what is not necessarily so in the creative process and in the process of reading.

1.1.6.   I shall not go into the difficult problem of what kind of reader or readers we may construct for a specific text. I shall proceed on two assumptions:

   (*a*) that we may speak of an ideal "maximal" meaning of a text, based
         on the assumption that all possible interconnected constructions of
         meaning are necessary and that there is a maximal functionality of all
         elements and of all orders of elements in a text;

(*b*) that no matter which is a better reading or on what grounds we may accept a certain reading, all readings, "right" or "wrong," including "misunderstandings," or willful distortions, as well as partial readings, employ similar techniques. That is, even if we may disagree on particular readings, we may construct a general theory of how readings proceed. Furthermore, we may construct a general theory of how texts are built in conjunction with an understanding of the processes of reading which such texts require.

1.2.   The Hierarchy of Patterns

1.2.1.   A text presents a highly complex network of patterns of all kinds. Any element of any aspect of language as well as any element of anything that may be presented in language (the so-called "secondary modeling systems") may serve as a basis for a pattern. We link up dispersed elements in the text to construct plot, character A and character B, the writer's view of peasant society, style, parallelism of various kinds, etc. Within such larger patterns there are numerous smaller sub-patterns, little chains of elements repeated or linked up in various ways. Thus, the pattern of character A is a conglomerate of many sub-patterns: A's biography, style, activity, relations to her mother, relations to other persons, ideas, etc.

1.2.2.   A *pattern* is a link of two or more elements in a text constructed by any means whatever. These elements may be continuous with each other, as syllables in a meter, or discontinuous, as events in a plot. The principles of pattern construction may be largely classified into two kinds: (a) *principles of equivalence* (such as meter, alliteration or "situational rhyme"); (b) *reality-like principles* (such as character, the nature of human psychology, or the order of a physical setting). Literary theories usually discuss the first kind rather than the second. The enormous variety of structures in prose, however, is based to a large extent on the endless variety of phenomena in the real world and in "possible worlds" used as principles for pattern constructions in literature. In general terms: we not only use literature to understand the world, but we use the world (as well as many "possible worlds") to understand and construct works of literature.

We may also speak of a third kind of pattern construction, based on a mixture of the two, namely (c) *principles of literary institutions*, such as literary genres, which use aspects from both kinds: e.g., the rigid strophic structure of a sonnet on the one hand and the thematic pattern of a tragedy on the other.

1.2.3.   A more formal way of dividing patterns may be the following threefold division: elements in a text are linked by principles of *equivalence* (*a* is parallel to *b* in the sense p); *inclusion* (*a, b, c* may be perceived as parts of M); or *extension* (*b* is an extension of *a* in the sense p, such as cause, space, time). For each of these principles we shall have to employ norms either from the literary tradition or from knowledge of the world or both. Thus, equivalence of repeated sounds, words, or grammatical forms is one thing and equivalence of two presented situations from the point of view of a character's behavior is quite another.

1.2.4.   Patterns may be built of *homogeneous* or *heterogeneous* material. Thus, rhymes or alliterations are made of homogeneous elements: "inherent" (or qualitative) aspects of sound. But if we take plot, it is a highly complex construct built by a reader from a large variety of heterogeneous elements.

Thus, one event may be presented directly in an event sentence: "A killed B." Another event may be presented as a chain of sentences running through a whole chapter, such as: "The phone rang. She picked up the receiver. Her hand trembled. She ran to the closet. She took her coat. She ran out the door." etc.; the reader may conclude from the whole passage that there was a threat or that she left Chicago or both. In spite of the fact that, in their linguistic form, many of the sentences in such a chapter present event statements, these do not serve as events on the level of the reconstructed plot; in the construct of plot we receive a statement from the process of interpretation, i.e., a sentence which was not presented as such in the text but has to be constructed by the reader.

Furthermore, an event may be based on non-event material. For example, in an argument between two lovers about the weather or whether to close or open a window, a reader may detect a crucial point in the story, a crisis in their relationship. This is an event on the reconstructed level, though not based on any event-material in the language.

1.2.4.1.   In heterogeneous patterns, we may distinguish between "*proper*" elements and "*extrinsic*" elements. Thus, events are "proper" material for the construction of plot but the reconstructed plot will be based on extrinsic material as well, such as dialogue, character description, mood, ethical and behavioral norms of a society, etc.

1.2.4.2. A further example may be taken from the domain of ideas. Thus, at a certain point in *War and Peace*, the reader is led to think about the historiosophic question: Who makes history, a leader or the people? The reader has to scan the whole text for answers. He will construct a pattern which runs throughout *War and Peace* and is no less important and no different in structure from plot patterns. This pattern of ideas, too, will be based on "proper" elements, such as ideas expressed by the narrator or by characters (qualified by the reader according to his construction of the positions of the respective speaker-characters); but it will also be based on material extrinsic to ideas, such as the general plot of the novel, the characterization and behavior of leaders (Kutuzov and Napoleon) as compared to the behavior of representatives of the people, etc.

Any question whatever may send us back to the text to collect material dispersed throughout it which may contribute to an answer to the given question. Linking up such elements is not a passive process; the reader has to readjust, reorganize and reinterpret the various kinds of information he obtains as he advances along the text. In other words, the reader has to supply a construct.

1.2.5.   The patterns of a text create a complex network of *hierarchies*. Without such hierarchical constructs, it would be impossible to grasp a work of literature as large and complex as *War and Peace*. Such hierarchies, however, are not stable and architectonic but are *reversible*. I shall not discuss this issue in detail here. One example may suffice. For a reader to realize properly a certain point in the development of plot or re-live the correct tension, it is not enough for him simply to link the events which led up to this point. He must also construct the characters of the persons involved in the event, the social and moral norms which regulate their behavior, etc. In this case, such patterns as "character" or "norms of behavior" are subordinated to a single point in the pattern of plot. But at a later stage we may wish to construct a certain character and then an abstraction from the whole plot in which the character participated may be subordinated to a conclusion about this character. Such a hierarchy may be constructed either by a specific interest of the reader at a given moment or by a pattern foregrounded in a section of the text.

The availability of a whole *network of patterns* which may at any point be subordinated to any one specific pattern (plot, character, ideas, etc.) is a basic feature of literary texts.

1.3.   Two Levels of Organization of a Text

1.3.0.   It is a central principle of this model of the literary text that the patterns in any text are organized on two levels: the level of the *Text Continuum* and the *Reconstructed Level*.

1.3.1.   Characters, plot, ideas, time, space, style, etc., are built by the reader from *discontinuous* elements in the text and are reorganized according to their inherent principles (e.g., time elements are reorganized in their chronological order, ideas in their logical order, streets or trees in a spatial order, etc.). This Reconstructed Level is the one that is usually discussed in interpretations of a text and in literary theories. Unfortunately, in many theories and interpretations it is not always clear whether the scholar discusses something given in the text or something constructed or understood by himself as a reader.

1.3.2.   A writer, however, does not present us with plots, ideas, rhymes, etc., but with a linear text, a language continuum which unfolds step after step before the reader and from which all those patterns have to be constructed. The reader has to shift from sentence to sentence, paragraph to paragraph, scene to scene and he has to justify such shifting. Any close observation of a text will show a high degree of organization of the *Text Continuum* which is distinct from the organization of the fictional world on the *Reconstructed Level*.

A long text cannot possibly be of one piece. It is usually divided into many small segments with a whole network of motivations for the introduction of such segments and for their closure, shifters from one segment to another, transitions from one semantic focus to another, etc. We know, of course, the formal means of text segmentation, such as the division of a novel into chapters or a poem into strophic groups. Much more interesting and complex is the segmentation of a text based on semantic groupings, as we shall see in this paper.

1.4.   The Concept of Junction

1.4.1.   As we observe the typical patterns of literature, such as rhyme, meter, plot, ideas, characters, etc., we find that there is no language material which is purely of one of these kinds. A rhyme, for example, is a pattern of sounds but we have no sounds without words in language (except for the marginal cases of Dada or "trans-sense language," *zaumny yazyk*, of Russian Futurist poetry). Words, however, have other aspects as well: denotations, connotations, syntactic properties, evocation of images, "concrete" qualities, etc. When a poet finds a second word to match his first word in a rhyme pattern, this new word has to fit several patterns at the same time: with some of its inherent sounds it has to fit the rhyme pattern according to the rhyming norms of this poet or of a given period or genre; with its syllabic and prosodic features, it has to fit the metrical pattern of the line in which it is embedded; with its syntactic properties, it has to fit the sentence; with its semantic properties, it has to fit the imagery and the ideas of the poem. In short, a rhyming word is a *junction* in which several patterns meet. The rhyming word has to link up with and contribute something to all these patterns, within the norms proper to each kind of pattern and, at the same time, contribute something new and interesting, again, within the norms required by this poet or genre (or norms newly developed in a given text).

1.4.2.   A brief sample can be seen in John Crowe Ransom's poem, "Survey of Literature." The first line reads:

> In all the good Greek of Plato

In English, there are few precise rhymes for "Plato." Ransom uses a rich rhyme, adding the consonant P to the required -ÁTO, and rhymes *Plato—potato*. Indeed, the word "potato" fits the rhyme, as well as the surprise value of Modernism, but is semantically and stylistically rather distant from "Plato." To enable such a rhyme, a new semantic domain has to be introduced, determining the nature of the whole line:

> I lack my roastbeef and potato.

This, in turn, results in an ironic tone and thematic clash between the topics of the two lines, which must be supported by some higher principle in the text or, as in this case, carried throughout the poem. Thus, the word "potato" participates in several patterns simultaneously: the rhyme, the meter, the syntax, the theme of the line, the semantic clash and the tone of the whole poem.

Indeed, Ransom, a professor of literature, uses this quirky joke of a rhyme to kick up the traditional survey of great books into the realm of gluttony. One word generated this double helix, ironizing all of culture and culminating in a formalist delight: "Only consonants and vowels." Here is the poem:

> *Survey of Literature*
>
> In all the good Greek of Plato
> I lack my roastbeef and potato.
>
> A better man was Aristotle,
> Pulling steady on the bottle.
>
> I dip my hat to Chaucer,
> Swilling soup from his saucer,

And to Master Shakespeare
Who wrote big on small beer.

The abstemious Wordsworth
Subsisted on a curd's-worth,

But a slick one was Tennyson,
Putting gravy on his venison.

What these men had to eat and drink
Is what we say and what we think.

The influence of Milton
Came wry out of Stilton.

Sing a song for Percy Shelley,
Drowned in pale lemon jelly,

And for precious John Keats,
Dripping blood of pickled beets.

Then there was poor Willie Blake,
He foundered on sweet cake.

God have mercy on the sinner
Who must write with no dinner,

No gravy and no grub,
No pewter and no pub,

No belly and no bowels,
Only consonants and vowels.

1.4.3.   A rhymed strophe from Mayakovsky's *Cloud in Trousers* may serve as another example (literal translation, line by line):

Ведь для себя не важно
и то, что бронзовый,
и то, что сердце – холодной железкою.
Ночью хочется звон свой
спрятать в мягкое,
в женское.

V. Mayakovsky, Cloud in Trousers

Vedj dlja sebja ne vazhno	For yourself it's not important
I to, chto bronzovyj,	That you are of bronze,
I to, chto serdce—	That your heart—
kholodnoj zhelezkoju	a cold piece of iron,
Nochju khochetsja zvon svoj	At night, you want your ringing
Sprjatatj v mjagkoe,	to hide in soft,
V zhenskoje.	In feminine

Metrically, those are four lines, rhyming a b a b, though graphically divided in six lines. The two rhyming pairs here are (CAPS represent the rhymeme, i.e., the repeated sounds):

brÓNZOVYJ—ZVÓN SVOJ and ZHelÉZKOJu—ZHÉnSKOJe.
[made of bronze—your ringing; a piece of iron—feminine]

Each rhyming word here fits into the rhyme pattern according to several rhyming norms which were prevalent in Mayakovsky's poetry at the time: the rich rhyme, involving several sounds; the discontinuous rhymeme (based on a number of sounds throughout the word which are not continuous to each other); the diverging endings of the rhyming words; the use of a compound rhyme member; rhyming members with unequal numbers of syllables; linking of two semantically remote words, such as "small piece of iron" and "feminine." However, such a description of the rhyme norms, developed in a sophisticated manner by the Russian Formalists, is true but not sufficient. The poet had to find a way of including such thematically disparate rhyming words in the lines of one poetic text. We have to consider the norms of Mayakovsky's elliptical syntax and futurist metaphors to account for this conjunction of distant domains. Thus, *zhelezkoju* ("as a small piece of iron") would not be possible without the metaphor using the instrumental case. And the word *zhenskoe* ("the feminine") is introduced by means of the concretization of a non-concrete noun and the nominalization of an adjective. *Zvon* ("ringing"), a concretization of a non-material metonymy of metal, can then be hidden in a concretized softness, linking in one image the two opposite semantic domains: metal and softness.

Thus we can say that a rhyming word is a junction on two levels. It is a junction of concrete patterns within the given context—thematic as well as verbal—as well as a junction of general norms governing the domains of these patterns.

1.4.4.   The same could be said for an event. There is no pure event material in language. Each passage of a text presenting an event has to contribute at the same time to a number of other patterns: the characters participating in this event, the setting in which the event occurs, etc. Such a passage is, clearly, a *junction* in which several heterogeneous patterns meet, intersect and interact. Here is a passage from L. Tolstoy's *War and Peace*, involving general Bagration and seen through the eyes of one of the heroes of the book, Prince Andrey:

> Prince Bagration screwed up his eyes, glanced back over his shoulder and see-ing the cause of the confusion turned his head again indifferently, as much as to say: "Is it worth while bothering with trifles?" He reined in his horse with the ease of a good rider, and slightly bending over disengaged his sabre which had caught in his cloak. It was an oldfashioned one, of a kind no longer in gen-eral use. Prince Andrey remembered the story of how Suvorov had presented his sabre to Bagration in Italy, and the recollection was particularly agreeable to him at this moment. They reached the battery from which Prince Andrey had surveyed the field of battle.

This passage may be called "the episode with the sword." It is one unit of the text (a "scene"), based on a semantic principle: nothing immediately be-fore or after speaks about this sword. However, on the Reconstructed Level, the episode of the sword is a junction: it contributes to several heterogeneous and discontinuous patterns, each reappearing throughout the novel. Among them are: the characterization of Bagration; the characterization of Andrey; Andrey's relationship with Bagration; Tolstoy's meticulous attention to the changes in armament and warfare; the question of whether the Russians can beat the French, asked during a battle of defeat but recalling a period when the Russians did stand up to the French (under General Suvorov).

It is interesting to note how all this semantic material was introduced. In the previous sentence a Cossack was killed and his horse still trembled. The ensuing confusion called for Bagration's attention. He moved his head, caus-ing his sabre to be caught in his cloak; thus, the reader's attention is called to this unusual sword through the eyes of an observer, Prince Andrey. Andrey, paying attention to this peculiar sword, recalls then that it comes from a pre-vious war in which Bagration participated with Suvorov. It is a character who takes us in his memory to another place and another time.

Thus one, continuous chain of the Text Continuum, leading from one minor event to another in a rather realistic procession, and emphasizing the point of view of Andrey, created this minor scene. Then, as a whole, the scene functions as a junction for various patterns on the Reconstructed Level; each of them abstracts from the scene such elements or conclusions as fit its nature or its set of questions.

1.4.5.   The task of the poet is not a simple one as it would seem from descriptions of the technique of rhyming or the outline of a plot. He cannot simply add a rhyme or an event. He has to unfold the text so as to introduce new junctions which link up with several patterns in the text, according to the norms of his poetics and the logic of the poem's themes and images, as well as provide the desired rhyme or event.

There is, however, a considerable difference between the two cases, the rhyming word and the scene. In the first, the unit which served as a junction was a unit of language, a word, whereas in the second case it was a piece of the text constituted by a semantic principle, using a *frame of reference* or a piece of the fictional world of the novel. The difference between these two kinds of junctions is one of the basic reasons for the differences between poetry and prose.

1.4.6.   We see now that higher constructs in literature are not like the simple architectonic model we have of the smaller units of language. In language we may say that a number of phonemes link up to make a morpheme and a number of morphemes link up to make a sentence. Each higher pattern is exhaustively inclusive of the lower ones. And each lower element enters as a whole unit into the higher pattern. All such units are predetermined in the structure of the language. In literature, however, no pattern is based on a continuous set of units which enter in their entirety into this particular pattern; rather, a pattern abstracts from the text those aspects which are relevant to its nature. A rhyme links only the rhyming words and abstracts from them those sounds which may be considered equivalent. Plot will abstract from specific scenes or situations their event-aspect rather than their style, setting or ideas, and only such event-aspects which may fit the particular plot-construct.

1.4.7.   Unlike language, in literature not all elements appearing in a text belong to the literary organization. Thus, all sounds belong to the phonology of a language, all phonemes of a word belong to its morphemes, but not all sounds in the text belong to the sound structure of a poem. Only such sounds as may be linked into patterns of rhyme, alliteration or sound orchestration will be activated by equivalent sounds in other places. If they cannot be linked in such a way, the sounds will be considered neutral or transparent from the point of view of literary organization. Such neutral material or material irrelevant to a given pattern dominating a passage will appear throughout any prose text.

1.4.8.   Seeing segments of the text as junctions, as units with their own continuous consistency, rather than as "motifs," directly serving plot or any other kind of structure of the text, is quite different from the accepted description of the text continuum. Thus, the concept of "motif" implies that a certain plot (*fabula*) consists of a chain of such units which have merely been presented in a different order (*sjuzhet*) in a text. But as we see from the notion of the junction, a piece of the text may serve simultaneously as a unit (a "motif") for plot as well as for several other heterogeneous patterns. Similarly misleading is the description of narrative as a deep structure, which is then mapped onto a rather accidental surface structure: if a piece of a text serves as surface for some "deep" structure (e.g., of plot), it serves at the same time for other, heterogeneous, "deep" structures (characterization, ideology, representation of warfare, etc.).

A text is not merely a reshuffling of elements for a structure of plot or ideas, but the presentation of an unfolding continuum which has its own logic and its own organization and from which a reader is led to construct both "form" and "meaning," plot, style, structure, ideas, world view, genre properties, and so on. Mallarmé's famous saying that poems are made not of ideas but of words—which was used for an apology for sound orchestration and "form"—could be directed against rhymes and meter as well: poems are not made of rhymes or meter either but of "words." The only material used are "words" (i.e., language), not events, meter, rhyme or ideas. The writer has to present his words, however, in such an order as to enable the construction of all those patterns, thematic as well as formal.

1.4.9.   We can observe a typical example from the opening of the first chapter of *War and Peace*:

> Anna Pávlovna had had a cough for some days. She was, as she said, suffering from *la grippe*; *grippe* being then a new word in St. Petersburg, used only by the elite. (7/15)[1]

---

1   The numbers in parentheses refer to the original Russian text (*Tolstoy* 1964): page/line.

This passage serves as a characterization of Anna Pávlovna, as a concrete description of the period, as an observation of the language, as well as a contribution to creating a distance of time (and attitude) between the writer and his contemporary reader on the one hand and the characters presented on the other. Of course, each of these patterns constructed from the given sentence will be reinforced and repeated or developed in other parts of the text. Thus, the distance in time between the author's contemporary readers and the characters in the past, illustrated through the language of the characters, can be seen a few lines later:

> He spoke in that refined French in which our grandfathers not only spoke but thought. (8/8)

This sentence, while contributing to the time-distance pattern opened above, is a new junction, contributing at the same time to the characterization of Prince Vassily and to the linguistic pluralism of Russian society.

1.5.   The Three-Tier Construct of Meaning

1.5.1.   The two tiers of patterning of a literary text involve both semantic and non-semantic material. Whenever semantic material is organized, a *three-story construct* is involved. The three tiers are: the tier of "sense" (senses of words and meanings of sentences); a Field of Reference (FR); and Regulating Principles (RP). If meaning is to be taken as anything which may be understood by a reader, meaning is a resultant of the interaction of these three tiers (see Chapter 3).

1.5.2.   While using a language we know the senses (denotations) of words and the resultant "meanings" of sentences. We apply these senses of words and of sentences to a Field of Reference (FR). From the FR we obtain further information about the referents discussed, specification of the meanings presented, as well as justification or falsification of the truth values of the sentence. Thus, if I say "it was a gray day," those who were there could see whether I meant that the sky was clouded or that the day was dull, or both. Metaphors in language exist precisely as an interaction between the sense of a word and the frame of reference to which it is applied (see Chapter 2). In everyday life we save a lot of what we want to say by simply relating our words to existing frames of reference and to information our listener has or may easily obtain from those frames of reference.

1.5.3. I distinguish between a large *Field of Reference* (FR) and specific *frames of reference (fr)* within it. A *frame of reference* is a continuum of any kind—in time and space or in theme or in ideas—which may accommodate a number of referents. A room about which I speak is an *fr* and so is a scientific theory. When speaking about one or the other or applying sentences to them, I rely on the reader's knowledge of a certain selection of referents within each framework.

In real life, as in literature, we encounter numerous small *fr*s. A Field of Reference (FR) is a hypothetical continuum of a large number of such *fr*s. Thus, in the FR of a novel we have a number of *fr*s (of time and space) in which a character appears when he is two years old, when he is 20 and 70 but not in between. Nevertheless we assume a hypothetical Field of Reference (FR), only parts of which were actually presented in the text, which comprises one continuous lifetime of this character. The same holds for a science, such as physics, where not all details are discussed in one continuous field but where specific frames of reference are developed which we assume to belong to one larger field of "Physics" as a whole.

1.5.4.   *Regulating Principles* present the attitudes of the producer of the text or speaker of the words. Such phenomena as irony, point of view, set toward the text, etc., belong to this domain. The Regulating Principles tell us "in what sense" to take the senses of the words. They are not merely based on the nature of the speaker, his position vis-à-vis the topic at hand but also on his or her position in a given situation; for example, he may be excited because of a recent event which makes him exaggerate some of the things he relates.

1.6. The Internal Field of Reference

1.6.1.   The one exclusive feature of a literary text is that it is a text which creates an *Internal Field of Reference* (IFR), that is, at least part of the words and sentences create a Field of Reference to which the same sentences refer. Within this IFR we know only what the sentences relating to it have presented us with (the fictional persons and situations). We cannot go beyond the text to find out whether the speaker lied or didn't lie, whether there was such a Natasha, whether she loved, how red the roof was, etc. In any other text we can, in principle, find additional texts or sources of information about the same FR to which the given words relate.

This is not to say that sentences and words in a literary text refer only to one IFR or only to the Internal FR. Some of them may refer at the same time to one or several External Fields of Reference (ExFR) as well. Clearly, in *War and Peace* many words and sentences refer at the same time to places in Europe or dates in modern history, claiming truth values outside the novel. General sentences about human nature are applicable inside as well as outside the literary text. Moreover, many general constructs made by the reader on the basis of a text will refer to an External FR: generalizations and images of a society, of history, of man, of Russia. This double relationship is crucial, for example, in Solzhenicyn's novels where we relate not only the internal information to the ExFR (Soviet Russia under a certain regime) but vice versa, information from the ExFR is brought in to illuminate the IFR.

1.6.2.   In the use of language in everyday life we have the illusion that only the level of "sense" is given by means of language; the Field of Reference is presented in external reality; and the Regulating Principles are given in the social conditions of the speech situation. In a literary text, however, we have to reconstruct both the Field of Reference and the Regulating Principles from the same body of language which carries the senses of words and meanings of sentences. Since this is the case, there is an interdependence (if not a circularity) between these three tiers. For example, the assumption that a certain passage is ironic influences the meanings of the sentences to be taken ironically by the reader, but only such an understanding of the sentences approves of the hypothesis that the passage is indeed ironic. As soon as we get a sentence which does not seem to be ironic we may have to revise or discontinue the Regulating Principle (irony) which we constructed previously.

1.6.2.1. For example, in our chapter, after telling us that the Vicomte tells his story, Tolstoy writes:

> The story was very pretty and interesting, especially at the point where the rivals suddenly recognized one another; and the ladies looked agitated.
>
> "Charming!" said Anna Pávlovna with an inquiring glance at the little princess.
>
> "Charming!" whispered the little princess, sticking the needle into her work as if to testify that the interest and fascination of the story prevented her from going on with it. (21/15)

In this case we may assume that the story was pleasant and interesting only through half of the first sentence. In the second half and especially in what follows, we start doubting whether Tolstoy meant it seriously or ironically. We may say that, in this passage, two Regulating Principles converge. From the point of view of the women listening to the story, the literal meaning is true: it was indeed a pleasant and interesting story; but from the point of view of the narrator who mocks these women and presents a different level of seriousness on political issues, the words are certainly meant ironically. Thus, the resultant meaning of the sentence is interdependent with the constructed and clashing Regulating Principles under which the sentence should be read.

2. INTERNAL AND EXTERNAL FIELDS OF REFERENCE IN *WAR AND PEACE*

2.1. Referential Grounding

In daily life, we use words applying them to a Field of Reference we know a lot about, to a world in which we have lived for years. We do not present entirely new information but call up or take a position on or reshuffle some elements of previous knowledge. One of the difficulties of writing a text of fiction is that it presents words as if they were being used in a real life situation, whereas the writer often had no previous opportunity to present all the details of the frames of reference to which these words should apply. In short, the Internal Field of Reference created in a work of literature needs *referential grounding*. Thus, major characters are often introduced only after minor characters have appeared and a setting has been presented; major places may be presented as a continuation of minor places which have been detailed in the beginning; etc. "Exposition," known to traditional theories of literature, is only one way of referential grounding—the presentation of the past of characters and events which are central to the story—but this is by no means the only possible technique for referential grounding. Grounding is a metonymic rather than a chronological-causal dimension given to referents in the IFR. They appear as continuous to the grounding referents.

2.1.1.   The party given by Anna Pávlovna, which constitutes the first large episode of *War and Peace*, serves, among others, several purposes of such grounding. Thus, the major characters are introduced through it, though only after the reader has acquired an adequate image of the *fr* (the party) and after several minor characters have been presented to which these major characters are linked by several links.

2.1.2.   This, however, is not sufficient. Tolstoy links his IFR to the ExFR known to the reader from history. He uses a famous chapter in history much as a Greek tragedy uses myth. Indeed, the IFR of the party did not exist in history. It projects, as it were, a plane parallel to the plane of real life in historical time. But, in literature, unlike Euclidean geometry, parallel planes may meet and overlap at several points. Several places, names of persons and dates pertain at the same time to the ExFR in history and to the author's IFR which is discontinued from it. By this device the reader brings to the text a wealth of information and attitudes which help him to grasp the party and the situation in which the characters are set, in spite of the fact that he is immediately confronted with a large number of characters, all of them presented rather sketchily in a kaleidoscopic view.

2.1.3.   As is well known, Tolstoy worked on this chapter for a whole year. The Russian scholar E. Zajdenshnur has published fifteen versions of the opening of *War and Peace* (1961: 291–369). In all of them Tolstoy tried to find a place where many people of various origins and attitudes could meet together. Eventually, he preferred the party to the battlefield. To have not a one-family novel but what he called an "epopeia," he had to make many people meet. A party provides an excellent motivation for that purpose.

Anna Pávlovna's party is conveniently chosen because it is given by a person who is at one and the same time linked to the Tsarist court (which opens a store of information from higher circles) and low enough to invite aristocrats of lesser importance.

The party has to be presented in such a way that many persons express themselves briefly and we move on to other characters. This is achieved through a special technique, as we shall see below.

For such characters, unknown to the reader and not related to each other by any obvious plot, to be palpable, they have to say something about something very important. Hence, we have a crucial political event in real history reopening the questions of "war and peace" with which the characters may take issue and thereby reveal their positions. Therefore, the novel starts in July, after the Russians have learned of Napoleon's annexation of Genoa and Lucca.

2.2.   Three Planes of Reality

2.2.1.   In the episode of the party, there are three Fields of Reference or, in other words, three planes to which the words refer. There is, basically, the Internal Field of Reference: Anna Pávlovna's party—a definite, fictional place and time—and a group of characters meeting there. Then there is the External Field of Reference: Europe in 1805. The relationship between IFR and ExFR is a peculiar one. Clearly the time and place of IFR are continuous to the time and place of ExFR although they are disconnected. Thus, the party is held specifically in July 1805, though it is not determined exactly when in July; it is held somewhere in Petersburg, but it is not clear exactly where. Even if it were clear, it would be impossible to demand truth values of continuum in time and space between ExFR and IFR. It is, however, a basic assumption of the semantics of the text that the characters and the ideas to which the characters relate are continuous in both fields. The characters speak to each other and about each other as well as about referents in the ExFR.

2.2.2.   In addition to the *presented present* in the IFR, there is a *projected future* and a *projected past*. This is due to the quasi-realistic assumption that a character in a text is a semantic unit which has a past and probably a future or that such past and future are presupposed.

The party is an *fr* based on a continuum of time and space: fr_1 (t,s). We may also consider each character as an *fr* in its own right, based on the unity of a person, without any unity of time and place: fr_1 (-t, -s). Thus words in this chapter are junctions which may refer not only to the basic *fr* (t_1, s_1), the basic scene of the chapter, but to other places and times which are located in *frs* of the characters. Moreover, such characters may meet in the projected past or in the projected future, some points of which, again, coincide with points in time and space of the ExFR.

2.2.3.   The third, the highest plane or FR is the time and position of the narrator. No sentences refer directly to him—the narrator is a zero if accounted for by direct semantic descriptions, it is rather a narrating voice. Nevertheless he plays an important role in the novel. His different time is established by such remarks as the one on the French language of "our grandfathers" or on the word "*grippe*" which was "then" (i.e., in Anna Pávlovna's time) a fashionable word (cf. 1.4.9 above). Many of the conceptions of the situation are necessarily related by the reader to the position, point of view and understanding of the narrator and his time. Moreover, the text is interspersed with remarks by the narrator on the events narrated.

2.2.4. This threefold referential structure may be seen in the following diagram:

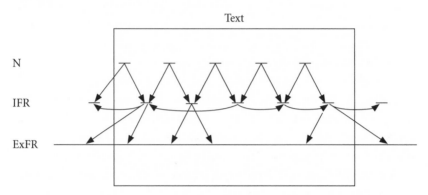

In other words, we have here the narrator's time, the fictional time and the historical time. Each "time" (FR) has its own spaces, values, characters, language.

One major tool for segmentation of the text is the mechanism of the narrator's interference. Thus, one way of dividing the text into pieces is the shifting from one to another of these three planes: from the narrator to the characters to the outside world and back again.

2.3. Information and Segmentation Through Interaction of the Three Planes

2.3.1.   Within the IFR, the reader is presented with a stock of information from the ExFR: (1) Some facts and dates (actually it is of no consequence which dates and facts are mentioned provided they create the connection between the internal and external historical situation). (2) Some abstractions, e.g., the general situation of hesitation between war and peace. (3) Norms of relating to this general situation, both in its specific historical details (such as Napoleon, the French Revolution) and in the general ideological dimensions of society, war and peace.

The historical ExFR is used as a store of information and as a point of departure for orientation within the IFR. For example, if Pierre says something about Napoleon it is immediately clear that Pierre is a "revolutionary"; this we know simply through our understanding of the political positions of that period.

2.3.2.   A number of specific links connect the three planes of reference of the text. Thus, the first sentence immediately establishes the dependence of a personal relationship on the issues of war and peace: Anna Pávlovna declares, though jokingly, that if Prince Vasily will not admit that it is war, he will not be her friend. This basic dependence of personal positions and relationships on the state of the "World" is well established throughout the episode, concluding with Andrey's abandoning his pregnant wife.

2.3.3.   Shifting between the three planes enables not merely one kind of segmentation of the text but also shifting from minor issues to major issues, from concrete details to generalizations and vice versa. We could say that the shifting semantic perspective is enhanced or made possible by this mechanism. Thus, long political speeches are not presented here at all, though the reader—and the audience at the party—are constantly being prepared to listen to them. For Tolstoy, such speeches would be boring. They are simply used for shifting from the political issues referring to the ExFR to the characters within the IFR.

2.3.4.   In the beginning of the episode, segmentation is achieved by cutting off the stream of the dialogue by comments of the narrator. At first the comments seem to be presented, as it were, in parentheses: our story starts with a speech by Anna Pávlovna; after her talk the narrator comments on it, explains how the whole thing came about and only then does Prince Vasily answer; but he answers as if no break occurred between her part of the dialogue and his; i.e., he answers within the "Internal" plane of reality.

On another occasion the narrator's comment is used to skip parts of the dialogue (a "cut" in presenting the IFR):

> In the midst of a conversation on political matters Anna Pávlovna burst out:
> "Oh, don't speak to me of Austria." (9/20)

2.3.5.   The bulk of the chapter consists of dialogues between characters. Tolstoy presents them, as it were, in a scenic way. He lets his characters talk but then he observes their way of talking and subsequently remarks on his observation, explaining it through characterization and description of the speaker. The general direction of this procedure is as follows:

Speech → Observation → Characterization → Description

Cutting across this gradual transition is another semantic transition: from a detail (D) to a generalization (G) in the domain of this detail. We may observe the following passage in which the narrator comments on Prince Vasily's speech:

> He spoke in that refined French ($G_1 = D_1$) in which our grandfathers not only spoke but thought (G_2), and with the gentle, patronizing intonation (D_2) natural to a man of importance who had grown old in society and at court (G_4). He went up to Anna Pávlovna (D_3), kissed her hand (D_4), presenting to her his bald, scented, and shining head (D_5), and complacently seated himself on the sofa (D_6). (8/8)

The description is divided in two sentences, linked by an anaphora ("He"). The following diagram represents roughly the structure of transitions from Details to Generalizations in this passage:

N: Sentence 1   Sentence 2

Obs.: $G_1 = D_1$ $G_3 = D_2$ $D_3 \rightarrow D_4 \rightarrow D_6$

          ↓   ↓   ↓ ↗

Char: G_2 G_4 Descr.: D_5

Figure 2. G – generalization; D – detail; N – narrator; Obs. – observation; Descr. – description; Char. – characterization.

G_1 and G_3 are generalizations when related to the preceding sentences (Vasily's speech) but become details ($G_1 = D_1$; $G_3 = D_2$) when related to what follows. Each generalization may express several things and carry several functions. Thus G_2 expresses the time distance between the narrator and the characters, the social status and the character of Prince Vasily.

2.3.6. Thus, instead of unfolding the IFR in a logical manner which would have taken a great deal of space, Tolstoy starts in medias res, shows the reader directly the speeches of some characters unknown to him yet and then, through the narrator's comments, enlarges the semantic framework and the scope of information. This technique enables Tolstoy to create a wide network—of time, characters, society, places—in barely suggested threads.

For the sake of concreteness one would have needed a much greater detailing of each of the presented generalizations. Indeed, for each generalization (representing a different *fr*), there is some concrete detail given in the immediate text; but such details are merely glimpses of observation, not developed to any descriptive extent. Such details are embedded not in the framework of the semantics of the particular generalization but in the fr_1 of the party, an *fr* in which all such *fr*s intersect. The effect of a concrete "fictional world" is achieved not in the topics raised but in the *front fr*: the party.

3. SEGMENTATION AND ITS MOTIVATIONS

3.0.   In addition to the three-plane division which contributes to segmentation of the text, there is a further mechanism for segmentation. Since the bulk of the semantic material of this chapter is on the second plane, i.e., on the level of the characters (presented in the *front fr$_1$*), the author needs a further device to cut their dialogue into small pieces. Indeed, no dialogue or monologue is allowed to unfold and develop in detail and length as Dostoyevsky would have done it. The reader is led from one circle of people to another.

I shall first show some specific devices of this segmentation and then summarize the principles of segmentation and motivation in the whole episode.

3.1.   Local Motivation

3.1.1.   In the first part of the episode we have only two characters: Anna Pávlovna and Prince Vasily. Here the dialogue is not just rambling, moving from one issue to another but concentrated around changing topics in shifting segments. For example:

> [A.P.]: "Don't tease! Well, and what has been decided about Novosiltsev's dispatch? You know everything."
>
> "What can one say about it?" replied the prince in a cold, listless tone. "What has been decided? They have decided that Buonaparte has burnt his boats, and I believe that we are ready to burn ours."
>
> Prince Vasily always spoke languidly, like an actor repeating a stale part. Anna Pávlovna Schérer on the contrary, despite her forty years, overflowed with animation and impulsiveness. (9/1–10)

The passage continues the previous tension between the two characters: Anna Pávlovna tried to lead the discussion into political questions, whereas Prince Vasily is bored and, as we shall see later, intends to shift the interest to his own personal affairs. The passage opens with a dialogue: Anna Pávlovna shifts attention from "teasing" to politics, asks a political question and Prince Vasily answers. From the dialogue, the reader gets some information about the ExFR as well as some implicit information about the IFR. He implicitly grasps the contrast of positions of the two persons, the contrast of tone, emotional involvement, etc. The text takes up this implicit contrast, leading the reader from the explicit references relating to world affairs to the implicit relations in the IFR. In the last sentence, the narrator gives a description of Vasily's speech and Anna Pávlovna's speech. The narrator's remarks parallel the structure of the preceding dialogue. However, since the text does not unfold in a logical order but rather by concatenation, the description of *his* speech comes first, linked directly to *his* replica. Thus, the structure is chiastic:

Dialogue: *She → He*
Narrator: *He → She*

From the description of her speech we shift to a generalization of her character (according to the principles described in 2.3.5).

3.1.2.   The next passage starts with a new theme linked directly to the subsidiary theme of the previous sentence: the nature of her excitement. What has been a third level subordinated topic in the previous passage becomes the main topic not only of the sentence but of a whole segment of text:

> To be an enthusiast had become her social vocation and sometimes even when she did not feel like it, she became enthusiastic in order not to disappoint the expectations of those who knew her. (9/11)

Again, there is a shifting of topics within the passage: from the nature of her excitement with its contradictions, we turn to her own awareness of this situation and then to other features of her character and age. The next passage uses this by-now well-established feature of Anna Pávlovna's character, her being an "enthusiast" and her excitability, to introduce a long passage on the political situation in Europe:

> In the midst of a conversation on political matters Anna Pávlovna burst out:
> "Oh, don't speak to me of Austria." (9/20)

3.1.3.   The general principle of this technique may be formulated as follows: *any point in the text continuum may be used as a suprasegmental.* Thus, information on Anna Pávlovna's character is used as a motivation for the introduction of a new passage. Indeed, Tolstoy uses Anna Pávlovna to present the reader with a *summary* of the whole political situation of Europe, though this summary is presented in an almost parodic manner through the naïve and excited talk of Anna Pávlovna.

3.1.4.   Since, in the text, Anna Pávlovna is self-conscious of the advantages and defects of her nature, she herself discontinues the same segment by means of the same motivation: "She suddenly paused, smiling at her own impetuosity." (16/16)

3.1.5.   On close examination we see that Tolstoy never introduced new semantic themes without preparation. The excitement of Anna Pávlovna has been well-established in previous passages in what could be called a *semantic chain*: various remarks in this direction have accumulated throughout the first pages of the chapter:

> "Heavens! what a virulent attack!" (8/4): "Can one be calm in times like these if one has any feeling?" (8/21): "Ne me tourmentez pas" (9/1): Anna Pávlovna . . . overflowed with animation and impulsiveness. To be an enthusiast had become her social vocation. (9/9)

3.1.6.   The principle of concatenation has led us from polite talk to a political dialogue to characterization of the persons involved in the dialogue to a presentation of the political situation in Europe. Logically it is a reversed order. But this is the situational order of literature.

3.2.   Long-Range Motivation

3.2.1.   In addition to such *local motivations* for the introduction and the discontinuation of specific segments, there are also *long-range* as well as *global motivations*. The shifting from a dialogue of some persons to other persons, from one topic to another, from political to personal affairs and vice versa, is made possible by the general semantic conditions of the *fr*. Such global motivations in this episode are: the nature of a party, the political situation referred to, the social bias of the participants, or the use of known historical information.

3.3.2.   In addition to the feature of a typical party—a global motivation—there are some specific additional long-range motivations. Thus, the functions of a hostess carried out by Anna Pávlovna are elaborated into an image of a manager of a spinning factory:

> And having got rid of this young man who did not know how to behave, she resumed her duties as hostess and continued to listen and watch, ready to help at any point where the conversation might happen to flag. As the foreman of a spinning mill, when he has set the hands to work, goes round and notices here

a spindle that has stopped or there one that creaks or makes more noise than it should, and hastens to check the machine or set it in proper motion, so Anna Pávlovna moved about her drawing room, approaching now a silent, now a too-noisy group, and by a word or slight rearrangement kept the conversational machine in steady, proper, and regular motion. (17/3)

This image is developed further: "Anna Pávlovna's reception was in full swing. The spindles hummed steadily and ceaselessly on all sides." (17/31)

The image is a junction and fulfills several functions in the text: (1) it serves the characterization of Anna Pávlovna; (2) it serves as a device of irony; (3) it is connected to the pattern of similar images of the mechanical wheel as opposed to the natural principle which divides characters in Tolstoy's work; (4) it serves as a metaphor, i.e., a stylistic device; (5) it serves as a supraseg-mental principle for motivating the composition of the chapter.

3.2.3.   Indeed, the guests are divided into three groups. You cannot show a party with everybody talking simultaneously, unless it is a film and we cannot focus on specific speakers. Anna Pávlovna goes from one group to another, tries to link such groups and to take care of the normal humming of her machinery.

Her function in this respect clashes with that of Pierre. Pierre is, on the one hand, an illegitimate son, i.e., a "lower" character; on the other hand he is the (bastard) son of a rich and influential person, i.e., a potentially "higher" character. Pierre is a newcomer and, like any newcomer, wants to get information; he is young and revolutionary and clumsy and therefore does not know the rules of the polite game. Thus, Pierre's character, too, serves as a motivating force for the introduction of new things or for the disruption of the polite flow of dialogue.

3.2.4.   In addition to the image of the spinning factory, there are minor motivations for continuing or discontinuing, linking groups of people, etc. E.g., Anna Pávlovna presents the Vicomte as an expensive dish to her guests:

> As a clever maître d'hôtel serves up a special choice delicacy, a piece of meat that no one who had seen it in the kitchen would have cared to eat, so Anna Pávlovna served up to her guests, first the vicomte and then the abbé, as peculiarly choice morsels. (18/30)

3.2.5.   There are several disturbances of a rather silly nature like the Princess's knitting, Hippolytes's silly jokes, Prince Vasily's having to go to the British Ambassador and so on. As a result of all such disturbances made of semantically minor or "irrelevant" material, the dialogues are kept short and lively, are actually purposeless and used simply to characterize the society. There is no time for serious political discussion in this tumultuous party.

3.3.   On Classifying Motivations

3.3.1.   We may now summarize. Motivations may be classified as to their extension: there may be immediate (local), long-range, and global motivations. Immediate motivations are responsible for the introduction of one specific segment (such as the introduction of Anna Pávlovna's political outburst). Global motivations cover a whole text or a certain part of it and depend on the nature of the FR of the given text. Long-range motivations are those which establish a principle repeated many times within a given text. Such a principle is not necessarily used throughout the text and may be used in conjunction with several other principles.

3.3.2.   Motivations may also be classified by the material used for their construction. There may be formal motivations, such as divisions of a text into chapters or strophes; and motivations of a semantic nature. The latter may be built of local material, such as the shifting of a secondary topic of a previous sentence to become the main topic of a following paragraph; or of a constructed pattern, such as the constructed psychology of a character which is responsible for his behavior and speech.

3.3.3.   Furthermore, we may distinguish between motivations for introducing a segment and motivations for its nature. Thus, the image of Anna Pávlovna as a foreman of a spinning factory is responsible for the mere introduction of segments presenting groups of people talking at a party; but Anna Pálovna's excitement is responsible for the nature of the segment surveying the political situation.

3.3.4.   A similar example, though a more complex one, is the story to be told by the Vicomte de Mortemart. After a rather elaborate preparation, throughout which the reader and the guests are promised "to be served" the interesting Vicomte, we hear finally that the Vicomte is going to tell a story about the Duc d'Enghien (18/15). The story is, however, delayed several times until page 21/6.

When the Vicomte gets around, at long last, to telling the story, his words are not recorded at all. We are presented merely with a brief summary of the topic of his story, shifting immediately to gossip about the personal aspects of it. This abbreviation is motivated by the listeners, the ladies of the evening, who have no interest in politics as such. In this case, motivation for the introduction of a certain story, even after an elaborated build-up, is not enough to have the story presented if there is no good motivation for the nature of the presentation.

4. ORDER AND DYNAMIZATION

4.1.   Logical Order

4.1.1.   Besides the principles of segmentation discussed above, there is also a logical order imposed upon the fluid text. One obvious division is the division of the party into three circles. This, of course, helps to break up the unmanageable crowd into separate discussions in groups. Nevertheless, it is clearly an artificial device, since Anna Pávlovna takes all the trouble to bring these groups together (after presenting them to the reader one by one).

4.1.2.   A further device of ordering is the summary statement at the beginning of Chapter II:

> Anna Pávlovna's drawing room was gradually filling. The highest Petersburg
> society was assembled there: people differing widely in age and character but
> alike in the social circle to which they belonged. (13/28)

Here the technique is reversed as compared to the first chapter: first comes a generalization (about the society as a whole) and then a detailing, by groups and individuals. The middle part of the whole episode looks like a list of characters belonging to Petersburg's aristocracy (see Table 1). Each segment is basically devoted to a particular character; the lead is then transferred to another character in a new segment.

Nevertheless, if we observe the opening passage of chapter II closely, we will see that all the names mentioned here—Prince Vasily, his daughter, the beautiful Hélène, the young Princess Bolkonsky, Prince Hippolyte, Mortemart, the Abbé Morio—have been introduced and mentioned in the previous chapter, not systematically but à propos other matters. Thus, each of them separately has had his own referential grounding, and is at least known to the reader.

4.1.3. The symmetrical order of the structure of chapters II-IV is not easily felt, due to the large number of disturbances caused by silly things, concatenations and associative transitions from one topic to another, abounding here as in the first chapter.

As Table 1 shows, the whole episode is well planned and schematically divided into large segments centered on particular characters or topics. Nevertheless, the impression is of a disorderly party and a natural flow of associations without any backbone of plot. This impression is due to: (1) the associative and, as it were, unplanned transitions from one theme to another or from a theme to a person and vice versa; the fact that a segment starts with one theme and shifts into another toward its end or provides, toward its end, a lead for the next segment and (2) the nature of the planning itself: planned segmentation does not overlap exactly with chapter divisions; motivations and headings of divisions are not necessarily given at their head.

4.1.4. The logical order is not a framing order, it is not presented as such from the beginning. The fact of the party is introduced only after the first dialogue, and several key themes have been presented to the reader. The image of the hostess as the manager of a spinning factory is presented after she actually behaves in this manner. The generalization about the kind of society attending the party is given only at the beginning of Chapter II, after a sampling of this society has been shown. The division into three circles is given even later, at the beginning of Chapter 3.

Nevertheless, the list of characters is presented to the reader in a continuous way: in the first chapter, they are referred to only in the words of the two speaking characters, i.e., outside the presented *fr.* Throughout Chapters II and III, when they appear on the scene, the list continues, disregarding the formal overall different structures of the respective chapters.

4.2. Dynamization

4.2.0. In sum, several overlapping principles of segmentation work throughout the whole episode. The author picks up one, then another, or uses several of them together to shift from one segment to another, without seeming to be systematic (though he was).

4.2.1. From a global observation, we see that the episode is well planned. The impression of a fluid, irregular and natural situation, the Rousseauist element in Tolstoy, is enhanced by the principles of dynamization. The major forms of

Table 1. Schematic Outline of the Episode

Semantic Parts	Chapters	Segments
A. Prologue to the Party:		
Prince Vasily + Anna P.	(I)	1) Phatic function + characterization
		2) Politics
		3) The problem of his children
B. Characters	(II)	4) Everybody comes → a list → Presentation to aunt
		5) Princess B.
		6) Pierre
		7) The hostess
	(III)	8) 3 circles
		9) (a) Vicomte
		10) (b) Hélène
		11) Her circle: the Princess + Hippolyte
		12) The Vicomte's story
		13) (c) Abbé + Pierre
[as all are gathered enters:]		14) Andrey [Vasily gets up]
		15) Vasily + Hélène leaving
	(IV)	16) Mother of Boris [returns to circle]
C. Political Argument		17) Opening resumed: Genoa + Lucca
		18) Andrey + Vicomte
		19) Pierre—the argument about Napoleon
		20) Hippolyte
D. Epilogue	(V)	21) Leaving: Pierre
		22) Andrey, Hippolyte, the Princess
E. After the Party		23) Hippolyte + Vicomte
		24) Pierre at Andrey's

dynamization are: (1) disruption of an established logical order; (2) shifting of theme in the text continuum; (3) the introduction of little threads of plot; (4) semantic chains running discontinuously through parts of the text.

4.2.2.   The first category is easily seen throughout the episode in the large number of disruptions of announced themes. It works even in such a planned matter as the three circles. There is, first, a generalization about the three circles, then they are presented one after the other. The little thread of plot, however, which creates an anticipation for Mortemart's story leads into the third part of the second circle (9). Thus, this part becomes disproportionately more conspicuous than the others. The first two circles are, from this point of view, conceived as corridors leading up to "the point."

4.2.3.   The second category, *shifting*, can also be seen throughout the text. We have shown above how a secondary topic in one segment becomes a primary topic in a succeeding segment. A different kind of concatenation is caused by a logical unfolding of a disrupting theme. Thus, the pregnant princess, having caused a disturbance in the story and having further delayed the long expected story of the Vicomte, finally sits down.

> There was a general movement as the princess, smiling and talking merrily to everyone at once, sat down and gaily arranged herself in her seat.
>
> "Now I am all right," she said, and asking the Vicomte to begin, she took up her work. (20/7)

Now that the text focused on the princess, there is bound to be a gentleman who pays attention to her, and of all people it is Hippolyte: "Prince Hippolyte, having brought the workbag, joined the circle and moving a chair close to hers seated himself beside her." (20/11) This is cause enough for Tolstoy to switch to the description of Hippolyte (segment 11).

4.2.3.1.   A chain of this kind of shifting may be illustrated in the dialogue between Anna Pávlovna and Prince Vasily. The political tirade of Anna Pálovna which we have analyzed above starts with her bursting out on the issue of Austria. Before her tirade there was a cut in the scene motivated by the narrator's interference. He says clearly, "In the midst of a conversation on political matters Anna Pávlovna burst out: 'Oh, don't speak to me of Austria.'" (9.20)

The reader has no idea what Prince Vasily said that could have caused such an outburst on her part. Moreover, it seems at first that Prince Vasily is bored and uninterested in Anna Pávlovna's politics. He is simply polite and plans to leave soon for the party of the British Ambassador. Then, more than a page later, the name Vienna pops up again.

> "I shall be delighted to meet them," said the prince. "But tell me," he added with studied carelessness as if it had only just occurred to him, though the question he was about to ask was the chief motive of his visit, "is it true that the Dowager Empress wants Baron Funke to be appointed first secretary at Vienna? The baron by all accounts is a poor creature."
>
> Prince Vasily wished to obtain this post for his son, but others were trying through the Dowager Empress Márya Fedorovna to secure it for the baron. (10/24)

It turns out that Prince Vasily had a family matter to discuss with the hostess. The issue is not introduced directly but through mentioning Baron Funke, as if he were another person in the list of persons mentioned earlier in Anna Pávlovna's gossip. In what follows Anna Pávlovna is used by the author for skillful maneuvers to shift away from the topic of interest to Prince Vasily. Eventually, when she returns to the topic of his family, she talks about his daughter rather than the son and only afterward does she mention the two children and the third (the disturbing one) thus shifting to the third son, Anatole, and from here to the issue of finding a match for him. Through this match for Anatole, we are led into a discussion of the Princess Bolkonsky, then her father, the old Bolkonsky, then her brother who is not yet mentioned by name (though later he will be introduced as Prince Andrey, to become a major character of the book), his wife Lise, and even General Kutuzov.

Listing this chain does not nearly exhaust all motives discussed or touched upon in the coextensive text. It is rather one chain running through a certain part of the text, while at each point there are chains or patterns intersecting with the one listed here.

4.2.4.   The little tensions of plot created in this story are harmless. They cannot become semantically dominating patterns of the chapter. The rest of the material cannot possibly be subordinated to them. They are used, however, for the sake of creating little anticipations and leading the reader by the nose on rather uninteresting matters of no consequence. Prince Vasily announced right away that he will leave the soirée later, for the British Ambassador's party (8/23). This is a good enough reason to try to influence him to stay, which Anna Pávlovna does skillfully, using his interest in a match for his son. Prince Vasily's departure later, again executed in several installments, actually serves as a frame to close the noisy party, leaving in the end only a few people who resume the real discussion of politics, announced at the very beginning.

4.2.4.1. Similar anticipations are built up around: (1) the two interesting Frenchmen who are to come to the party (10/18); (2) Bolkonsky, the son, who will come too (13/12); (3) Lise, his wife, who mentions that her husband is leaving her, which reopens the whole issue of war and personal destiny and—later on—the issue of the relationship between her and her husband (15/25).

With such little sets of anticipation built up, a number of delaying techniques are used to disrupt the promised results. It is easy for Tolstoy to pick up one principle in order to disrupt another, using characterization of behavior or the misunderstanding in dialogue for that purpose. It is like picking up changing threads in a multi-colored carpet to weave a colorful abstract pattern.

4.2.5.   A large number of semantic threads are spread throughout the episode. When the narrator names a whole list of people from the Petersburg aristocracy coming to the party, all of them have been introduced previously. Practically no important information is given without any grounding. Typically, Andrey Bolkonsky is introduced à propos some observation about his wife but his name is not mentioned with the first reference to him in the story. Similarly, information on persons is spread out through the skillful, brief and dispersed introductions of such persons within stories of others.

This is true for a large number of semantic elements in the story. Thus: "But Pierre now committed a reverse act of impoliteness." (16/33) Pierre's misbehavior, clearly used as a motivation for the nature of a new segment, is built upon his previous misbehavior and against a whole pattern of conventional behavior well developed in the episode.

4.2.5.1. Anna Pávlovna's attempt at finding a match for Prince Vasily's son uses a repetition on the issue of matchmaking. It opens with the following sentence:

> They say old maids have a mania for matchmaking, and though I don't feel that weakness in myself as yet, I know a little person. . . . (18/28)

and it closes, resuming the same theme:

> Ce sera dans votre famille, que je ferai mon apprentissage de vieille fille. (13/25)

4.2.5.2. Despite the extremely condensed amount of information in this episode, there are numerous repetitions. For example: "'You think so?' rejoined Anna Pávlovna in order to say something and get away to her duties as hostess" (16/31) and in the next paragraph: "she resumed her duties as hostess" (17/4).

5. MULTIPLICITY OF INFORMATION

5.1.   Shifts of Theme

In addition to the external means of segmentation, such as the dramatic technique of dividing a chapter into scenes by either introducing a new character or making a character exit, there are also shifts within the speech of one speaker or within one theme.

We have mentioned a number of those above and we may now summarize the major types: (1) A piece of speech by a character is presented; then the narrator comments on the character's intonation and behavior; then he shifts from that to a general characterization, sometimes a brief biographical note on that character. (2) Most of the interlocutors speak at cross purposes. This is not done in the mode of absurd drama emphasizing the lack of communication between people; it is rather well motivated as a clash of interests of the two interlocutors, e.g., Anna Pávlovna leading into political matters and Prince Vasily trying to shift the discussion to his personal concerns. (3) A large number of thematic shifts has a global motivation, the major motivation being the interdependence of politics and the issues of war and peace with the personal affairs of the characters. (4) The introduction of a secondary topic, first embellishing or explaining the main topic, then to become a major topic for the following passage.

5.2.   Diverted Concreteness

This shifting, multi-directional, fluid text continuum, built by means of several well-defined and well-organized principles of motivation and along a well-planned and well-disguised schematic order, allows for the inclusion of a great amount of information in a relatively short space. This density of issues is typical of the openings of fictional worlds. Naturally, the major topics introduced are not developed at all. They are merely openings for future great themes of the novel. It seems that in this episode, Tolstoy is more interested in the way people react to the important information, both on a political and a personal level, than in the information itself.

Moreover, this technique enables Tolstoy to make many remarks of a general nature which are introduced simply as explanations of concrete observations. Had the order been reversed, such a generalization would have needed a great deal of elaborating and detailing to be acceptable to the reader. The realistic effect is achieved due to the *fr* of the party, in which all such concrete details are embedded, though the bulk of information relates to other *frs*, both political and personal, about which the characters speak and think. Thus, we can say that the party serves for purposes of *diverted concreteness* much in the way a metaphor serves in poetry to present concreteness in an *fr* other than that of the basic topic.

5.3.   Point of View

5.3.1.   I shall not discuss here the intricate issue of point of view in this episode and in Tolstoy's work in general. I mention its principles only to explain the technique of shiftings throughout the discussed text.

Clearly, the overall effect is of an omniscient author, not only omniscient but also omnipotent. He manipulates the division of information throughout the chapter, the concatenations, the cutting or introduction of new segments, the ironization of the characters and so on.

This is achieved without making the narrator obvious. Only in the beginning is the distance between the characters and their time, on the one hand, and the time and the position of the narrator and his readers, on the other hand, clearly established. It is a distance of two generations.

Later, however, within this framework of an omniscient narrator, Tolstoy uses his omniscience extremely sparingly. The reader never moves from one character to another without being led by a third character, e.g., by the hostess. The reader is never presented with a view of the behavior and position of a character except through the eyes of other characters present at the situation. The omniscient framework enables Tolstoy simply to shift the point of observation from one character to another, from one circle to another. But the observation itself is internal, from within the IFR. This, indeed, is *suspended omniscience.*

5.3.2.   On the whole, we could say that point of view in this text is divided into three aspects: (1) The *point of judgment* is in the narrator's present. (2) The *point of observation* is in the past, i.e., from inside the present of the party, moving from one character to another, from one circle to the another. (3) The *selection of information* is given from each given speaker's point of view and motivated by the speaker's character. This is a threefold network of points of view used interchangeably throughout.

5.3.3. This technique is well represented on the level of language. Thus, in some cases the narrator supplies general information on "our grandfathers" or on human nature. But in most cases he does not know exactly what the characters feel, he simply formulates their feelings from the point of view of an external observer: "said Prince Hippolyte in a tone *which showed* that he only understood the meaning of his words after he had uttered them." (20/32); "And among all these faces that he found so tedious, none *seemed* to bore him so much as that of his pretty wife." (22/27); "Hélène was so lovely that not only did she not *show* any trace of coquetry, but on the contrary she even *appeared* shy of her *unquestionable and all too victorious* beauty." (19/14); "and the vicomte lifted his shoulders and dropped his eyes *as if* startled by something extraordinary." (19/21) [all italics mine—B.H.] In such cases the narrator does not know exactly what the characters feel and think but has external impressions of them or suspicions. In other cases, however, Tolstoy is not shy of telling clearly what the feelings of a character are:

> Influence in society, however, is capital which has to be economized if it is to last. Prince Vasily *knew this*, and *having once realized* that if he asked on behalf of all who begged of him, he would soon be unable to ask for himself, *he became chary* of using his influence. But in Princess Drubetskáya's case *he felt*, after her second appeal, something like qualms of conscience . . . *This last consideration moved him.* (25/14)

6. OUTLOOK

As we have seen, there are basically two kinds of techniques of presenting the text continuum: (1) Overall principles of segmentation, overlapping with each other and dividing the whole text into smaller parts. (2) A number of principles of step-by-step transitions and dynamic uses of chains of semantic material of one form or another. This provides for the high degree of linkage with which each semantic detail is connected. It is a technique which leads the reader in a number of simultaneous ways step by step through the several chapters. It is not, however, based on building up a major narrative pattern on the level of the reconstructed text.

Actually there is only one major pattern for the whole episode: the nature of the party and the nature of the society participating in such a party. But this is a pattern underlying the text, rather than running through it, as plot would. In addition, a large number of patterns is opened up, to be used in large or small degrees throughout the novel: characters, relationships between characters, political circumstances, ideas and attitudes. But none of these has been built up throughout the episode to a degree sufficient to be able to establish a hierarchy, either in the sense of dominating the meaning of this episode or in the sense of dominating its structure. There is no single idea or structure dominating this episode. It is a cacophony of voices, themes, persons, a big market fair laying ground for the rich network of a fictional world which is about to unfold in the novel. The composition of the whole part is based primarily on the level of segmentation.

REFERENCES TO CHAPTERS 1–8

Amichai, Yehuda, 1994. *A Life of Poetry, 1948–1994*. Translated by Benjamin and Barbara Harshav (New York: Harper Collins).

Black, Max, 1962. "Metaphor," in: *Models and Metaphors* (Ithaca: Cornell UP).

Brooke-Rose, Christine, 1958. *A Grammar of Metaphor* (London: Secker and Warburg).

Brooks, Cleanth, 1965 (1939). "Metaphor and the Tradition," in: *Modern Poetry and the Tradition* (New York: Oxford UP).

Brooks, Cleanth and Robert Penn Warren, 1960. *Understanding Poetry*, 3rd ed. (New York: Holt, Rinehart and Winston).

Brown, Roger, 1958. *Words and Things* (New York: The Free Press of Glencoe). Esp. Chapter IV: "Phonetic Symbolism and Metaphor".

Caton, Charles E., 1971. "Overview: Philosophy," in: Danny D. Steinberg and Leon A. Jakobovitz, ed., *Semantics*, Cambridge UP.

De Beaugrand, Robert, 1980. *Text, Discourse and Process*, Ablex.

Delbouille, Paul, 1961. *Poésie et sonorités* (Paris: "Les Belles Lettres").

Dostoevsky, F., 1879–1880. *The Brothers Karamazov*, transl. David Magarshak (Harmondsworth: Penguin Books), vol. 1.

Golomb, Harai, 1968. "Combined Speech," *Ha-Sifrut* 1: 251 ff. [In Hebrew]

Grammont, Maurice, 1933. *Traité de Phonétique* (Paris: Delagrave).

———, 1967. *Le vers français* (Paris: Delagrave).

Jakobson, Roman and Linda Waugh, 1979. *The Sound Shape of Language* (Bloomington: Indiana UP). Esp. Chapter IV: "The Spell of Speech Sounds."

Katz, Jerrold J., 1972. *Semantic Theory* (Harper and Row).

Kreuzer, James R., 1955. *Elements of Poetry* (New York: Macmillan).

Masson, David I., 1967 (1960). "Thematic Analysis of Sounds in Poetry," in: Seymour Chatman and Samuel R. Levin, *Essays on the Language of Literature* (Boston: Houghton Mifflin).

Mooij, J. J. A., 1976 *A Study of Metaphor* (Amsterdam: North Holland).

Ortony, Andrew, 1979. *Metaphor and Thought* (New York: Cambridge UP).

Perry, Menakhem and Meir Sternberg, 1968. "The King Through Ironic Eyes," *Ha-Sifrut* 1:263. (In Hebrew, English translation forthcoming.)

Reinhart, Tanya, 1980. "Conditions for Text Coherence," *Poetics Today*, 1:4, 161–180.

Ricoeur, Paul, 1977. *The Rule of Metaphor* (Toronto: Toronto UP).

Rilke, Rainer Maria, 1955. *Sämtliche Werke*, ed. Ernst Zinn, Erster Band (Frankfurt: Insel).

Searle, John R., 1979. *Expression and Meaning* (Cambridge: Cambridge UP).

Staiger, Emil, 1946. *Grundbegriffe der Poetik* (Zurich: Atlantis).

Toland, John, 1977. *Adolf Hitler* (New York: Ballantine Books).

Tolstoy, L.N., 1961. *Vojna i mir, in Sobranie sochinenij v dvadcati tomax*, Vol. 4 (Moscow).

Ullman, Stephen, 1962. *Semantics* (New York: Barnes and Noble).

Weinreich, Uriel, 1980. "Explorations in Semantic Theory," in: *On Semantics*, Univ. of Pennsylvania Press.

Zajdenshnur, E. E., 1961. "Poiski nachala romana 'Vojna i mir': pjatnadcatj nabroskov (1883–1984)," in *Literaturnoe nasledstvo 69: Lev Tolstoj 1*, 291-396 (Moscow: AN SSSR).

FRAMEWORKS

9 THE ELUSIVE SCIENCE
OF LITERATURE

Remarks on the Fields and Responsibilities
of the Study of Literature

[Tel Aviv 1968]

1

Why a science of literature? Is such a science possible? What kind of science can it possibly be? Or should we merely talk of a body of knowledge, a complex of studies, theories, methodologies, interpretations? What place should poetics occupy in such a science-or-not-quite-science? What kind of poetics? And why should one write about literature at all? Haven't our libraries turned into bewildering Towers of Babel, into jungles of languages about the languages of art in language, or poetries about poetry?

Such and similar questions urge themselves upon us at the onset of a new journal at this junction in time. The editor is hard put when writing his introductory notes: obviously, he should not presume to impose his own "approach" as "the ideology" or "manifesto" of the journal. Indeed, in this paper he will try to keep his personal positions at bay, not to take a stand on specific matters, nor engage in concrete discussions of issues in the philosophy of science or the methods of criticism. The following remarks intend merely to draw a map of the field, to clarify some of the major crossroads, difficulties, and objectives.

This paper, under the title "Poetics, Criticism, Science," was first published in Hebrew in the first issue of *Ha-Sifrut/Literature*, 1968, and in English in the first issue of *PTL, Journal for Descriptive Poetics and Theory of Literature*, 1976.

2. THREE LEVELS OF RELATING TO LITERATURE

The social uses of literature are part of our usage of texts in general. We live in a world of words. We turn such words into emotions, understandings, actions, and again into words. Our experiences of the world and of our own bodies are drawn into the same circle, translated into words and into new emotions, understandings, etc. Moreover, we cannot use texts unless we employ additional knowledge, feelings, experiences from other texts or from our non-verbal environment. The ways and modes of this behavior are still to be explored, though in recent years they draw more and more attention from scholars of texts, sociologists, anthropologists, psychologists.[1] Without claiming that human behavior with literary texts is an activity *sui generis*, I would like to discuss this activity for the moment.

Our responses to literature and our "uses" of literary texts are of a great variety. We may distinguish three major levels of relating to literature:

1. *The response of a reader or a listener to a specific work of literature.* This response may be immediate or mediated, brief or extended, cursory or intensive, one-time or repetitive. We may speak of the reader's "enjoyment" or "aesthetic experience," the "realization" or the "understanding" of a text, or other modes of response. We may argue that there is a special kind of aesthetic experience or, on the contrary, that such experiences are composed of other basic kinds of emotive and cognitive responses; that it is a pure activity, or a complex mixture of heterogeneous mental actions. Among those mental activities we may include such heterogeneous impulses as the passive absorption of long passages in a novel or the active construction of hypotheses in detective stories and of complex metaphors in modern poetry. We will think of empathy with characters, recognition of pieces of represented reality, learning of the habits of remote or imagined societies, activation of thought processes, enjoyment of games in language, puns and sound patterns, and so on. Moreover, in the reader's experience of a work of literature there may be intermingled verbal reactions, activities of a critical nature, reflections on the artistic organization of the work, remarks on the author's "subtlety" or "perspicacity," "cunning" or greatness. A plethora of attitudes offer themselves, yet the overall purpose of this activity is the personal absorption or "enjoyment" or "experience" of works of literature.

---

1   See for example the concept of *Textverarbeitung* developed in Wienold's book *The Semiotics of Literature* (1972).

2. *The mediation in words between literature and an audience.* The purpose of this form of talking or writing about literature lies in conveying one's own impressions, understandings and evaluations of works and of writers to others and in influencing an audience to read or appreciate certain works of literature or to understand them in a certain way. The modes of mediation are numerous and play multiple roles in the makings of a culture: from table talk and remarks on writers and novels during a party, through reviews in journals and awarding of literary prizes, to serious critical articles and teaching in classrooms.

Mediation as such plays an important role in the preservation of any culture. In teaching and in writing reviews and criticism we convey to the next generation and to larger audiences the transferred values and texts of a culture (or try to promote a counter-culture and an anti-aesthetics), we sort out new and old creations, judge among them, try to select the better ones or the more "relevant" ones. Actual criticism may be atrocious, may tear down a fine play on Broadway or impede publication of Joyce's *Dubliners*; great books were often misunderstood by contemporaries. But it is a necessary process if the vast cultural production can at all be preserved in the limited memory of one society. However, important as such functions may be, their main purpose is not the understanding and evaluation of literature for its own sake—though understanding may be used as part of the process of influencing, explaining, judging, conveying attitudes about literature and about books to a society or to a part of it—the main purpose is lending one's voice to the judgment of literature and the shaping of culture.

3. *The serious study and analysis of literature.* As any scholarly discipline does, this mode aims at an objective and systematic understanding and description of an aspect of the world around us, in this case: literature, a field created in human culture, in all its varieties, forms, appearances. It develops a body of knowledge and a system of methods to describe and explain such phenomena in ways which can be verified, argued with, improved upon, or refuted and replaced.

These distinctions are not aimed at defining the "science" of literature, but rather at providing a preliminary orientation. The discussions in the philosophy and methodology of science are wide open, schools of thought are as many as in literary criticism, and there is no scientific, absolute philosophy of science. It would make no sense for me here to enclose the whole field of the study of literature within one school of thought in philosophy and one methodology. As is well known, the English word "science" has strong connotations of natural sciences, whereas in German, Dutch, or Hebrew, it is perfectly acceptable to talk about the science of literature and the science of religion. Yet the "social sciences" preserved their scientific label even in English. It is, after all, a matter of semantics. I use the word "science" here as an abbreviation for "theory + field research + methodology + interpretation."

It is not quite clear to what extent one may talk about the study of literature or other social sciences in the same sense one talks about natural sciences, or should they rather have separate principles and methods as some philosophers and scholars would assume (see the German term *Literaturwissenschaft* and the arguments around Hermeneutics).[2] In any case, there is no reason for the inferiority complex (or the superiority shoulder shrugging) of literary critics *vis-à-vis* the linguists or social scientists. Are the human mind, society, verbal communication, the health of our body, or economics, less "complex," or "organic" than a poem is? Are they more readily open to systematic observation? Are they more tractable for model-building and generalizations?

Of course, there is no reason to assume that the word "science" should imply any kind of absolute truth, devoid of the difficulties and problems obsessing the methodologies of other social sciences. It is a *horizon* rather than a strait jacket. It delimits conveniently the purposes of such a systematic field of knowledge, which has as its primary aim the understanding of a field of reality and the construction of theoretical models for that purpose, and is clearly distinct from subjective, impressionistic, ideological or didactic criticism. The expression "science of literature" seems to me to be preferable to the catch-all label "criticism" and is a short-cut for a whole series of terms such as: "a systematic and integrated study of literature" (Wellek & Warren), "a body of knowledge," plus "theory," plus "methodology," plus "research," etc. Clearly, the degrees of rigor, exactitude, and methods used vary greatly from poetics to interpretations to history to the psychology of reading, as they vary in all sciences. As two philosophers of science have recently written: "It is a fiction of long standing that there are two classes of sciences, the exact and

---

2   On the classical distinctions between the humanities and the natural sciences, see Wellek & Warren (1949: Ch. 1). The philosophical assessment of the new revival of hermeneutics in German scholarship can be seen in the writings of H. G. Gadamer, J. Habermas, or K. O. Apel. A well-balanced and thorough critical reassessment of the whole issue can be found in the writings of Siegfried J. Schmidt.

the inexact [. . .]. This widely prevalent attitude seems to us fundamentally mistaken; for it finds a difference in principle where there is only one of degree, and it imputes to the so-called exact sciences a procedural rigor which is rarely present in fact."[3]

In any case, this third kind of endeavor (science) should be set apart from the second kind (mediation), though in English both may be habitually covered by the term "criticism."

The three levels may be distinguished by the roles of the participants in an act of communication about literature. On the first level, there is no act of communication about the text, or, rather, there is intrapersonal communication in the reader's mind, the addresser and the addressee being the same person. On the second level, a single person communicates (in the name of his/her feelings, professional authority, or social status) to an audience. On the third level, persons representing an inter-subjective position (a consensus of a social group, an accepted logical structure, a system, a methodology, an appeal to science or to logical reasoning or to "objectivity") communicate with an audience in the name of that common ground. The participants in an act of communication about a literary text are, then, respectively:

(1) ONE (to himself);

(2) ONE to MANY;

(3) one (representing MANY) to MANY.

The distinction between these three levels does not imply that such human activities may be always entirely separated. We may have glimpses of scientific insight when simply reading a poem, or, vice versa, enjoy a text quoted in a factual scholarly study. The point is that the purposes are different and one activity should not be judged by the goals of the other, such as the naïve talk about whether criticism or the study of literature does enhance the enjoyment of poetry or improve society. A better understanding may of course help in teaching, reviewing, judging, or enjoying literature, but this is not its primary and direct purpose.

---

3   O. Helmer and N. Rescher, 1969. "Exact vs. Inexact Sciences: A More Instructive Dichotomy?" in: L. I. Krimerman, ed., *The Nature and Scope of Social Sciences* [New York] 181–203. Quoted from Schmidt [1975a: 33].

3. THE POSSIBILITY OF PLURALISM

When our purpose is in the third domain, we are confronted with an enormous variety of approaches, theories, methods, terminologies, a veritable *embarras de richesses*. In journals of literary criticism and research the student finds a bewildering number of authorities: Frye and Aristotle, Wellek and T. S. Eliot, Barthes and Tynianov, Jakobson and Freud; names of schools or trends in literary criticism, philosophy and other disciplines: Hermeneutics, Formalism, Structuralism, Phenomenology, New Criticism; or such expressions as social relevance, cultural history, tradition, symbol, system, semiotics, etc., all of which are called upon as authorities for certain beliefs or modes of approaching the subject discussed. To the uninitiated it seems that this speaks against the assumption that writings about literature may be or may become a science.

It seems that there are two basic ways of escaping this jungle: either one takes the framework of one school of thought as a kind of creed or scientific belief, and considers everything else as "non-scientific" or "gibberish" or "jargon"; or one adheres to the liberal (or cynical) view of "pluralism." (Of course, there is a third way out: leaving the whole lot of them aside and enjoying poetry itself. But surely we do not want to give up the fascinating search for understanding and rational discussion of such unbelievably elusive and impressive things, as works of literature are.)

4

We shall look at the second possibility first. A generation ago, R. S. Crane, one of the major figures of the Chicago School of Criticism, observing the history of literary criticism and approaching it realistically, argued for a theory of pluralism:

> literary criticism is not, and never has been, a single discipline, to which successive writers have made partial and never wholly satisfactory contributions, but rather a collection of distinct and more or less incommensurable "frameworks" or "languages," within any one of which a question like that of poetic structure necessarily takes on a different meaning and receives a different kind of answer from the meaning it has and the kind of answer it is properly given in any of the rival critical languages in which it is discussed (1953: 13).

Thus the famous New Critical attack of L. C. Knights on A. C. Bradley's approach to Shakespeare ("How Many Children Had Lady Macbeth?") is, according to Crane, not really a better or more correct way of looking at Shakespeare, simply because the respective writings of Bradley and Knights were not *"answers to the same question about the same object"* (emphasis mine—B.H.). "Bradley is talking about the plays as reflections of their author's imaginative view of what is tragic in life, whereas Mr. Knights is talking about them as effects in the right reader of certain determinate arrangements of words on the printed page" (16). As Crane saw it, the opposition between these two critics "is not one of conflicting interpretations of the same facts, to be settled by an appeal to a common body of evidence, but of *two distinct worlds of discourse,* in which the 'facts' cited by each critic in support of his position have been determined differently for the two of them by their prior decisions to constitute the subject-matter of Shakespearian criticism in essentially different terms" (17, emphasis mine—B.H.).

In Crane's view the truth about literature cannot be enclosed within any particular scheme of terms and principles of method. A methodological relativism, called "pluralism" (since it is not to be identified with historical relativism and is rather a panhistorical museum of approaches), is essential to criticism as such. The history of criticism is seen as an endless process of discovering new aspects in works of literature by means of new sets of terms. As a result "real knowledge of literature has been advanced though never in a straight line" (27).

Crane does not forsake the use of logical or scientific criteria within each critical "language." His is a pluralism of questions rather than of answers. Indeed, he tries to improve upon this ideology of general *laissez-faire* by claiming that there are "standards for distinguishing the better from the worse in the performances of critics or for making comparative valuations among the different existing languages of criticism" (32). For our purposes, however, Crane's position is interesting for its radical formulation of this rather American (1950!) ideal of pluralism. To sum up, again using Crane's words:

> The pluralistic critic [. . .] would take the view that the basic principles and methods of any distinguishable mode of criticism are tools of inquiry and interpretation rather than formulations of the "real" nature of things and that the choice of any special "language," among the many possible for the study of poetry, is a practical decision to be justified solely in terms of the kind of knowledge the critic wants to attain (31).

5

Indeed, shifts of interest from one aspect of literature to another have enhanced new ways of talking about literature or changed the hierarchy of interest at the expense of "lesser" aspects. Thus the emphasis on interpretation or "close reading," which was uniquely developed in the United States (New Criticism) and elsewhere (E. Staiger) in the nineteen forties and fifties, was due to specific historical conditions. In America it was the background of the Southern critics' reaction to the general and sociological talk about literature and to the prominence of science. It was a response to the Marxist atmosphere among New York critics and the claim that Marxism is a scientific method. In the German language it was a reaction to the "metaphysicalization" of the German science of literature, the oversimplified and over-generalized typologies of *Geistesgeschichte*, which saw literature as an expression of national, even regional/tribal spirit, which have deteriorated into the phraseology of Nazi criticism. It seems that the new critics wanted to hold to the very concrete facts; they wanted to emphasize the special values of a poem, to free it from its being used merely as a document (of the writer's biography, national or social history, or theoretical classifications), and to see the act of interpretation as an art. E. Staiger's book is called *Kunst der Interpretation*. They tried to grasp the hold which a poem has on a reader's experience ("dass wir begreifen was uns ergreift," as Emil Staiger wrote); to account for the uniqueness of an individual poem in terms of the material from which poems are made, i.e., language, with all its ambiguities, sound and semantic patterns, contextual complexes, etc.

Thus, specific historical conditions, the mentality of a group of critics who came to the fore, a special view of the aesthetic object in language, as well as a revaluation of the hierarchy of importance of questions to be asked in the study of literature—all these combined have made interpretation into a central preoccupation of literary critics and teachers. Indeed, in the writings of I. A. Richards, Emil Staiger, Cleanth Brooks, their contemporaries and followers, interpretation became a high art. It is clear that our knowledge of the great richness of a poetic text as an "organic whole" or a "concrete universal," our ability to look at its subtleties and its contextual links and effects has changed radically with the achievements of this trend. Moreover, this direction has helped to popularize the study of literature in the universities and to immensely raise the level of students' ability to read literature. However, as so often happens in the history of criticism, the overstressing of one aspect, individual interpretation came at the expense of interest in literary history and

literary theory. Moreover, it was bound to deteriorate, since without systematic frameworks of literary history and poetics, an individual interpretation
must lose its orientation in time and space, its logical basis and general validity. Indeed, our journals and libraries became flooded with interpretations
lost in subjectivism, cultural "overkill" and *ad hoc* extemporations, beautiful
or insightful as they may be.

Nevertheless it would be wrong to confuse the contribution of this direction of literary criticism with the historical conditions or ideological background which helped develop it. "Close reading" is not a reactionary act, even
if its origins are in political conservatism. On the other hand, the current opposition to this direction, the criticism of the over-extended minute analysis
and of the undisciplined subjectivity devoid of any theory, history, study of
social background, etc., cannot cancel the validity of interpretation itself as
one of the basic goals of the study of literature.*

6

Similar observations may be made about a very different school of criticism.
The so-called Russian Formalists emerged just before and after the revolution
of 1917. Their rise was enhanced by the coincidence of a number of factors: (a)
the disappearance of the old intellectuals after the Russian Revolution and the
opening of academic institutions to a new generation; (b) the historical accident of a group of students of philology interested in literature and thus being
able to combine the knowledge of linguistics with the study of poetry; (c) the
influence of the poetics of Futurism upon the young scholars; (d) the dynamics
of the internal development of the study of literature, with the expected reaction to a criticism preoccupied with extrinsic aspects such as the biography of
the writer or his role as a social critic; (e) the polemical position of the Russian
Formalists *vis-à-vis* a rather crude sort of Marxism.

It would, however, be wrong today to reduce the achievements and
methods of the Russian Formalists either to the poetics of such a radical
and extreme school of poetry as Russian Futurism or to an ideology of aesthetic "formalism," or to anti-Marxism or, on the contrary, to the impulses
of a revolutionary movement. The questions posed and modes of discussion

---

* Since this was written, in 1968, the hierarchies have changed, but the structure of the problem is the same.

developed by the Russian Formalists are valid and valuable far beyond those conditions of their emergence and may be useful within quite opposite ideological frameworks.

Clearly, these two schools—though both opposed to reducing literature to extrinsic factors—have delimited very different objects of inquiry. For Staiger and some of the New Critics the goal was the elucidation of the single poem, its ambiguous, rich and complex meaning and organization. The Russian Formalists, on the other hand, were interested primarily in the description of literary systems as existing in history (a genre, a literary "school," the works of a writer), of which a single poem is merely a document or an expression (as *parole* is to a *langue*). New Criticism and Formalism shared a mutual interest in the "language of literature" as a rather absolute mode (with a common origin in the aesthetic point of view of symbolist and post-symbolist poetry). They differed in that the Russian Formalists had a more systematic and more detailed theory, and they did not divorce the analysis of the "poetic language" from the study of literary history and reception. Therefore, even an analysis of a single text looks radically different in each of these trends due to its different aims, language of description, and status within the system of inquiry.

7

We shall not discuss here the difficulties and flaws in Crane's approach: whether works of literary criticism are really written in entirely separate languages or separate "worlds of discourse"; whether such languages are indeed "incommensurable"; whether we cannot distinguish between several languages confronting similar problems and decide which may be preferable; or how we can get the notions of the "kind of knowledge" that we want to attain and how we can have the intuitive knowledge to judge among better or worse approaches. Without going into a discussion of such difficulties, it is worth emphasizing that Crane has touched upon a very basic issue in comparing different "approaches" or critical "schools" or "languages."

Indeed, in many cases arguments between schools are actually pseudo-arguments; they are not arguments about different possible answers to one question but about different questions to be asked. For instance, whereas a Marxist approach may be valuable to the understanding of processes in the history or sociology of literature, a formalist approach may be illuminating on rhyme and semantics in poetry. The quarrel between the two is rather a quarrel about politics of criticism, about economics of science: what is or is not worth discussing at the present moment of the development of a science or the needs of a society. A real argument arises only if and when the two schools confront the same problem. Thus Marxism does not seem to have a different way of discussing the semantics of poetry. On the other hand, Russian Formalism developed an alternative theory of literary history and it is up to the scholars to judge which—Marxism or Formalism—is more correct or what combination of the two may be acceptable.

8

The position of pluralism, realistic though it may seem, confines literary criticism to a kind of *musée imaginaire* which is quite akin to the *musée imaginaire* of art itself. It is not a new paradigm, taking the place of an old one, which dominates the field, as Kuhn has seen it in the natural sciences, but a coexistence of all available paradigms.

Though on the face of it, pluralism seems to reflect reality, two major confusions should be pointed out. Firstly, there are indeed many different questions to be asked about literature, but we must be able to distinguish the variety of questions from the variety of possible answers or methods within one domain, answering one set of questions or analyzing one object of inquiry. Interpretation of a poem will remain a legitimate task of the study of literature, the methods of interpretation however may be radically changed with the advances in literary semantics and in the theory and logic of interpretation. We must distinguish between the coexistence of different paradigms for different subfields of a science on the one hand, and competing paradigms of one discipline on the other. For example, structural versification as developed in Russian Formalism and in the subsequent Slavic school and "generative metrics" developed in recent years from generative grammar in the USA, are two "languages" discussing one kind of object, and it is perfectly legitimate to ask which of these paradigms answers similar questions better and is better suited for a scientific and relevant discussion of poetic rhythm. Similarly in the theory of literary history we have several major paradigms, such as (a) the German school of *Stilgeschichte* describing art history in terms of a cycle of two or three basic types (Wölfflin, Waltzel, Strich); (b) the Marxist view of literary history as a reflection of class history; (c) the Russian Formalist view of literary history as a process of automatization and de-automatization, as a movement of shifts in a set of changing genres, and as a result of the responses of each generation to the challenges of the previous one; or (d) Harold Bloom's rather similar though individualistic and quasi-psychoanalytical view of literary history, moved by the "anxiety of influence" experienced by major poets. Such theoretical models approach one problem—the history of literature—though, indeed, they pose very different questions or unfold different aspects of this history. A scientific theory of literary history would ideally have to confront such approaches. It would probably find that in all of them there is some kind of truth, that is, it would have to describe to what extent, in what forms, in what periods and in what languages one tendency is stronger than the other, or to what extent there is an interdependence between such mechanisms of literary history, or to what extent one theory supercedes the other.

Secondly, the "questions" themselves are not to be seen as an open-ended marketplace, but as organized within a reasoned, stratified structure of the field as a whole.

9

The immense spread of writings about literature is self-defeating. It is impossible to have a thorough grasp of the whole field or any part of it. The pluralistic view of the variety of existing "approaches" may be realistic; but at a closer look one is struck by the immense number of repetitions and rephrasing of similar observations in other terms. Jakobson's assessment of the situation in linguistics can easily be transferred to the study of literature (as can many of his synoptic views in that brilliant essay):

> Yet a careful, unprejudiced examination of all these sectarian creeds and vehement polemics reveals an essentially monolithic whole behind the striking divergences in terms, slogans, and technical contrivances. To use the distinction between deep and superficial structures that is current today in linguistic phraseology, one may state that most of these allegedly irreconcilable contradictions appear to be confined to the surface of our science, whereas in its deep foundations the linguistics of the last decades exhibits an amazing uniformity (1975: 4).

The explosion of writings is not unknown to other sciences and fields of knowledge. A science cannot be one integrated whole graspable by one mind.

But working in a specific science is made possible through the clear organization and structuring of that science, which makes all information available whenever needed. The tightening and structuring of the mass of knowledge about literature, along with concerted efforts at synoptic and comprehensive theories, should enable us to reduce the amount of repetitions and make the available knowledge comprehensible, usable and cumulative.

The strangeness of other people's "languages" is an unjustified psychological barrier between scholarly communities in different countries. It is amazing how many major achievements in the theory of literature are unavailable to many serious scholars. For example, the real breakthrough in poetics started by the Russian Formalists and their followers, which had a decisive impact on contemporary European literary theory, is little known and even less utilized in American literary criticism.

10. THE SUBDISCIPLINES OF THE SCIENCE OF LITERATURE

The English word "criticism" has covered too many kinds of activities, from the newspaper review and impressionistic essay in a literary magazine to scholarly studies or theoretical frameworks (such as Northrop Frye's *Anatomy of Criticism*). The use of one single term for such a variety of activities and objectives was quite often detrimental to major fields of this study. Thus, critics interested primarily in great writers, or in evaluation, or in the analysis of single poems and novels, have seen all other possible concerns of the study of literature as subordinate to their own interests and judged them accordingly. Thus, many critics interested in describing writers and interpreting their works see literary theory merely as a terminology and a tool to describe insights of interpretation. A similar danger may appear in some of the recent theories of "poetics" which try to cover all possible studies of literature under this term, thereby overlooking the field of interpretation (as an "unscientific" methodology) or the assessment of "extrinsic" conditions of literary history.

A science is not necessarily one continuous field of study covering one continuous field of reality molded in one way, but rather a conglomerate, a cluster, or a galaxy of scientific activities with varying degrees of rigor and rather vague boundaries. Is it true, for example, in physics, that particles theory uses the same methodology as the study of semi-conductors? Why should the same methods be used, then, for prosody, literary history, and the interpretation of a poem? Indeed, methodologies should be made to fit the objectives of the various branches of the science of literature, and each of those should be based on the nature of the objects studied.[4]

11

The scholar of literature is confronted with objects given in the reality of human culture: texts. He has to consider the creators of such texts, the realizations of texts by readers, as well as groupings of texts and their historical appearances. Within such given objects and groupings, we may isolate, for the sake of analysis, various phenomena or objects of inquiry.

In the large field of the study of literature one may discern three focuses of interest:

(a) THE SINGLE WORK OF LITERATURE;

(b) LITERATURE IN ITS HISTORICAL EXISTENCE;

(c) POETICS, OR THE SYSTEMATIC STUDY OF LITERATURE.

The main branches of the study of literature are related to these centers of interest (see Figure 1).[5] In what follows we shall discuss them in a somewhat different order.

12. POETICS: THEORETICAL AND DESCRIPTIVE

Poetics is the systematic study of literature as literature. It deals with the question "What is literature?" and with all possible questions developed from it, such as: What is art in language? What are the forms and kinds of literature? What is the nature of one literary genre or trend? What is the system of a particular poet's "art" or "language?" How is a story made? What are the specific aspects of works of literature? How are they constituted? How do literary texts embody "non-literary" phenomena, express various themes and ideas?

As in any science, it is necessary to distinguish between a theoretical and a

---

4 A plea for the division of the field into three separate, autonomous and interdependent disciplines—literary theory, criticism, and history—was made by René Wellek (1949; 1963). The discussion in this paper proceeds beyond that triad, detailing and justifying the divisions somewhat further.

5 This figure is adapted from *Ha-Sifrut*, 1968.

Figure 1. The Main Branches of Literary Study

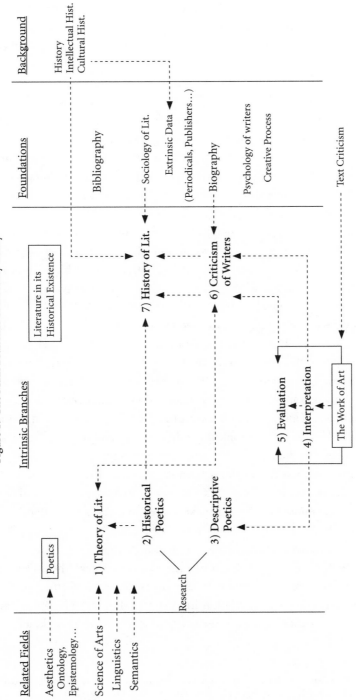

descriptive branch of poetics?[6] Theoretical Poetics (or "Theory of Literature") involves a theoretical activity, the construction of a system built according to the logic of an aspect, a question or a set of questions. On the other hand, Descriptive Poetics is a scholarly activity involving an exhaustive research of the literary aspects of certain specific works of literature.

To take a simple example, within the Theory of Literature we may have a chapter or a book on characterization in the novel. Such a study may divide the problem into secondary aspects, e.g., modes of characterization (direct description, characterization through dialogue, through style, by means of plot, etc.); classification of characters (major and minor characters, round or flat types, conventional stereotypes); the dependence of characterization on other aspects of the novel (such as plot); the dependence of characterization on the genre, the ideology of the writer, or the historical period, etc. Of course, such a systematic discussion would have to draw upon examples from concrete works of literature or from descriptive studies which may be relevant to the aspects discussed. But the structure of the argument is a purely theoretical and logical one. It cannot possibly exhaust the whole field of examples. It provides a model. Critics of this model may bring counter-examples in order to improve or change certain generalizations or revise the model as a whole.

On the other hand, a study in Descriptive Poetics will attempt an exhaustive description of its object. Thus, it should formulate results responsible for all the actual appearances of characterization within a certain framework, for example, in Dostoevsky's novels or in *The Brothers Karamazov*. It may analyze one isolated aspect or problem within a certain body of texts (art imagery in the poetry of Wallace Stevens, sound orchestration in Nabokov's prose, time in Joyce, etc.) or the poetics of a whole text or writer. A study of "The Novel as a Self-Conscious Genre" (Alter, 1975) or a study of the structural principles and predominant patterns of Shakespeare's sonnets (Stephen Booth, 1969) are typically concerned with Descriptive Poetics.

Descriptive Poetics is based on fieldwork, much in the same way as the research work of a sociologist or a linguist is. It is nevertheless a systematic study based on a question or a set of questions derived from the theory of literature. Indeed, the relationship between Theory of Literature and Descriptive Poetics is a very intimate one. It is impossible to make a descriptive

---

6   This distinction is clearly established in the tradition of Russian Formalism and Slavic theory of poetics. See for example Zirmunskij (1928) and Ivanov (1968).

study without a theoretical framework, as much as it is impossible to build a theory without material from descriptive studies.

13. HISTORICAL AND DESCRIPTIVE POETICS

Descriptive Poetics may be divided into two quite distinct disciplines: Historical Poetics and Descriptive Poetics in a synchronic frame. Thus, Historical Poetics will be concerned with the history of the sonnet or the novel, with the development of the iambic pentameter in English poetry, with the unfolding of new techniques of stream of consciousness or modernist metaphors, etc. Historical Poetics will also be concerned with the system of genres as a whole, with problems of the evolution of the literary system, the changes in principles of the art of literature, the poetics of literary movements placed in historical periods, such as Imagism or Futurism, and the like.

On the other hand, Descriptive Poetics proper is concerned with the study of certain aspects of literature seen as a "simultaneous order," disregarding distances in time. Thus, a study of plot in the novel may deal with Kafka's *Castle* and *Don Quixote* as different modes of the same genre. In this respect the distinction of the two disciplines is not precisely the same as the distinction between synchrony and diachrony in linguistics, though it is derived from it. A linguistic analysis of a synchronic system is indeed concerned with the structure of language at one moment in time. But in poetics it seems worth including the synchronic description of one literary movement within historical poetics; and on the other hand, the nonhistorical or descriptive part of poetics is not synchronic but panchronical in nature.

14

Cutting across the distinction between Theoretical and Descriptive Poetics, there are further sub-divisions of the field of poetics, each developing its own methodology or rival methodologies. The most widespread and traditional division is based on a distinction between "levels" or "strata" in the work of literature. Prosody, stylistics, literary semantics, narratology, are examples of such sub-disciplines. Actually, these disciplines describe not just a level within a single text, but the intersection of a literary system and a text.

In recent years, the distinction between texts and systems became prominent. There are, however, systems which are not confined to one level of the text. Speaking about the "rhetoric" of fiction implies analyzing devices on all levels, unified by a certain tendency; and so does the study of a genre or of the poetics of a particular literary trend or writer. Moreover, when developing a model for the description of one writer's poetics we cannot simply use categories developed for the language as a whole: e.g., the distinction between metaphor and metonymy is not sufficient to catch the specific quality of one writer's figures. Thus, taking this direction we can see poetics as a hierarchy of concentric circles, receding from the most general models for the universals of literature down to the poetics of a single text. Within the domain of poetics we may also ask a number of general questions leading to the constitution of further sub-disciplines, such as psycho-poetics or socio-poetics.[7]

15. CRITICISM IN THE SPECIFIC SENSE

Poetics, both Theoretical and Descriptive, asks questions of a systematic nature. The object of inquiry is defined by the science itself, much in the same way as the theory of learning in psychology or the study of institutions in sociology or syntax or phonology of a specific language are. When discussing phonology, a linguist looks only at those aspects of the corpus of language under observation which answer the questions posed by the science of phonology or by a specific model within it. In a similar way a scholar of prosody looks only at the aspects of versification and considers other facts of the poetic text only insomuch as they influence the rhythm and form of the poem.

Quite a different form of studies are those concerned with objects given in reality, in the actual life of literature. We would like to confine the term "Criticism" within our scheme to this domain. Here we may include, for example, a monograph on an author, a description of a literary movement, a typological comparison between two authors, the description of literature in a certain society (e.g., the American novel today, or English poetry in the '20s). Within each of such studies the scholar finds a great variety of phenomena. In describing one poet, for example, he may have to deal with aspects of the poet's biography, experiences, prosody, style, themes and genres; he may have to deal with a body of texts which is not quite of one nature, he may have to discuss changes and shifts in this body, deal with exceptions, etc. It is not the

---

7   Some of these problems have been discussed by Even-Zohar (1974).

system of a science that dictates the set of questions to be handled, but reality itself that provides a set of heterogeneous objects, in which some kinds of order should be found. Indeed, a critic may wish to unify the writings of one poet, find some pervasive spirit, world view, or set of principles or line of development in them, but in reality not all poems and not all aspects of the poems may really belong to such generalizations, there are better and worse, more or less typical poems, and so on.

Criticism (in this narrow sense) is more like the writing of history, whereas poetics is closer to linguistics. The object of study in Criticism is given by the accidents of history, society and biography, whereas the object of study in poetics is provided by the theoretical framework. The methodological purity which is possible in any branch of poetics is precluded for the critic. He deals with a heterogeneous bunch of problems to be sorted out, interrelated and organized within his study, whether organized by biography or by problems. For each of those problems he needs different tools and methods and much depends on his judgment of which aspects to consider as more prominent or basic. Arguments against a certain study of this kind involve not merely methodological criticism of the analysis of specific aspects (such as the analysis of versification or ideas), but also a comparison between the model presented by the scholar and the actual body of literature discussed, as seen, intuitively or in other researches, by the critic. The assessment of the relative value of different aspects in this heterogeneous but unified object will leave much to personal judgment, will be dependent on general theories of how literature behaves, what are human motivations, literary institutions, etc.

16. LITERARY HISTORY

Criticism as described above is achronical in nature. Its counterpart may be called the History of Literature. This discipline again is defined by reality rather than by the system of a science.

Both Criticism and History will use various methodologies from other branches of the science of literature, primarily from Poetics and Interpretation, as well as non-literary methods and knowledge, generally called "background material." Thus, a critical monograph of a writer will employ methods of interpretation and evaluation of single works, will assess the poetics of this writer and its dependence on the poetics of certain literary trends, etc.; but it will also have to include non-literary facts without which the unity of the object of inquiry is unclear, such as details of the author's biography and psychology, the cultural, social and philosophical background of the period.

In addition to historical poetics, literary history will also have to describe such facts of the sociology of literature as the organization of literary groups and journals, censorship, changes in the tastes and moods of a society and in its intellectual attitudes, and other extra-literary factors influencing the emergence of new literary trends. Historical Poetics can, for example, describe in purely literary terms the evolution from the poetics of Impressionism to the poetics of Expressionism in German poetry in the beginning of the twentieth century. A history of literature, however, would have to explain why Expressionism became such a dominant factor in German literature after World War I, and for this purpose it would have to introduce, in addition to the explanation of the intrinsic dynamics of literary evolution, such facts as urbanization, World War I, shifts in the interests of intellectuals in politics and ideology, etc.

17. INTERPRETATION

Poetics as well as literary Criticism and History attempt the construction of *systems*, whether poetic or historical, explicit or implicit, for the description of large sets of works of literature or aspects within such sets. On the other hand, interpretation deals with one single object, one novel or one poem. In this domain we are asking questions such as: what is the meaning of this poem (that is, we attempt a translation of the poetic language into a more logical or discursive language); how is it made; what is the relation between different aspects of the poem, their mutual motivation, interaction, unity or disunity; we may also be interested in the unique quality of this particular poem.

Here, again, the scholar has to deal with heterogeneous categories to be described by heterogeneous methodologies. However, the links between such varied aspects are to be justified in terms of aesthetic or poetic principles which govern the unity of the one text. In its endeavor to find what seems to be an unrepeated singularity of one object, interpretation is a rather problematic field as a scientific discipline. In many practical interpretations the scholar has to resort finally to pointing to the poem itself, quoting actual lines in order to "show" the reader what he really means.

It is, however, plausible to argue that even in interpretation we do not really deal with a unique and single object (which cannot, of course, underlie a scientific description). Thus, on the one hand, we describe phenomena within the poem which are based on an organization of a number of elements expressing one principle (of style, or meaning), and on the other hand a poem can be seen as an intersection of "codes" or "systems" within literary history, poetics, and culture. Clearly, no interpretation is possible unless the critic (or reader) has such knowledge, at least implicitly, in his mind. A poem is "uniquely individual" only in relation to other things (and even then it may be more a matter of creating an *illusion* of singularity).

A great linguist has written about natural language:

> The variability of meanings, particularly their manifold and far-reaching figurative shifts, and an incalculable aptitude for multiple paraphrases are just those properties of natural languages which induce its creativity and endow not only poetic but even scientific activities with a continuously inventive sweep. Here, indefiniteness and creative power appear to be wholly interrelated (Jakobson, 1975: 21).

Works of literature, typically, make the most of this property of language, which even the linguists have not yet described systematically.

The high degree of contextual interpretation of language in a literary text makes the poem a very integrated unit, perhaps the highest or the single independent unit of literature. Literary theory is still far from explicitly understanding how such units work (though in individual analyses we can show it in high complexity). Applying the demands of a rigorous methodology, developed in linguistic phonology or in theoretical syntax or even developed in some fields of systematic poetics, to the field of interpretation, would cause unnecessary misunderstandings: the very different nature of the object at hand certainly requires a very different methodology.

There is another typical feature of this discipline. Contrary to the illusions of earlier critics that here they really confront an independent, closed, concrete object, which can be directly observable, it appears today that the analysis of one poem may depend on a number of unexpected informations from a wide open field which is not directly the object of observation: we have to draw upon poetic systems, as well as historical, cultural, linguistic, personal and accidental facts outside the poem, which cannot be systematically assessed in advance. The very range of such objects is a matter of argument for each specific interpretation. A rigorous methodology would not be able to define in advance the ways of working of a scholar confronted with a poem; much does depend on the scholar's intuition, availability of external knowledge, etc. We should not, however, confuse the context of discovery—the intuition or "art" of interpretation—with the context of explanation, or accounting for interpretational hypotheses. Even in such a difficult and heterogeneous mode, requirements for a logic of interpretation may be devised, which could provide us with rules for judging which statements in this domain are more or less objective, or well-founded. Such rules, however, must be much more flexible than those describing generalizations in prosody or the history of ideas; many statements about meanings in poems are interdependent with other statements: on literary and social norms, attitudes, hierarchies, psychology, the language of a writer, etc.

18. EVALUATION

Evaluation, too, is a field which has caused a great amount of misunderstanding in recent years. On the one hand, there are those who oppose it altogether as an objective or scientific field. Thus, Roman Jakobson compared a literary critic to a "grammatical (or lexical) critic"; Northrop Frye has mocked "all the literary chit-chat which makes the reputation of poets boom and crash in an imaginary stock exchange" (1957: 18). On the other hand, there are those who confuse the study of literature with critical evaluation and see the purpose of literary studies and interpretations solely in value judgment.

Here, again, it seems that we deal with words about a single object: the one poem or novel to be judged. But here again the singularity of the object is an illusory one, because judging involves placing it within a system of values. The analysis of actual evaluations from the point of view of actual historical systems of values may, of course, constitute a field of scientific inquiry.

In any case, in objects such as works of literature, which are historically defined by means of values (aesthetic or extra-aesthetic) inherent in them, avoiding the issue of evaluation would mean a gap in the study of the field. The study of such values and evaluations and of their employment for the analysis of particular works of literature should become as objective as possible and should take its place as one of the legitimate branches of the science of literature. This, however, should not be confused with other studies of literature. Our curiosity as to the nature and forms of literature in its varied appearances is perfectly legitimate independently of whether the studied objects are "great" works of art or not, or whether certain typical devices improve their value, or expose their failure.

19. FOUNDATIONS AND RELATED FIELDS

Biography, bibliography, textual criticism (in the sense of text edition and collation) are considered to be auxiliary disciplines of the study of literature. "Auxiliary" is perhaps a misleading term, since any science may become auxiliary for the science of literature, be it sociology, psychology or aesthetics. Clearly the science of literature as a whole cannot give up those disciplines. They provide the material basis on which literary studies can be made. Their separate status, however, is based on the fact that their object of inquiry is not a literary object as such and their methods are not specific to the science of literature. Thus, textual criticism deals with a body of language and not with an aesthetic object (which is the same text, as realized by a proper reader).

Many aspects of literature and literary texts may be dealt with by other disciplines as well: philosophy and neighboring sciences. The language of poetry may be discussed not only in poetics but in the philosophy of language, psychology, linguistics, semantics. Aesthetics and philosophical ontology may deal with the nature of literary objects as much as literary theory does, though perhaps using a different metalanguage and methodological framework. Moreover, as poetics comes across specific aspects of literature, it must necessarily discuss phenomena which are not confined to literature alone: metaphor is certainly not a purely literary phenomenon, neither is contextual semantics as a whole. The study of the structure of texts is not merely a literary discipline. The problem of understanding texts is shared by poetics, psychology, sociology and linguistics. Even the dynamics of literary history cannot be separated from the study of the dynamics of the history of cultural institutions. All such facts imply the necessary interaction between disciplines which intersect in the same object or pose similar problems in different objects. It is not that poetics as a whole is part of another science or a class of sciences, but rather that sub-fields of poetics intersect with various sub-fields of other disciplines. The isolationism, which characterized earlier modern poetics in its struggle for autonomy, is a thing of the past.

20. THE IMPORTANCE OF POETICS

This division of the science of literature into subdisciplines is not meant in order to appease contradictory trends in contemporary criticism but rather to claim that there are different kinds of objects in the study of literature, and they demand different methodological solutions and perhaps even different attitudes of their observers. The balanced development of these subdisciplines and their interaction are of absolute necessity for the well-being of each of them. As Wellek has argued convincingly, it is impossible to write literary history without using methods of poetics and interpretation (unless we write chronologically ordered facts about writers and paraphrases of their work), as it is impossible to construct theories and models in poetics without basing them on historical research and on interpreted texts.

It is, however, only poetics which can provide a systematic description of literature as a whole, can embody within one system the scientific assessment of its parts and heterogeneous phenomena, and can provide the rational tools and methods for the study of specific issues and texts. Whereas interpretations are valuable to readers interested in particular works of literature while criticism and history tell us about particular writers, periods, national literatures, it is primarily poetics which illuminates literature as a peculiar phenomenon of human culture. It is only through poetics that we can explain to our colleagues in other sciences what literature really is and *how* it is, and what is the nature of literary movements, the functioning of language and values in literature.

Furthermore, interpretation, criticism and literary history are still in a stage which may be called pre-scientific. A wealth of learning is brought to bear upon a single text or a period in the past; we are brilliant amateurs, skillful artisans; we delight in writing literary essays about literature, in paraphrasing the messages conveyed, explicating the background and evaluating the effects; we are easily tempted to talk via literature about human beings, societies, ideas, language and art, without the rigors of philosophy or the disciplines of sociology, psychology, linguistics. We are carried away by the text we describe, or the life of the writer we investigate, and the readers follow us, they know what we mean, because they have read the books we describe and illuminate. But so many sentences of such essays can be easily transplanted from the analysis of one writer to another; so many terms are vague, too general and interchangeable; we—so agile in conveying a writer's "meaning"—are so helpless and groping when describing the art of the text or the writer's particular nature; we know so little to say about the special quality of a writer's imagery beyond the general terms "metaphor," "image," or "tenor" and "vehicle"; we are practically unable to distinguish varieties of plot or plot-evasion beyond the most basic terms, unless, of course, we quote examples and *show* how it is, or write an interpretation of the individual case. One wonders often, if it is not a new impressionism (or, rather, a fair of impressionisms) which criticism offers us under the heavy armour of historical knowledge and scholarship.

There is only one solution: the vigorous development of a systematic poetics, "a poetics which stands to literature as linguistics stands to language" (Culler, 1975: 257). As it is impossible to describe a specific language without linguistics, so it is absurd to write literary history, criticism or interpretations without the tools for assessing the "language" of their objects: literary texts and institutions. Indeed, nobody writes criticism without a complex set of assumptions on poetics, and without an assortment of terms and methods. But assumptions which are vaguely implied, put the literary critic—splendid as he may be in his insights—in splendid isolation as an intelligent being.

Poetics is only one task of the study of literature, but it alone can provide the basis for all other branches of this discipline. It is not an easily available tool. We should not be impatient with its still primitive schemes when applied to specific texts. Much simpler objects than poems, such as the relatively small units of meaning, are not yet provided with a real scientific theory. As an editor of a recent representative anthology on semantics wrote: "in the area of philosophy of language perhaps as much as in any other philosophical field, chaos reigns, little is agreed on, new methods are to be eagerly seized upon, and we have hardly begun" (Caton, 1971: 3). And poetics deals with highly complex and flexible compounds of language and meaning, placed in history and reflected in the minds of readers.

It is, however, not a new discipline. We know a lot, much more than we can formulate explicitly. Possibly we should relax some of the demands of existing logic and prevalent scientific methodology in order to cope with the nature of such an object as literature. But whatever we are able to say today, we should try to do it as systematically as possible, giving up some of our essayistic reflexes.

A radical renewal of poetics, the first steps of which we witness today, should provide the tools for deep and detailed analysis and the language for description and explanation in all branches of the study of literature and make them as decently inter-subjective and controversial as the other humanistic disciplines are. Poetics is still young and wide open, and therefore it is so interesting to work in it.

21. SOME DIFFICULTIES OF THE
SCIENCE OF LITERATURE

As we have seen above, the division of the study of literature into separate branches does not merely classify historically developed methodologies and kinds of interest, but sets apart distinct objects of inquiry with necessarily different modes of analysis. We may now point out several inherent difficulties in the science of literature, which raise special questions and call for specific theoretical and methodological solutions.

1. In linguistics, it is quite clear what is human language and what is not. The delimitation of the field of inquiry of the science of literature is not clear at all. Indeed, there are tensions in linguistic theories, too, between the description of "norms" of a language, or "grammaticalness," and the description of "non-grammatical" or "deviant" usages of the language. However, it is clear that a deviant sentence, a non-sentence even, is still something in the English language. It is not clear in the same way with texts on the borderline of what is considered in a certain period to be "literature." Many writings by poor writers, or "graphomaniacs," would not be considered literature, though they may use literary forms.

The concept of what can or cannot be considered literature is a changing one, it is historically and socially determined. Therefore, many definitions of literature and many literary theories are circular: they describe a field which they have defined and delimited in advance. Value judgment interferes with definition.

A possible solution may be in seeing literature as a flexible aggregation of groups of texts which have been considered in different periods and by different groups of people as "literature." The study of literature then is a study of objects in language dependent on certain norms outside the objects themselves (or abstracted from them) which are constantly changing. A British analytical philosopher argued that the traditional aesthetic definitions of art are "irrefutable," i.e., that one cannot bring a counterexample to Croce to show art which is not "intuitive-expressive," because he would simply not consider it as art.

We may, perhaps, use the major traditional definitions of art, such as "significant form," "concrete universal," "organic unity," etc., turning such terms from definitions into questions: to what extent, in which works of literature, and in what forms and shapes are works "concrete" or "abstract," "expressive" or "fictional," etc.? Nevertheless, the difficulty remains: we do not have a clearly defined set of objects to be studied, delimited in advance by some definition of the science.

2. Another basic issue are the differences in traditions which literary theorists carry with them. Since it is impossible to know closely all the forms and appearances of literature, literary theorists tend, consciously or unconsciously, to rely on their particular limited knowledge of literary works and their particular aesthetic tastes. Their theories tend to be generalizations from the facts of their personal and cultural education and beliefs. The differences between cultures and periods, however, are enormous. Thus, the Japanese haiku may be considered an ideal form of poetry, but it would be wrong to look at one haiku as an ideal poem in the European classical sense. Haiku are published in enormous numbers. Harold Henderson wrote: "In 1957 there were about fifty monthly magazines devoted to haiku, most of them successful commercial ventures. The issues that I have been able to check contain a minimum of fifteen hundred haiku each [. . .] I believe the total is probably well over a million" (1958: 1–2). Of course, with such numbers, the individual poem plays a much less independent role than it does in Western poetry. And within the Western tradition itself there are serious differences. Thus, the emphasis which Russian Formalists, Roman Jakobson, and Slavic poets and scholars have placed on the sound structure of poetry, its meter, rhyme, sound orchestrations, etc., may be due to the important role which this aspect has played in the poetry-making of language-texts in those languages. On the other hand, the centrality of metaphor and figurative language in Shakespeare and in major bodies of English poetry has made figurative language central for English and American critics. Changes in public taste have rearranged literary histories and reshuffled the priorities of literary theories. In fact, very general and vague value judgments, derived from a group of ideal texts, served as the foundations for delimiting the larger field of observation and the basic theoretical notions and questions of literary critics. This seeming circularity can be resolved not by abandoning the issue of value judgments altogether, but by an analytical view of the interdependence of a set of value norms and a set of objects of literature.

As in the previous point, it is clear that we have to abandon biases based on an essentialist fallacy defining literature or defining aesthetic value in basically one way. This becomes clear especially today when many scholars refuse to see only elitist poetry as literature and consider various kinds of verbal and non-verbal texts which are part of our mass culture, such as detective stories, TV shows, science fiction, etc.

3. In the science of literature, not only is the set of objects to be considered an ill-defined set, but the individual object is ill-defined as well. It is not quite clear what a work of literature is. As we know from the phenomenological tradition, primarily from Roman Ingarden, there is a dichotomy between the language text and the "aesthetic object" realized by a reader from this text, which is changing in history.

As a result, texts are ambiguous, there are many contradictory interpretations, and we cannot speak of a work of literature as one single object. On the other hand, neither a subjective reading nor a statistical average reading can satisfy the scholar of literature. The object of inquiry is a plausible construct somewhere between the text and the interpretations made by "proper" readers. However, the extent to which a reader has to interfere or realize a text depends on the kind of text, the period and the kind of readers involved. Moreover, the reader has to construct an "implied author" and read the text in the light of such an author's assumed position or "intention" though this position has been abstracted largely from the text itself. Here again, there is not a circularity, but an interdependence between two or more constructs, to be disentangled by the scholar. In any case, a poem is not an objective fact which he can simply observe and classify.

4. The necessity for rational description which any scientific approach poses should not be confused with a view of the text itself as a rational structure. Those who accuse poetics of taking away the "soul" of poetry or of destroying the experience of reading literature simply confuse the method of science with the object it studies. There is no need to abandon the view of a poem as being created in largely intuitive and irrational ways, along with rational planning and structuring. The reconstruction of such an irrational process or of the unique imagination which imbues a text or a group of texts by one writer is again one of the goals of the science of literature.

5. The historian and the linguist, too, deal with texts. The psychologist and the sociologist analyze words, as well as behavior. But for them the texts and the words observed serve merely as evidence for the construction of con-

clusions about the phenomena analyzed in those sciences. A linguist is interested in the "*langue*" or the "competence" rather than in the "*parole*" or "performance" in a single sentence. A historian is interested in processes, or in facts and events, which left their traces in the analyzed texts. In the study of literature, we cannot forget, however, the intrinsic value of (some) individual works of literature and the interest in their singular nature (at least for some readers). As Wellek expressed it: "Literary study differs from historical study in having to deal not with documents but with monuments" (1963: 14–15). Of course, we may analyze such a "monument" merely as a *document* for generalizations about the process of literary history, or the poetic system, or the "rules of the game" of this particular text. But we have to deal with its nature as a monument as well. We cannot simply sweep the issue under the carpet.

6. A work of literature is one object made of many: words and sentences in a language, and items of meaning conveyable in words and sentences. Though there is a high degree of integration, the independent value of the small units brings in considerations and information from outside the text which cannot be overlooked in the study of literature. Unlike pigments of paint or notes in music, words exist as independent signs outside art. We cannot simply describe a poem as one organic whole without considering those autonomous elements and local contexts.

7. On the other hand, no description of the independent values of the constituent units can suffice to explain their values and functions in a work of literature. If natural language is highly context sensitive, this quality is certainly made great use of in literary texts. It does not follow that one has to give up any attempt at systematic description of literary units. True, we cannot have a dictionary of elementary units in literature or of meanings of words in poetic texts. We can, however, have a grammar of the forms in which units combine, the principles of transformation which they undergo in various semantic and aesthetic contexts.

8. Unifying a text can be done only through using norms and models from outside the text, whether from the literary tradition or from the world or possible worlds. Understanding literature requires not just knowing the natural language in which it is written but a number of other systems such as psychology, sociology, religion, a world view, and parts of such systems, which the Russian semiotic school of the nineteen sixties has called "secondary modeling systems." This would imply that a literary text is not only a closed form but is wide open to anything embodied in language or capable of being transformed

into language. Therefore, a literary scholar engaged in an interpretation may have to resort to any number of extra-literary informations and, therefore, to other sciences as well.

9. The basic units of a natural language are clearly defined. We know the forms, sizes, and selection of phonemes and morphemes of a language. Literary units, however, such as metaphors, images, characters, events, points of view, are often highly complex constructs which a reader has to make. Thus, a metaphor is not simply one word which has changed its meaning; in modernist poetry we know when a metaphor starts; we don't know, however, in advance when it will end and which materials of the text may be drawn into it or whether it may not be transformed into an "object" in the "world" of the poem. Events may not even be presented as such in the text but may be conclusions forced upon a reader. Whether an event may or may not be constructed from a certain passage depends on whether a certain plot hypothesis of the larger text requires such a construction.

Thus, we cannot codify and list a dictionary of basic units which a computer would be able to identify when scanning a text, as it may be able to identify words in their graphic forms. Even the objective existence of certain elements in a text is not sufficient to make them literary units. Thus, we cannot simply count the sounds of a poem. The sound becomes part of a literary unit only if there is a higher pattern of an alliteration or sound orchestration—which may include this particular sound. In short, there is a strong interdependence between the existence and the forms of textual units, on the one hand, and the possibility of constructing larger patterns to which they may belong, on the other.

10. Most of our terms are "static," they seem to describe fixed categories and units. A literary text, however, is "dynamic" (in the sense of Tynianov and Mukařovský). The text is presented to us as a sequel of signs. We use time to write it and to read it. It does not appeal to us as one simultaneous experience (as Staiger thought) but rather as a process, in which later parts have to be integrated with earlier ones, earlier informations get readjusted, reunderstood or reversed. This process does not necessarily represent a sequel in time, making literature an "art of time" rather than of space, as Lessing thought (having in mind a one-to-one relationship between signifiers and signifieds). But there is always a duration of the text, employed by the author for the sake of building up an aesthetic experience. Now, on top of the dynamic patterning of the text, there are, clearly, intentions to construct resultant "static" units,

such as an image of a whole poem, an idea, a world view, or the nature of a character. The tension between the dynamization of a text and the subsequent compound "static" integration is a typical feature of literature.

11. There are great difficulties in generalization and prediction in the science of literature, even in poetics. Paradoxically, any generalization is good only for the area in which this generalization holds, it breaks down when it doesn't hold. Thus, we may formulate a poetics of a volume of stories by a writer based upon most of the stories. We cannot, however, guarantee that it will hold for all of the stories, or for all of the good stories, or equally for all parts and aspects of the pertinent stories. A story (or a part or aspect of it) which does not belong to this poetics would need a different description. A group of works (of one genre, one writer, one literary trend) may constitute a separate "language"; but such "languages" are highly fluid, are not separated from each other, are actually combinations of quasi-subcodes in changing degrees and forms.

This should not preclude the possibility of constructing generalizations for such "codes" or "languages," knowing however, that their validity is a self-limiting one.

In short, there is a high degree of interdependence of any kind of norms and generalization on one hand, and the incidents of literary texts and literary history on the other. We cannot study any norm or any fact separately from such interdependences.

22

There is a tremendous gap between the units isolated and terms clarified in literary theory on one hand, and our knowledge of the highly complex contextual relations in particular texts on the other. We can clearly recognize a page of Proust or Faulkner, but our theories reach only to the smallest units of a text (meter, rhyme, stylistic elements) as well as to the highest (narration, composition, point of view). The large area in-between is still no-man's-land for literary theory. When describing a page we grope in the dark, or use our well-trained intuitions.

Such is the present state of the art, which calls for a close interaction of theoretical models with the analysis of specific texts. There is a danger that the logically minded theoretician will fly away from the truth of literature, will simplify it for the conveniences of method to such a degree that no interesting observations will be made. At the other pole, there are too many essays, steeped in culture, which tend to turn all terminologies into metaphors, forgetting the virtues of a simple, straightforward argument based on a method as logical and as systematic as possible at the present time.

23. THE PRESENT SITUATION AND THE UNIVERSITIES

The special difficulties confronting the science of literature, the highly complex and flexible nature of its objects and groups of objects should not be overlooked. There are, on top of it, certain phenomena in the organization of the study of literature which impede the development of this science. We shall make a few selective remarks in this direction.

1. The achievements of sciences were made possible by a combination of bold generalizations and theoretical models, on the one hand, and very minute and specialized studies on the other. Our world view in physics as in linguistics has been changed radically when the smallest units, atoms or phonemes, were split and analyzed. The development of a new theory or the achievement of new knowledge is a product of many scholars working in one direction, each on his very particular, detailed project. No such specialization has been achieved in literature. The state of our knowledge in metrics, for example, has not advanced considerably in recent years because the minute studies required for that purpose would not give young scholars a job. And the situation in literary semantics is much worse, in spite of some bold generalizations.

Scholars of literature are generalists rather than specialists, contextualists rather than systematizers. The value which an older generation has placed upon a scholar devoting many years to one critical edition of a book has not been transferred to poetics. Of course, no specialization is of any value unless it depends on a large theoretical model or contributes to its development. The rather amateurish and eclectic state of the theory of literature is due to the scarcity in specialized studies as well as in sufficiently detailed and operative theoretical models and the cooperation between the two.

2. The study of literature confronts issues which are at the same time of interest to other sciences: linguistics, semantics, sociology, psychology, philosophy, etc. Indeed, the study of literature was time and again invaded by the methodologies of neighbor sciences. Time and again it has been shown that such an invasion may be fruitful at the first period but becomes encumbering

at a later stage because the borrowed terminology is turned into a set of metaphors, and because there always remain phenomena peculiar to literature which are not accounted for by the foreign science. Nevertheless, a permanent cooperation with such fields seems to be of absolute necessity for the scholar of literature. He cannot proceed without making hypotheses about the psychology of the reader, about semantic integration in language, about moral norms in an imaginary society, etc.

3. A special difficulty at the present stage consists in the university structure of the study of literature. It is a perennial complaint of literary theoreticians that academic teaching of literature does not reflect the state of the science. In 1950, the German scholar Ernst Curtius had written: "The academic organization of philological and literary studies reflects the aspect of the humanities of 1850. As seen from 1950 this aspect is as obsolete as the railway system of 1850 is" (1955: 45). Similar criticism, in a new vein, was strongly pronounced by Wellek and Warren in the last chapter of their *Theory of Literature*. That chapter written in the 1940s is by no means outdated, though it is not reproduced in the paperback editions of the classical book.

The situation is more crucial today, as the universities are the social institutions for the development of science. Unfortunately, theory of literature as well as systematic poetics play a marginal role in university programs. They are used as embellishments, or as secondary tools, and at best as examples of some ideology (the "approaches" approach). Literature departments are the only departments in the humanities built not according to topics but according to writers or groups of writers. Students in linguistics, psychology, sociology, anthropology, etc., study courses on issues and topics, such as social institutions, semantics, syntax, developmental psychology, theory of learning, etc.

Students of literature are not trained systematically in their own profession, even in its present state of knowledge. They are more often than not unable to work exactly on aspects of prosody, stylistics, the poetics of narrative, or genre theory. As a result, no seminars, even graduate seminars, can be based on a systematic knowledge of poetics and take up more advanced and specific problems.

By extension, no wonder why literary critics and teachers confronting theoretical issues start time and again from the very beginning.

4. As there is little systematic study of poetics in the universities, the market of books is strongly affected. Since English is the foremost language in which literature is taught and written about, the situation in English influ-

ences the whole discipline. Books are usually oriented towards university courses or are exorbitantly expensive. Since there are very few courses dealing systematically with prosody, there are few books on prosody available. And so in all other fields of poetics. There is, in short, an institutionalized (though perhaps unintentional) suppression of poetics in the present day situation of the study of literature as well as in the publishing world. This is, of course, a self-defeating device. Ph.D. dissertations become less and less meaningful, contributing the three hundred third interpretation of a writer to whom three hundred two books were devoted before, but not advancing the science of literature. No cumulative effect is achieved. The interest in reading journals and books of "criticism" has certainly dropped. No knowledge on literature or any of its aspects (as distinguished from books on writers and literary history) is readily available.

5. With the explosion of culture one would assume that the ideal of conveying the whole of a cultural tradition must be abandoned. We cannot possibly give the student the knowledge of everything valuable in the past. Instead of trying to make the student of literature a carrier of the treasures of a culture, instead of teaching him in the medieval way of an apprentice studying through practice the ways of reading texts, we should try to convey to him a systematic body of knowledge about literature and tools for further questions and analyses.

This is not a plea for abandoning the teaching of writers and their works or suppressing the teaching of close reading. As linguistics cannot be done without the knowledge of languages, so poetics cannot be done without the knowledge of a body of literature as variegated as possible. Poetics should not be turned into a stockpile of terminologies and methodologies but rather into an intellectual means for organizing the knowledge of works of literature.

Teaching of literature not only through the rich accidents of one text, but through the questions of a scientific order would clarify for the students (and their teachers!) the issues involved in understanding literature, the connections between literature and other fields of human knowledge, and will prepare future scholars who may break through to a new level in the description and explanation of these highly complex and familiar language constructs, which we are only in the beginnings of understanding.

[1968, 1976]

REFERENCES

Alter, Robert, 1975. *Partial Magic: The Novel as a Self-Conscious Genre* (Berkeley, Los Angeles, London: University of California Press).

Booth, Stephen, 1969. *An Essay on Shakespeare's Sonnets* (New Haven, London: Yale UP).

Caton, Charles E., 1971, "[Philosophy] Overview," in: Danny D. Steinberg and Leon A. Jakobovits, eds., *Semantics* (Cambridge: UP), 3–14.

Crane, R. S., 1953. *The Languages of Criticism and the Structure of Poetry* (Toronto: University of Toronto Press).

Culler, Jonathan, 1975. *Structuralist Poetics* (London: Routledge & Kegan Paul).

Curtius, Ernst Robert, 1955. *Europäische Literatur und lateinisches Mittelalter* (Bern: Francke).

Even-Zohar, Itamar, 1974. "Sifrut, Mada Ha-" ["Literature, The Science of"], unpublished; abbreviated version in: *Encyclopaedia Hebraica*, XXVI, 413–419.

Frye, Northrop, 1957. *Anatomy of Criticism* (Princeton: Princeton UP).

Henderson, Harold G., 1958. *An Introduction to Haiku* (Garden City: Doubleday).

Ivanov, V. V., 1968. "Poetika," *Kratkaja Literaturnaja Enciklopedija*, V (Moscow: 936–943).

Jakobson, Roman, 1975. *Linguistics in Relation to Other Sciences* (New York, Evanston, San Francisco, London: Harper & Row).

Kuhn, Thomas, 1966. *The Structure of Scientific Revolutions*, 3rd ed. (Chicago: Chicago UP). (Orginally published 1962.)

Mayenowa, Maria Renata, 1974. *Poetyka Teoretyczne* (Wroclaw, Warszawa, Kraków, Gdańsk: Ossoliński).

Schmidt, Siegfried J., 1975a. *Literaturwissenschaft als argumentierende Wissenschaft: zur Grundlegung einer rationalen Literaturwissenschaft* (Munich: Fink). (English version to be published by North-Holland.)

———, 1975b. *Zum Dogma der prinzipiellen Differenz zwischen Natur- und Geisteswissenschaft* (Göttingen: Vandenhoeck & Ruprecht).

———, 1985. "On a Theoretical Basis for a Rational Science of Literature," *PTL* 1: 2 (forthcoming).

Todorov, Tzvetan, 1968. "Poétique," in: *Qu'est-ce que le structuralisme?* (Paris: Seuil), 99–166.

Wellek, René, 1963. *Concepts of Criticism* (New Haven, London: Yale UP).

Wellek, René, and Austin Warren, 1949. *Theory of Literature* (London: Jonathan Cape).

Wienold, Götz, 1972. *Semiotik der Literatur* (Frankfurt/Main: Athenäum).

Zhirmunskij, Viktor, 1928. *Voprosy teorii literatury* (Leningrad: Academia).

10 A UNIFIED THEORY
OF THE LITERARY TEXT

[Berkeley 1972]

INTRODUCTION

Structuralist tendencies became strong in Israel primarily in linguistics and in poetics. For reasons explained below, we shall devote this survey to the latter field.

From the mid-1950s to the early 1960s a new trend in the study of literature began developing in Israel. Its major concern became theory of literature and poetics, with a strong emphasis on combining structural analysis with interpretations of individual texts. An Israeli school of poetics, with a consistent philosophical framework, developed a body of theory and research. The name "Neo-Structuralism" indicated a link with the tradition of Russian Formalism, especially as reformulated in the principles of Czech Structuralism. However, influences of Phenomenology and of Anglo-American New Criticism as well as of German theories of literature were felt in this reformulation of the theory of the literary aesthetic object. Later the affinities with the emerging European Structuralism became evident. In the conception of the Israeli

The following text is composed of chapters from a survey, "Structuralist Poetics in Israel," written by Ziva Ben-Porath and Benjamin Hrushovski in Berkeley in 1972, commissioned by the editor of *Semiotica*, Thomas A. Sebeck, for a volume *Structuralism Around the World* (never published). It appeared eventually in 1974 as *Papers on Poetics and Semiotics*, No. 1, published by the Department of Poetics and Comparative Literature, Tel Aviv University. The chapters selected here were written by B.H., summarizing his theoretical work in the 1960s.

school a phenomenology of the aesthetic object precedes the use of structural methods, and the linguistic analysis of the text is subordinate to the specific problems of literature.

The name Structuralism should be taken here in the widest possible sense, not as an exclusive technique, but as a general direction. It indicates both an interest in forms and structures and the use of structural methods for the analysis of traditional problems of literary criticism, such as themes, meaning, literary history, etc. Characteristic of this approach is the shift from locating poetics in the "language of poetry" to an all-encompassing "unified" theory of the literary text. In recent years, in conjunction with developments in other countries, the horizon was widened towards a theory of texts in general and a theory of the process of semantic integration in understanding language.

The methods of many Israeli studies suggest the conviction that finding and describing the complexities of literary phenomena should precede formulation of a pure systematic theory. Therefore, though the goal of most studies was theoretical, the theoretical statements grew out of work in descriptive poetics. Another trend, however, strove towards rigorous theory, linguistically oriented. Most of the writings of the Israeli school of poetics are in Hebrew, many of them based on Hebrew texts. Because of the language barrier, we feel obligated to present in detail several typical studies, hoping to make an understanding of them as independent as possible of a knowledge of Hebrew literature. An attempt to present a single unified body of theory would at this point be unjustified, and would certainly obliterate the differences of approach and method of various scholars.

TRADITIONAL HEBREW POETICS

Close interpretation of texts, with reference to subtleties of language, contextual meaning, and formal traits such as repetition, is an old and pervasive tradition in Hebrew writings, going back to the days of the canonization of the Bible. Hebrew law, legend, sermons and mystical texts, as well as the long tradition of Biblical exegesis, depend heavily on this hermeneutic technique. Even secular Hebrew literature written throughout the ages cannot be understood without consideration of its allusions to the Bible and other interpreted texts from the religious tradition. On the other hand, there is no trace of any systematic poetics in the Bible, in the Talmud or in Hebrew liturgical poetry. Hebrew traditional writings made no clear-cut distinctions between aesthetic, religious and historiographic functions and had no body of theory comparable to Greek and European poetics.

Except for scattered remarks, Hebrew poetics started with the impact of Arabic linguistics, poetics and philosophy. The poet, scholar and philosopher, Sa'adia Ga'on (882–942) wrote a dictionary of Hebrew rhymes in the tenth century. The most prominent early contribution to Hebrew poetics was that of Moses Ibn-Ezra, in two treatises written in Arabic (c. 1135) (see Pagis, 1970). Hebrew medieval poetics cannot be compared in scope, originality and value with the fundamental contribution of classical Hebrew linguistics in Spain and Provence. Nevertheless, there is a persistent tradition of treatises in Hebrew poetics, extending from the Middle Ages to the 19th century. Originating in Hebrew adaptation of Arabic poetics, this tradition felt the influence of later movements, notably the Italian Renaissance. Most of these poetics were derivative and didactic in nature. Under the influence of both Arabic and European rhetoric, these treatises were primarily prescriptive. Often illuminated by interesting examples and remarks, they consisted mainly of catalogues of categories, classifications of meters and poetic devices.

LITERARY THEORY AND THE BEGINNINGS OF STRUCTURALISM

After the establishment of the State of Israel and the end of the War of Independence, a growing interest in literature for its own sake arose in Israel. The German and Hebrew poet and critic Ludwig Strauss, influenced by such German critics as W. Kayser and E. Staiger, called attention to literary types, genres and forms. Lea Goldberg, an exquisite poetess and aesthetically oriented literary critic who became the first chairman of the Department of Comparative Literature at the Hebrew University, published a book on the short story in the European tradition. A short-lived journal, *Behinot* (11 issues, 1952–56), edited by the critic and aesthetician S. Zemach, was devoted wholly to literary criticism and reviewing, and published translations of English and American New Critics. A parallel shift took place in Hebrew poetry. There was a revulsion from what was felt to be "rhetorical" and empty versification, towards a "precise" poetic language and a poetry of the individual, modeled after T. S. Eliot, W. H. Auden and English modernism.

In this atmosphere, interest in the language of poetry arose in some circles around what was then the only higher academic institution in Israel, the

Hebrew University in Jerusalem. Thus, within the framework of linguistics, some teachers, especially of the younger generation (such as D. Tene and U. Ornan), dealt with the style and semantics of Hebrew literature.

Linguistically oriented poetics, with a plea for a "science of literature" in the formalist-structuralist tradition, was represented in the lectures on the language of poetry and the literary text given by B. Hrushovski in the middle 1950s and in the early 1960s. During the latter period a group interested in structural poetics centered around these lectures. Among them were students of diverse backgrounds, pupils of the philosopher of language Y. Bar-Hillel, the English literature critic Dorothea Krook, and others. Several members of this group became the core of the Department of Poetics and Comparative Literature, founded in 1966 at the new Tel-Aviv University, and of its journal, *Ha-Sifrut* (1968–1987).

Ha-Sifrut (Literature), launched in the spring of 1968, became an organ of literary theory and poetics. However, as the only journal for the academic study of literature in Israel, it also contains critical and historical articles on Hebrew and comparative literature by writers of diverse approaches.

Since most of the work in poetics in recent years was published in this journal, we shall lean heavily in this survey on publications in *Ha-Sifrut*.[1] It may be noted that critics who cannot usually be identified as structuralists often contributed studies of structural aspects to *Ha-Sifrut*. In many cases it is hard to make clear-cut distinctions between "pure" structuralists and scholars of related interests. Moreover, in recent works of literary and academic criticism in Israel a stronger concern with questions of language and poetics is felt.

In addition to the work of Israeli authors, *Ha-Sifrut* has surveyed writings in many languages, primarily in the field of literary theory. From the Israeli vantage point, it was possible to confront theories of literature of several traditions: Russian, English, German, French, Scandinavian and others (Roman Jakobson, Wayne C. Booth, E. Lämmert)—see the papers by Ziva Ben-Porath, Menachem Brinker, Joseph Ewen, Uri Margolin, Tanya Reinhardt. The journal published translations of several classical contributions to poetics, as well as original writings by foreign authors (translated from manuscripts) (such as Seymour Chatman, Thomas Sebeok, Beatrice Silverman Weinreich). The

---

1   Each quarterly issue of *Ha-Sifrut* contained 200 or more double-column pages. Since Hebrew, written without vowels, is relatively short, this is equivalent to about 500 pages of an English journal.

language of the journal is Hebrew, but some idea of the work done is available through the English summaries.[2]

FROM THE LANGUAGE OF POETRY
TO THE LITERARY TEXT

In the 1950s and in the early 1960s, literature as literature meant naturally focusing on the "language of poetry," a vague term which covered a whole range of issues discussed by the Anglo-American New Critics, some German "style critics," Roman Jakobson and the Russian Formalists. The obvious source for a "scientific" treatment of the language of poetry was European structural linguistics, as well as the beginnings of semantics, such as they were at that time.

The linguistic approach was especially fruitful for the study of prosody and of elementary units of style. However, it became clear very soon that there are inherent differences between language and the "language of literature" and therefore between linguistics and poetics. The notion of "system" could be applied to the study of prosody or to the description of the style of literary trends and of markedly individual poets. Literature could be seen as a very complex "system of systems." Even the smallest element, such as rhyme, had to be discussed as a meeting point or a junction of several systems. Thus, in Russian and in Hebrew Modernist rhyme a group of heterogeneous principles influenced the choice of rhyming words: the system of sound requirements in rhyme (as opposed to the "classical" system), the system of poetic diction determining selection of words, the attitude toward neologisms, principles of poetic syntax, the attitude toward thematic relations between rhyming words, etc. It is possible that in a given poetic style such heterogeneous principles were influenced by one, more abstract, poetic or aesthetic attitude. But this is not necessarily the case. There are clear cases of autonomous development of separate principles of poetic style (such as Baudelaire's use of "classical" strophic forms in combination with themes and images which are more akin to those of German Expressionism of around 1920). It became clear that in poetry we cannot use indiscriminately the absolute term "norm." When speaking of a poetic system it became necessary to make a gradual distinction between at least four kinds of "norms": a) an absolute *law*, mandatory for all instances of

---

2   In several cases the English summaries are quite extensive, but in other instances they are too short and misleadingly simplified.

a certain phenomenon; b) a *tendency*, which is predominant in a certain style or writer but whose actual appearance in each instance is neither obligatory nor indicative of authenticity or poetic value; c) *symptomatic* devices which, though they may be infrequently used, are typical and "essential" representatives of a given style (thus, so-called "Modernist" rhymes may appear only occasionally in a writer's work, but they become the symptomatic "markers" for his new style. The same applies to some "typical" kinds of "Modernist" metaphors, which often occupy a small part of the poetic text); d) *"permitted"* expressions, including so-called "poetic licenses" or otherwise possible deviations from a predominant tendency, which are neither symptomatic nor linked to any "essential" traits of the writer's work.

Another difficulty with the notion of system was the problem of its scope, the area in which a certain system functions. It turned out that in the history of literature, as well as in the writings of one writer, a certain norm or even a whole complex "system" holds only as long as it holds. There may suddenly appear works which do not fall under these norms. A "language" of a writer is neither as obligatory nor as distinct from the "language" of another writer as, say, English from French.

The more the study moved from prosodic to semantic and thematic elements of literature, the more it became clear that we cannot confine the discussion to the "language of poetry," or to the smaller components within the limits of a sentence. As some of the Danish Structuralists have suggested, the linguistic sign is a contextual sign. In opposition to this and to I. A. Richards's concept of "context," a concept of "text" was developed. It is not a *context* but a *text* with which we are dealing. In many respects the text is the primary literary unit which determines the form and functions of the elements which compose it. A text is a highly organized piece of language. Any detail in a poem is not determined by some vague context but by a conjunction of patterns of the complete text. The notion of *text*, though developed in Israel independently, was quite akin to the same term in Soviet semiotics in the 1960s and in some of the Western poetics of the same period. The similarities derive perhaps from a strong common influence of Russian Formalism and Czech Structuralism on these schools of literary theory.

However, in Israel, the theory of the text was combined with the phenomenology of the literary object as proposed primarily by Roman Ingarden. For the linguist, it is perhaps possible to provide an objective analysis of a corpus of language, but it would be impossible to have an "objective" poetics. Some of the meanings of the aesthetic object are not presented as such in the literary text but are rather provided by the reader in the process of understanding or, as Ingarden put it, "concretization." A text is a piece of language to be "realized" by a reader according to some inherent requirements of this text, as well as according to the literary tradition and other psychological and historical circumstances. This attitude implies that no structural analysis of a poem can be done before having an interpretation or a set of possible interpretations of this poem. Thus, the common practice of basing an interpretation on the study of meanings and "structures" of a work seems to be reversed; structure became dependent on interpretation.

Ingarden's (and Dufrenne's) dichotomy between *l'oeuvre d'art* and *l'objet esthétique*, the second being a "pertinent" realization of the first, was accepted. Another principle of the phenomenological school was also accepted: the concept of the "aesthetic object," rather than the concept of the "language of poetry," as central to the study of poetics. Even though literature as a whole may be seen vaguely as a system, its units are not simply pieces of a language continuum but independent and transferable objects. However, Ingarden's division of a work of literature into clearly distinguished "strata" (which was accepted, for example, as the basis for R. Wellek's and A. Warren's *Theory of Literature*) was attacked in a series of papers and lectures. A transition from elements of "meaning" or style to substantial parts of the "world" of the work of art was shown. Many metaphors, especially in Modernist poetry, as shown in the works of Rilke, Mayakovsky, Alterman and numerous others, "grow" with the unfolding of a poem and may become basic parts of the situation, objects or persons in the "world" of a poem. In some parts of such a developing image, the links with the basic situation may be metaphorical, whereas in other parts they may become realistic. The so-called "realization of metaphor" is only one form of a whole range of phenomena in this field. We can speak of "figurative situations," "figurative events," transitions from elements of style to elements of the world and the composition of a work of art, etc. As opposed to the static conception of the aesthetic object (reflected in the work of Ingarden, as well as in the terminologies of many schools of criticism), the concept of the "dynamic" nature of the language of poetry was developed, based on the seminal ideas of Tynianov and the Czech Structuralists. Since the aesthetic object is seen as being dependent on the process of reading, the stages of this process and the order of verbal elements in a text became extremely important.

At all times, theoretical thought by members of the Israeli group was strongly linked with detailed observations of specific literary texts. It was felt that a much more thorough knowledge of the complex and subtle nature of the literary object is needed before meaningful systemizations can be made. Hence the role of interpretations in the development of the new poetics. In this respect, a great deal was learned from the experience of New Criticism, especially since the major foreign language known to younger people in Israel was English.

In the early 1960s, the outlines of a theory of the literary text were developed by Benjamin Hrushovski [Harshav]. For obvious reasons, this work will not be presented here in detail. However, at least some principles have to be given here, as a background for the studies discussed in the following chapters, some of which were applications or developments of this theory. These principles will be outlined in an informal, non-technical manner, and, unfortunately, without illustrations.

PRINCIPLES OF A UNIFIED THEORY OF THE LITERARY TEXT

A work of literature is a certain set of language elements, called the *text*. A text implies a whole network of linkings between elements, to be done by a reader, some of which are presented by syntactical or logical means or as traditional literary forms, and some of which have to be provided *ad hoc* by the reader himself. There is a great variety of smaller "units" in any literary text. Unlike the units of language, all literary units are patterns of at least two language elements (in rhyme, metaphor, plot, etc., etc.). Whereas linguistics deals with a corpus of language exhaustively, poetics deals with it selectively, e.g., *all* the sounds in a text or in a language are described by phonology, whereas in poetry only those sounds are relevant which participate in sound patterns of one kind or another. The same is true for all features of the literary text. Thus, no matter how we define an "event," in linguistic, logical or thematic terms, we cannot simply scan a text for and identify its "event units"; only such "event elements" are pertinent which participate in higher patterns, called plot, subplot or the like. Thus, killing a person may be a crucial event if the person is a major character but may be just part of a "description" if presented in a battle scene. On the other hand, "events" important to a plot may be presented not through event elements at all, e.g., the break-up of a relationship, which the reader constructs from a dialogue on unrelated matters (such as the weather). In short, whether a certain element of the text becomes part of a literary unit or not is decided not by the nature of this element but by a higher pattern into which it can be organized. We may speak of the degrees, forms, etc., of the patternability of certain elements in a literary text. There is a basic mechanism for creating patterns in a literary text, permeating all elements of the text, its sound organization, meanings, forms, etc. Thus, an attempt can be made to create a "unified" theory of the literary text, encompassing problems traditionally discussed under the headings of metaphor, plot, prosody, ideas, composition, etc. As a matter of fact, each of these particular fields, strongly developed in recent years, has come to a kind of dead-end, largely because it was discussed independently of the text organization, and too much was relegated to "context," a vague and undefined concept.

A large part of the organization of a text lies in patterning of meanings. The more we shift the discussion of literature from the traditional concern with the language of poetry to the discussion of prose, the more it becomes clear that most patterns in literature are patterns of meaning (though by no means exclusively so). And conversely, meanings in literature are meanings of patterns. Thus, the study of the literary text becomes intimately linked with the study of meaning and the understanding of language in relationships larger than a sentence.

By "meaning" we mean anything that is conveyed in the text, i.e., anything that may be understood by a reader. The units of meaning are not identical with language units (words, sentences), though they are located *in* words and sentences and in combinations of (parts and elements of) words and sentences. A text doesn't only "say" things explicitly, but *conveys* unstated meanings as well. A text is a body of language full of gaps, ellipses, unlinked units, to be read and understood, i.e., to be filled out and reorganized in the mind of a "proper" reader.

Understanding, whether "correct" or "wrong," whether complete or partial, is based on the same kind of techniques, rules and principles. Hence it is useful to assume, with Piaget, an "epistemic" reader, who does not impose his idiosyncrasies but who constructs all and only such meanings which can be justified from a given text. Understanding involves a) knowledge of normative units (lexical senses of words, syntactical contributions to meanings, presuppositions), as well as b) a process of semantic *integration*: linking, relating, judging, adjusting separate elements of the text, filling out gaps, etc.

We may distinguish between the psychological act of understanding, which is largely intuitive, and the reasoned *accounting* for and justification of specific meanings which were understood. Understanding proceeds usually through guesses and approximations; it is not a final act and does not usually exhaust all possible meanings of a text. Nevertheless, we may speak of an ideal "maximal" meaning of a text, based on an assumption that all possible interconnected constructions of meaning are necessary and that there is a maximal functionality of all elements and all orders of elements in a text.

Understanding is based on a process of *linking* elements in the text, whether they are connected syntactically or not, and combining, readjusting and specifying their semantic potentials into *complex meanings* or, usually, *chains of meanings*.

The equivalent in the text to "linking" (in the process of understanding) may be called a *pattern*. Assuming that any legitimate or possible link is based on material given in the text, we may discuss meanings in the observable object, the text. Thus, instead of speaking of "wrong" linking (or "misunderstanding"), we may speak of "unjustified" or "doubtful" patterns.

A pattern is a link of two or more elements in the text, constructed by any means whatsoever: word repetition, sound parallelism, identification of a mutual referent, abstracted synonymity, continuity of meanings, etc., etc.

The establishment of meaning, or understanding, involves *a three-tier construction*. The three tiers are: the level of "sense" (or designation), a field of reference, and regulating principles.

A speaker does not say entirely new things. He may use knowledge of previous language and reality pertinent to the meanings of his new sentences. Saying something and understanding it involves "zeroing in" on a field of reference (FR) and on a specific frame of reference (fr) within this field. We are thereby opening up a store of information which may be used to comprehend in full and specify what is conveyed by the new words.

The Regulating Principles (RP), such as: irony, point of view, tone, circumstances of an utterance, etc., tell us *in what sense* to take the "sense" (the designations of words, assertions, etc.).

The Field of Reference a) provides criteria for judging the truth value of statements; accepts or denies references to "literal meanings" of words, and thereby accepts or changes their meanings; b) provides material for specifying the meaning, such as: what kind of "red" (of bricks, of the sky, etc.), or in what sense "new" and so on.

FRs are of different kinds: "real," (in space and time) or "ideal" (relationships of concepts, a philosophy, etc.); "present" or "absent"; "known to the reader" or "new."

A literary text is a certain established, permanent and transferable set of language elements, a language object disconnected from a world of reference and from a situation of communication—disconnected, but not unrelated.

A literary text is a text which creates an *Internal Field of Reference*. The truth value of sentences or the referability of words is judged by whatever is given in this Internal FR. Meanings are linked with each other assuming such an IFR. Metaphors become metaphors only in relationship to such an FR. Though much of the language of a literary text behaves as if it were used in relationship to a known, real FR, actually no such real space and time are given in advance.

In short, the same body of language provides a) material for the construction and filling in of an FR; b) the "senses" which relate to this FR; c) the regulating principles by which these senses are to be read, including the "voice" and "point of view" of a reconstructed speaker or narrator or author.

The Internal FR is constructed using models of known external FRs. Thus, it is not only that we use literature to understand the world, but we have to use the "world" in order to be able to understand literature and, in general, to connect meanings in language. Of course this does not mean that the Internal FR has to be similar to any known "external" FR. Whether the rules of reality obtain or not in an Internal FR is established from the text itself. As the FR unfolds, we have to assume a "reality key" to know whether or not the fictional world is "realistic," "fantastic," "legendary," etc. Certain expressions may be metaphorical in a realistic FR, or "real" (i.e., referential) in a fantastic FR (e.g., a person becoming very small or very big is a metaphor—grotesque, hyperbolic, or otherwise—in a realistic text, but it is a "real" event in *Alice in Wonderland*).

It seems that defining a literary text as a text with an Internal FR is the only possible definition which distinguishes literature (including oral literature) from other forms of language. The existence of an Internal FR does not imply by any means that in a work of literature there is only one FR or that the words may refer only to this Internal FR. A considerable range of verbal expressions relates to FRs external to the given text, either in historical reality or in ideas or in the history of literature (allusion). An expression relating to such an external FR may bring back to the internal FR a store of information, qualifying meanings, etc.

A text is not presented in the form of one continuous Field of Reference. We may distinguish a whole series of *frames of reference (frs)*, which are pieces of the text continuous in meaning in some respect, in space, in time, or in ideas. There is a whole range of "shifters" which transfer the reader's attention from one small *fr* to another, from one space or time to another. Two contiguous *frs* may be constructed by the reader as belonging to one larger FR, e.g., separate episodes in one person's life, two places in a space continuity, etc. In some cases such a continuity cannot be established by the reader in the immediate context and creates two separate sets of FRs, to be linked at a later stage or to be linked by some larger principle. For example, the disconnected episodes in Sartre's novel describing the eve of World War II in different places in Europe are linked by the reader by means of the idea "Europe at the eve of war." If, however, the "sense" of a word (its designation) cannot fit its immediate *fr*, then it becomes metaphorical. Also, senses which refer realistically to one *fr* may be transferred metaphorically to another fr.

The "sense" matter of words may be used by the reader to refer at the same time to several *frs* or even to several FRs. Thus, in John Updike's *Rabbit Redux*, there is an argument over Vietnam between a conservative working-class husband and his wife's lover, a radical. The words used are understood by the reader to be referring at the same time to the situation in Vietnam and to the tension between the two men; when the husband says, "You people are destroying America," we understand him to say as well, "You are destroying my family."

We may speak of the transferability of semantic material from one *fr* to another, within the internal FR of a work of art as well as outside it. We may also discuss the degree, the form, and the extent of *"referability"* of semantic material to one *fr* or another.

How are patterns constructed? The reader links elements of language with each other, according to a number of principles. Patterns may be:

a. *Formal* or *implied*, i.e., connected by linguistic devices or traditional literary forms or informally connected but linked necessarily if the text is to be read as one unified "world." We use such implied links even for connecting the simplest elements of meaning; an opened door in one sentence and a table in another sentence are understood to belong to the same room even if no formal link was made and the word "room" was not mentioned.

b. *Continuous* or *discontinuous*. Meter or a descriptive passage could serve as examples for the first, rhyme or plot for the second.

c. Of *homogeneous* or of *heterogeneous* material. Thus, rhymes are made of homogeneous elements: "inherent" aspects of sound; whereas the idea of history in Tolstoy's *War and Peace* is made of heterogeneous material: statements by the author, utterances by characters, presentation of historical figures, the reader's conclusions from plot, etc. Such heterogeneous constructions by a reader play an important role in all areas of the literary work. Even rhythm is a heterogeneous construction, using "proper" elements (meter, quantitative features of sound) as well as "extrinsic elements": syntax, meaning, tone, genre-attitudes, etc.

d. *Stable* or *temporary.* Some patterns are constructed only temporarily, e.g., misleading explanations in a mystery novel, misleading positive impressions of a character, or certain visual details of imagery which have to be changed subsequently. Such temporary patterns are not just meant only for the first reading. They have to be constructed by the reader on subsequent readings as well, that is, even when he knows that the final meaning is different. Such temporary patterns play an important role in building up the reader's experience of the text.

e. *Unequivocal* or "*hovering.*" The first is rare in literary texts; the latter is prominent, for example, in symbolic overtones implied in certain kinds of scenery, which should not be explicated in full.

f. *Certain* or *possible.* The first implies something that can be convincingly constructed in an analytical interpretation, whereas for the latter we have no absolute proof, though some readers may feel strongly that such a possibility exists. One should not confuse this dichotomy with the previous one, since we may be quite certain about a "hovering" meaning and in doubt about an unequivocal one.

g. *Closed, semi-closed* or *open.* A rhyme, when finished, is a closed pattern. Alliteration is open as long as we read on, and new sounds may be added to it. Plot or biography of a character are most of the time open patterns. On the other hand, the psychology of a character is at each point a "semi-closed" pattern: in each situation the reader has to sum up the nature of a character, though he knows that this summary will be reopened as the story proceeds.

h. Established through "*purely-literary*" or "*reality-like*" principles. This distinction was central to the theory and underwent a series of refinements which cannot be discussed here. The basic idea is that besides the "purely-literary" patterns discussed in traditional structural analyses there is a whole range of "reality-like" principles without which the organization of a literary work of art is unthinkable. We link heterogeneous and disconnected events, situations, expressions, etc., by means of such concepts as the psychology of a character or the psychology of men in general, ideas, world views, etc.

Thus, the understanding, as well as the organization of a text and the "aesthetic experience," involve creating a whole network of patterns in the process of reading. The reader, having sufficient ground for the creation of a certain pattern, links a variety of elements, which may be discontinuous and heterogeneous. However, a pattern linking several elements of a text may employ only parts of these elements. Thus, a rhyme uses only a part of the sound-structure of the participating words; a characterization may be based on one hand on the narrator's or other person's generalizations about this character (qualified by the reader's understanding of the speaker's position) and on the other hand on abstractions and interpolations from dialogues and situations. Any name, abstraction, or question may send the reader back to scan the text for material for possible answers, which he combines into one composite pattern. Any meaning-transaction involves: 1) establishment of a link (through abstraction); 2) extraction of usable meaning-stuff or construction of missing parts; 3) mutual adjustment (specification). Since many semantic units in a text are not given in one language-unit but are presented as a pattern of elements, and since each element has to be embedded in its own context in the text-continuum, each element of such a complex meaning may take on a particular form and shade of meaning, such that the "meaning" of the whole pattern or *chain* becomes not one but changing. In literature we deal with *meaning-chains* (a plot, a character, an extended image, and idea) which are not reducible to one static statement.

On the other hand, the units of a text—both units of language (words, sentences, paragraphs) and literary units (scenes, dialogues, images, chapters)—may serve as *junctions* for several (heterogeneous) patterns. Thus, a rhyming word is a *junction*: some of its sounds participate in the rhyme-pattern, other sounds (stress, syllables) participate in the meter, its syntactic properties link it to the sentence, its concrete aspects to the image, its abstract meaning to the ideas, etc. A certain scene may contribute to the unfolding of plot, to the characterization of several personages, to the ideas, to the building up of the fictional reality, etc. A writer cannot introduce a pure event, as he cannot introduce a pure rhyme or a pure idea; he has to use words and sentences, which carry more than the needed event, rhyming sound, idea, etc. The additional elements, "irrelevant" to the pattern at hand, have to fit properly and interestingly with the other, heterogeneous patterns of the text. Moreover, any junction, any unit of the text, or any pattern may also serve a *multiplicity of functions* in the work of art.

The patterns in any text are organized on *two levels*: the *level of the text-continuum* and the *reconstructed level*. Characters, plot, ideas, time, space, etc., are built by the reader from discontinuous elements in the text and are reorganized according to their inherent principles (such as: chronology—for time elements, logical order—for ideas, etc.). This reconstructed level is the one that is usually discussed in criticism, often without making clear the differences between what is given in the text and what has been added, understood, or constructed (however necessarily) by the reader.

On the reconstructed level, the patterns enter into *hierarchical relationships*. But such hierarchies are by no means stable, one-directional, or architectonic. Since they are constructed by a reader from the material available in a text, they may be fluid, and may be inverted in the course of the unfolding of a text. They are always hierarchies "in respect of." Thus, characters may be subordinated to plot when we focus our attention on plot, but the same plot becomes subordinated to character as soon as we became interested in this character. This process is a consequence of the inherent circularity of a literary text.

In building the reconstructed level, the reader has to fill in many gaps, guess, create hypotheses, etc. For this purpose, he may use any outside model (from the world, from history, myth, legend, from literature, from theories of psychology, etc.). As Ingarden has shown, no presentation of reality in language can be detailed in full. One has to make a distinction between different kinds of indeterminacies (Ingarden's "Unbestimmtheitsstellen"); some are uninteresting, and some are *gaps* which the reader is encouraged to fill out, however hypothetically or temporarily.

As explained before, this is done by referring semantic material to the constructed Internal Field of Reference (and enlarging and specifying it thereby at the same time) and by means of a set of Regulating Principles, which are, in turn, constructed from the same text. Any part of the language-string may be raised to serve as a Regulating Principle (to become "supra-segmental"): a "Point of View," a tone, the nature of a character (serving as a qualifier of whatever he says), etc. This three-story construction exists in language in normal speech circumstances as well; however, there only the middle level is presented clearly in verbal material, the field of reference as well as the regulating principles seem to be given primarily in the situation. In a literary text, such a situation is reconstructed by the reader from the same verbal material, and there is a mutual dependence and circularity of the interpretations put on each of these three stories.

In traditional literary criticism the level of *text-continuity* has been practically overlooked. Apart from the problem of presenting a "world" to be constructed by a reader, a writer has to unfold his text step-after-step and justify the additions, shifts, stops, etc. The making of a page is as typical to the recognition of a writer (such as Faulkner or Hemingway) and as vital to the impact created on a reader as are the large patterns of plot, ideas, character. Basic to the unfolding of a literary work of art is *the principle of unprincipled advancement of the text*; a chapter may start as a description, shift to ideas, to a dialogue, to the past; proportions of presentation may change, etc. Another principle of literature is the disproportion of presentation of anything that is presented.

Basic to the analysis of the level of text-continuity are: the ways of *segmentation* of a text, the modes and forms of such segments, the *motivations* for introducing or discontinuing such segments and the *shifters* used for this purpose. We cannot detail here this part of the theory of the text (see Chapter 8).

Such is the general frame of thought from which specific descriptive notions are being developed to deal with traditional issues of literary criticism. On the other hand, it became clear that existing, "static" theories of meaning (which usually commit the "first-sentence fallacy," assuming that every sentence is a first one) cannot be automatically employed for the understanding of meaning in literature. On the contrary, their limitations seem to be indicative of their limited grasp of language itself, and the literary text, which is a tight complex of language employing to a high degree all possibilities which language offers, may serve as a convenient starting point for a new theory of meaning, which may be called Integrational Semantics.

THE READER, THE NARRATIVE TEXT, MULTIPLE SYSTEMS OF GAP-FILLING AND BIBLICAL POETICS

A major paper by Menakhem Perry and Meir Sternberg (1968) evoked a great deal of interest and debate. The authors analyze in detail the Biblical story of David and Bathsheba (II Sam., 11) and attack from this vantage point several major problems of Biblical poetics, the structure of fiction, and the theory of the literary text.

The point of departure is the theory of the literary object as depending on a relationship between a text and a reader. A reader who wishes to actualize the reality that is represented in a text, to construct the fictive world it projects, must answer, in the course of his reading, a series of questions such as: What is happening, and why? What is the connection between the events? What is the motivation of this or that character? etc. Many of the answers to these questions are not given *explicitly* by the text, but must be supplied by the reader himself, some of them temporarily, partially or potentially, and some fully and finally. The literary work leaves, in fact, a *system of gaps* which have to be filled by the reader in the process of reading. This is done through the construction of hypotheses, in the light of which various elements in the work are explained or fall into pattern. The validity of a hypothesis depends upon the number of elements in the text it makes use of and upon the degree of relevance between them that it creates. This phenomenon ranges from simple linkages or decisions carried out by the reader automatically to very complex systems of linkages, which are constructed consciously, laboriously, hesitantly, and with constant corrections or modifications in the light of additional information that is imparted in later stages of the work.

Gap-filling is by no means an arbitrary process. It is directed and limited by: a) the events, themes, ideas and linkages that are *explicitly* communicated in the work; b) the language and the structure of the work; c) the special laws of the world it projects, that have been impressed upon the reader in the course of his reading; d) the perceptual set that the generic characteristics of the work arouse in the reader; and e) the basic assumptions or general laws of probability that are derived from common cultural conventions and everyday life. In some cases the reader is forced to abandon e) in favor of c), but in most cases the reader tends to choose the hypothesis that is most probable and conventional within his cultural environment.

In telling the Biblical story of David and Bathsheba, the narrator limits himself to the rendering of external occurrences only (action and speech). He does not penetrate into the inner lives of the characters, although in this story, as in most stories dealing with adultery and treachery, the reader is interested precisely in the motivations of the characters. The narrator evades an explicit rendering or formulation of thoughts, but directs the reader to infer them from what is rendered explicitly. The suppression of the important facts, the pseudo-objectivity of the narrator, and the communication of the shocking events as if they were common occurrences create an ironic tension between the understated manner in which the story is communicated and the events themselves as reconstructed by the reader. The authors demonstrate a) that the filling of the central gaps in this story cannot be done automatically, but requires close attention to details of the rendered occurrences and of the language and style; b) that this process does not merely enrich the meaning of the story, but is rather a necessity for anyone who wishes to grasp what is happening; and c) that most of the gaps were opened by the narrator at central points or cruxes of the story.

The authors reconstruct carefully step by step the process of actualization of this story. As they show, one of the main gaps in the story is whether Uriah is aware of his wife's adultery. The text precludes a definite answer to this question. Each of the two possible hypotheses (yes or no) is supported by several general arguments, while other arguments expose its weaknesses and support the opposite hypothesis. Each of these hypotheses throws a different light on identical or different details of the text and organizes them in a different way, and each presents Uriah in a different way. On the other hand each of them throws an ironic light on David, but in different ways. The text deliberately exploits this inability to arrive at a definite choice between these two systems of gap-filling. The authors point out how the narrator makes use of the advantages of each of these systems in order to employ Uriah as a vehicle of cleverly veiled ironies which are directed at David. Also, the constant oscillation between the various hypotheses repeatedly directs the attention of the reader to the concrete texture of the work.

The co-existence of incompatible systems of gap-filling that are simultaneously constructed is not rare in literature (although most critics seem to overlook this important fact). The authors suggest that this phenomenon be called *multiple systems of gap-filling*. In some works the co-existence of these multiple systems of gap-filling is one of the main compositional principles.

The authors examine the two main hypotheses that have been discussed in the criticism of James's *The Turn of the Screw* (the Apparitionist hypothesis versus the Nonapparitionist hypothesis). The implicit ideal of English criticism to establish a single correct hypothesis is shown to be absurd. This ideal has led to the interminable controversy about "what really happens" in this *nouvelle*. In fact, the central compositional principle of James's story is the inability to decide between two central hypotheses.

Perry and Sternberg express their surprise that English criticism, which has regarded "multiple meaning" as one of the distinctive features of the language of literature, shied away from ambiguity on the level of events, in the field of reality represented in a work of literature.

The authors point out some basic differences between gap-filling in literature and in everyday life. In the literary work, this process is directed also by the *purely-literary patterns,* such as poetics of the story, its structure, its style, its rhythm, etc. Multiple systems of gap-filling may co-exist in everyday life too, but then we know that only one of the hypotheses is possible, though we do not always have enough information to decide which of them is the right one. On the other hand, in the literary work both hypotheses may be legitimate, because their co-existence may be aesthetically motivated in and through the artistic intentions of the work.

In a later issue of *Ha-Sifrut* an extensive discussion of this seminal paper was published, centering on the poetics of the Biblical narrative. The two critics, Boaz Arpali and Uriel Simon, attack primarily the application of modern analytical techniques to a chapter in the Bible, which is not an independent story but part of a larger continuum. Characteristically, Arpali entitled his paper: "Caution: A Biblical Story!" while Perry and Sternberg entitled their rebuttal: "Caution: A Literary Text!" Both in the two critical articles as well as in the extensive reply by Perry and Sternberg, a wealth of Biblical material has been examined and a series of principles of Biblical poetics has been formulated.

ANALOGY AND THE COMPOSITION OF THE NOVEL

In the first issue of *Ha-Sifrut,* Menakhem Perry (1968) published a study of analogy and its role as a structural principle in the novels of the Hebrew classic Mendele Moykher-Sforim (1832–1916). Mendele's novels were said to be deficient in many ways, primarily in their lack of "love intrigue," psychological change in characters, and tightness of plot. Perry argues that such observations are valid only as descriptive statements but must not be accepted as evaluative ones. As the analysis shows, the richness and interest of Mendele's novels lie in a network of patterns which compensate for the ostensible faults. The article draws on Hrushovski's early distinction between two types of patterns and linkages existing in a literary work of art: quasi-realistic patterns and purely literary ones. Having described the quasi-realistic linkages (plot and character) in Mendele's novels, Perry argues that owing to their looseness the reader is encouraged to look for the purely-literary patterns (primarily analogy). Mendele, the ostensibly super-realistic writer, uses a whole network of analogies (between fragments, parts of plot or lines of plot), thus superimposing—in Jakobson's terms—a principle of simultaneity over the continuum of the literary work. The effect and meaning of every part of the text become dependent on its relations with other parts.

In an examination of an analogy between two chapters of *The Travels of Benjamin the Third*, Perry shows the transformation of analogical materials: what appears in one part as a product of the imagination becomes in the parallel chapter an object which is real and concrete, and vice versa. On similar principles are based the analogical links between elements of style and language in one part of the novel and events and situations in the other part. A simile in one plot becomes a real object or event in the parallel plot. Words appearing in a metaphor or an idiom in one plot reappear as real events, based on their literal meanings, in the other plot. Thus, the novel progresses as a constant stream fluctuating back and forth between stylistic elements and plot patterns. In fact, the plot of *The Travels of Benjamin the Third* is based on the "literalization" and realization of idioms.

REFERENCES

Arpali, Boaz. "Caution: A Biblical Story! Comments on the Story of David and Bathsheba and on the Problem of Biblical Narrative." *Hasifrut*, 2:580–597 (1970).

Ben-Porath, Ziva. "The First-Person Novel and its Techniques According to Romberg." *Hasifrut*, 1:153–160 (1968).

Brinker, Menachem. "The Doctrine of *L'engagement* and the Evolution of Sartre's Aesthetics: 1938–1964." *Hasifrut*, 1:640–664 (1968/9).

Chatman, Seymour. "A Criticism of the Theory of Character in French Structuralism." *Hasifrut*, 1: 534–545 (1968/9).

Dufrenne, Mikel. *Phénoménologie de l'expérience esthétique*, 1953. English translation: *The Phenomenology of Aesthetic Experience*, Northwestern UP, 1973.

Ewen, Joseph. "Represented Speech: A Concept in the Theory of Prose and its Uses in Hebrew Fiction." *Hasifrut*, 3:140–152 (1971).

Hasifrut: Quarterly for the Study of Literature. (Since Vol. 4 (1973) new English title: *Ha-Sifrut/Literature: Theory of Literature—Poetics—Hebrew and Comparative* (In Hebrew, with English summaries)). Ed. Benjamin Hrushovski. Tel Aviv University, Vol. 1, No. 1: Spring 1968. The journal was published until 1987.

Ingarden, Roman. *Das Literarische Kunstwerk*, 1930. English Translation: *The Literary Work of Art: An Investigation on the Borderlines of Ontology, Logic, and Theory of Literature*, Northwestern UP, 1973.

Margolin, Uri. "The Narrative as a Continuum and as a Whole: A Critique of E. Läm-mert's *Bauformen des Erzählens*." *Hasifrut*, 1:293–306 (1968).

Pagis, Dan (1970). *Secular Poetry and Poetic Theory: Moses Ibn-Ezra and His Contemporaries* (Jerusalem).

Perry, Menakhem. "Analogy and Its Role as a Structural Principle in the Novels of Mendele Moykher Sforim." *Hasifrut*, 1:65–100 (1968).

Perry, Menakhem and Meir Sternberg. "The King Through Ironic Eyes: The Narrator's Devices in the Biblical Story of David and Bathsheba and Two Excursuses on the Theory of the Narrative Text." *Hasifrut*, 1:263–292 (1968).

Reinhardt, Tanya. "Three Approaches to Poetic Language." *Hasifrut*, 3:165–178 (1971).

Sebeok, Thomas A. "Semiotics: A Survey of the State of the Art." *Hasifrut*, 3:365–400 (1972).

Simon, Uriel. "An Ironic Approach to a Bible Story: On the Interpretation of the Story of David and Bathsheba." *Hasifrut*, 2:598–607 (1970).

Weinreich, Beatrice Silverman. "Formal Problems in the Study of Yiddish Proverbs." *Hasifrut*, 3:85–92 (1971).

SOURCES OF THE CHAPTERS

Chapter 1. "Fictionality and Fields of Reference: Remarks on a Theoretical Framework," *Poetics Today* Vol. 5 (1984), No. 2: 227–251. [E]

Chapter 2. "Poetic Metaphor and Frames of Reference: With Examples from Eliot, Rilke, Mayakovsky, Mandelshtam, Pound, Creeley, Amichai and the *New York Times*," *Poetics Today* Vol. 5 (1984), No. 1: 5–43. [E]

Chapter 3. "An Outline of Integrational Semantics: An Understander's Theory of Meaning in Context" [revised version], *Poetics Today* Vol. 3 (1982) No. 4: 59–88. [E]

Chapter 4. "The Structure of Semiotic Objects: A Three-Dimensional Model," *Poetics Today* Vol. 1 (1979), No. 1–2: 363–76. [E]

Chapter 5. "On Presentation and Representation in Fiction," *Wissenschaftskolleg zu Berlin: Jahrbuch 1983/84*, Ed., Peter Wapnewsky, Siedler Verlag, Berlin 1985, pp. 159–169 [E]. Also: "Présentation et représentation dans la fiction littéraire," transl. Anne-Marie Moulin, *Littérature 57* (Février 1985): 6–16. [F]

Chapter 6. "'Literariness' Revisited," in: Eimermacher, Karl, Peter Grzybek, Georg Witte, eds., *Issues in Slavic Literary Theory*, Bochum: Brockmeyer, 1989: 93–106. [E]

Chapter 7. "The Meaning of Sound Patterns in Poetry: An Interaction Theory," *Poetics Today* Vol. 2 (1980), No. 1a: 39–56. [E]

Chapter 8. "Theory of the Literary Text and the Structure of Non-Narrative Fiction: In the First Episode of *War and Peace*," *Poetics Today* Vol. 9 (1988), No. 3: 635–666. [E]

Chapter 9. "Poetics, Criticism, Science: Remarks on the Fields and Responsibilities of the Study of Literature," *PTL* Vol. 1 (1976): iii–xxxv. [E]

Chapter 10. "A Unified Theory of the Literary Text," in: *Structuralist Poetics in Israel* (with Ziva Ben-Porath), Papers on Poetics and Semiotics, No. 1, Tel Aviv University, 1974. [E]

INDEX